Writing ~~Badly~~ is Easy

Also by Amitava Kumar

FICTION

The Lovers (2017)

Home Products (2010)

NON-FICTION

Lunch with a Bigot (2015)

A Matter of Rats: A Short Biography of Patna (2013)

A Foreigner Carrying in the Crook of His Arm a Tiny Bomb (2010)

Husband of a Fanatic (2004)

Bombay-London-New York (2002)

Passport Photos (2000)

POETRY

No Tears for the NRI (1996)

Writing ~~Badly~~ is Easy

AMITAVA KUMAR

ALEPH

ALEPH

ALEPH BOOK COMPANY
An independent publishing firm
promoted by ***Rupa Publications India***

First Published in India in 2019 by
Aleph Book Company
7/16 Ansari Road, Daryaganj
New Delhi 110 002

ISBN: 978-93-88292-51-1

1 3 5 7 9 10 8 6 4 2

Printed at Replika Press Pvt. Ltd, India

'Amazon.com lists 4,470 titles under the heading of How to Write a Book.'
—Richard Bausch, 'How to Write in 700 Easy Lessons'

'Even if I'm telling urgent stories, I can still experiment with form and make it a creative process.'
—Katherine Boo's 15 Rules for Narrative Nonfiction

Press Information Bureau
Government of India
Ministry of Finance

21 JUN 2018 5:20PM by PIB Delhi

Rate of Exchange of Foreign Currency in Indian Rupee notified.

In exercise of the powers conferred by Section 14 of the Customs Act, 1962 (52 of 1962), and in supersession of the notification of the Central Board of Indirect Taxes and Customs (CBIC) No.49/2018-CUSTOMS (N.T.), dated 7th June, 2018 except as respects things done or omitted to be done before such supersession, the Central Board of Indirect Taxes and Customs (CBIC) hereby determines that the rate of exchange of conversion of each of the foreign currencies specified in column (2) of each of Schedule I and Schedule II annexed hereto, into Indian currency or *vice versa*, shall, with effect from 22nd June, 2018, be the rate mentioned against it in the corresponding entry in column (3) thereof, for the purpose of the said Section, relating to Imported and Export Goods.

I find the prose on this page less intelligible than the one on the next page.

In fact, what you see on the next page is art.

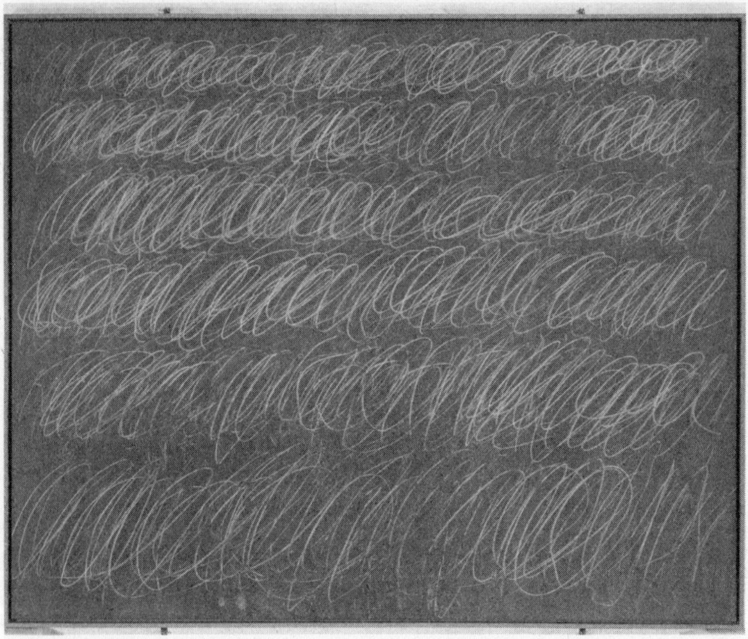

Cy Twombly, *Untitled*, 1968

Oil based house paint, wax crayon on canvas

68 x 90 in

CONTENTS

AUTHOR'S NOTE

All good writing must turn its face to the world. People, places, roads, rooms. But after a long practice of the craft, writers can be found writing about writing. In early 2009 I began working on this book and was writing short pieces that I planned to later include in it. One of these pieces I titled 'Rules for Writing'.* There were ten rules. Rule number 9 read: *Finish one thing before taking up another*. And then there was rule number 10: *The above rule needs to be repeated.* I present those rules, 1-10, in Appendix A at the back of this book, but what needs to be said here, right at the outset, is that I didn't finish what I had started.** I didn't finish writing this book after I had begun work on it. Instead, I published three other books. It took time for the idea and the form of this book to get settled in my mind. And it is probable that this book that I've now finished writing is better because the idea of it has stayed with me for so long, but of course there is no reason to be certain of that. And even if this is indeed the right time, it is better to begin with the recognition that (*a*) it is often difficult to follow rules (see above), and (*b*) I'd be lost without those rules, especially rules 2 and 5. This book is about what works in writing and what doesn't. It belongs to the genre of books by writers on writing. I love reading interviews with writers, particularly when they describe their work-

---

*First published in Amitava Kumar, *Lunch with a Bigot: The Writer in the World*, Durham: Duke University Press, 2015. See pp. 119-24.

**'The road to hell is paved with works-in-progress', Philip Roth, *New York Times Book Review*, 15 July 1979.

routines.* I don't want a lecture about the long lonely slog that resulted in a book; a small, useful tip will do just fine, thank you. It is faintly ridiculous this desire because there is no better trick than simply sitting down and writing. But we continue to wait for minor miracles—and sometimes we are rewarded, as I believe I was, for instance, when my eyes fell on the magical title of the following essay: 'Do You Want to Be Known For Your Writing, or For Your Swift Email Responses?'**

*Such interviews or essays demystify writing. As a reader you are able to see writing as a practice and as a process.

**Melissa Febos, 'Do You Want to Be Known For Your Writing, or For Your Swift Email Responses?', *Catapult*, 23 May 2017.

I

Against Babu English

BABU ENGLISH

The search for lessons in style is everywhere. An inadvertent result of the Wikileaks exposé, the *Indian Express* reported, was that it led to criticism of the long-winded language used by diplomats in India. According to the report, the Ministry of External Affairs in Delhi asked trainee diplomats to read the leaked cables 'and get a hang of the brevity with which thoughts and facts' had been expressed.* When *The Guardian* reported on this bit of news it added its own inch of context: 'India's bureaucracy has a well-deserved reputation for obtuse language and an ability to resist any reform. Both, it is often said, were inherited from the British Raj.'** We can blame history but even the British were amused by the ornate style that has come to be called Babu English. Here, for instance, is an example presented by the British Library:

82 *BABOO ENGLISH AS 'TIS WRIT.*

Here is another in much the same strain :—

" HONOURED AND MUCH RESPECTED SIR,—With due respect and humble submission, I beg to bring to your kind notice that for a long days, I have not the fortune to pay you a respect, or not to have your mental or daily welfare, therefore my request that you will be kind enough to show me some mercy and thankfulness, by pending some few lines to your wretched son and thereby highly oblige. In accordance by your verbal order, I am still lingering for your hopeful words, which I cannot put out from my memory or think not to be disappointed by you.

---

*Shishir Gupta, 'Cablegate: Keep language crisp like Americans, govt to babus', *Indian Express*, 6 December 2010.

**Jason Burke, 'WikiLeaks cables offer a lesson in brevity for Indian diplomats', *The Guardian*, 6 December 2010.

The aforementioned quote is from a book published in 1891. But why go so far back in time? Just consider the language used in the courts in India. If you have been reading about the judgments delivered by the honourable judges you will know that their principal feature is the use of obscure, archaic phrases.

Communication is not a goal, it seems, only a bewildering attempt at pomposity.

If such judgments do perform a public role, it is in forcing us to imagine the use of a new language that is unpretentious and elegant.

Here are the opening paragraphs—which I need to cite at length to demonstrate just how badly written they are—of the sessions court judgment delivered in 2012 in the Aarushi Talwar murder case:

> The cynosure of judicial determination is the fluctuating fortunes of the dentist couple Dr. Rajesh Talwar and Dr. Nupur Talwar, who have been arraigned for committing and secreting as also deracinating the evidence of commission of the murder of their own adolescent daughter-a beaut damsel and sole heiress Ms. Aarushi and hapless domestic aide Hemraj, who had migrated to India from neighbouring Nepal to eke out living and attended routinely to the chores of domestic drudgery at the house of their masters.
>
> The *mise en scene* is Flat No. L-32, Jalvayu Vihar, Sector 25, N.O.I.D.A., a suburb of New Delhi. The *Dramatis Personae* are Dr. Rajesh Talwar, his wife Dr. Nupur Talwar, the accused of this case, Ms. Aarushi and Hemraj, who were bludgeoned and thereafter, jugulated to death on the intervening night of 15/16 May, 2008, Mr. Umesh Sharma and Mrs. Bharti Mandal.
>
> The parties are *ad idem* that the case is based on circumstantial evidence. Skipping expatiation on prosecution

> story, a vignette of facts as unveiled is that on 15.05.2008 at about 09:30 P.M. only Dr. Rajesh Talwar, Dr. Nupur Talwar, Ms. Aarushi and Hemraj were last seen in the house by Umesh Sharma, the driver of Dr. Rajesh Talwar and in the morning of 16.05.2008 Ms. Aarushi was found dead in her bedroom, which was adjacent to the bedroom of accused persons and in between these bedrooms there was a wooden partition wall. The dead body of domestic servant Hemraj was found on the terrace of the house on 17.0.2008 and there is nothing to suggest that intruder(s) perpetrated this fiendish and flagitious crime.*

Did the judge assiduously follow a manual of bad writing to produce such monstrous prose? And can we really blame the British for such horrors? What would George Orwell, a proponent of clear prose, have to say about such writing? I'm tempted to say that he would find it 'flagitious', but he would probably use plainer language to describe it. 'Avoidable ugliness' could be one of his milder terms of rebuke. 'Sheer humbug' could be another. Orwell's advice in his classic essay, 'Politics and the English Language', provides a simple recipe for achieving clarity and coherence:

---

*Sessions Trial Number 477 of 2012. *The State of U.P. through the C.B.I. vs. Rajesh Talwar and another*. Judgment downloaded from http://online.wsj.com/public/resources/documents/AarushiVerdict.pdf

I cannot stop myself from quoting such verbiage. Here is the opening line from another judgment delivered by the Supreme Court of India in May 2016: 'The batch of writ petitions preferred Under Article 32 of the Constitution of India exposits cavil in its quintessential conceptuality and percipient discord between venerated and exalted right of freedom of speech and expression of an individual, exploring manifold and multi-layered, unbounded and unfettered spectrums, and the control, restrictions and constrictions, under the assumed power of "reasonableness" ingrained in the statutory provisions relating to criminal law to reviver [*sic*] and uphold one's reputation.' A commentator calls this language 'pompous, Punjabi-Victorian bastard English'. See C. P. Surendran, 'Defamation judgment shows India's courts put failed writers to shame', *Daily O*, 14 May 2016. https://www.dailyo.in/politics/defamation-judgment-language-cji-ts-thakur-supreme-court-english-language/story/1/10622.html

'A scrupulous writer, in every sentence that he writes, will ask himself at least four questions, thus: What am I trying to say? What words will express it? What image or idiom will make it clearer? Is this image fresh enough to have an effect? And he will probably ask himself two more: Could I put it more shortly? Have I said anything that is avoidably ugly?'*

---

*George Orwell, 'Politics and the English Language'. The essay is easily available online. For example: http://www.orwell.ru/library/essays/politics/english/e_polit
The only ones who can match our judges and other practitioners of officialese are our spiritual leaders. Here's an example of nonsense, a tweet by Deepak Chopra: 'Attention and intention are the mechanics of manifestation.' #CosmicConciousness
Another example of a mixture of blandness and banality is *Exam Warriors* by Narendra Modi (New Delhi: Penguin Random House, 2018). Example: 'Every individual is blessed with unique abilities. These abilities are best channelled through quality time management.' Here the RSS-pracharak shows a tin-ear for language and a taste for management-speak. Elsewhere he demonstrates a Hindu propagandist's fervour for mantras and yoga, not to mention a taste for militancy with the emphasis on warriorhood. My basic objection, however, is to Modi's claims to authority: How many examinations has he cleared in his life? Does he share anywhere in this book, with any degree of honesty, his own struggles with the demands of bureaucratic education, let alone his failures?

LANGUAGE IS YOUR FRIEND

I discover the limits of my language when I'm writing grant proposals and other applications. Formal demands cramp our style. In school, we are often asked to write letters addressed to officials or the principal: 'Dear Sir/Madam, I am writing to request…' Language use in such exercises is a set of rigid rules. There is a usefulness to such exercises but there is no spark of creativity in the writing. We can participate in such dull rituals when it is absolutely unavoidable but I want to make a case for writing that is bright or witty or entertaining. Allow me to quote in full the letter of application—playful, sharp, insistent, alive—sent by a twenty-three-year old Eudora Welty to the *New Yorker* magazine when she was applying for a job:

> March 15, 1933
>
> Gentlemen,
>
> I suppose you'd be more interested in even a sleight-o'-hand trick than you'd be in an application for a position with your magazine, but as usual you can't have the thing you want most.
>
> I am 23 years old, six weeks on the loose in N.Y. However, I was a New Yorker for a whole year in 1930-31 while attending advertising classes in Columbia's School of Business. Actually I am a southerner, from Mississippi, the nation's most backward state. Ramifications include Walter H. Page, who, unluckily for me, is no longer connected with

Doubleday-Page, which is no longer Doubleday-Page, even. I have a B.A. ('29) from the University of Wisconsin, where I majored in English without a care in the world. For the last eighteen months I was languishing in my own office in a radio station in Jackson, Miss., writing continuities, dramas, mule feed advertisements, santa claus talks, and life insurance playlets; now I have given that up.

As to what I might do for you—I have seen an untoward amount of picture galleries and 15¢ movies lately, and could review them with my old prosperous detachment, I think; in fact, I recently coined a general word for Matisse's pictures after seeing his latest at the Marie Harriman: concubineapple. That shows you how my mind works—quick, and away from the point. I read simply voraciously, and can drum up an opinion afterwards.

Since I have bought an India print, and a large number of phonograph records from a Mr. Nussbaum who picks them up, and a Cezanne Bathers one inch long (that shows you I read e. e. cummings I hope), I am anxious to have an apartment, not to mention a small portable phonograph. How I would like to work for you! A little paragraph each morning—a little paragraph each night, if you can't hire me from daylight to dark, although I would work like a slave. I can also draw like Mr. Thurber, in case he goes off the deep end. I have studied flower painting.

There is no telling where I may apply, if you turn me down; I realize this will not phase you, but consider my other alternative: the U of N.C. offers for $12.00 to let me dance in

Vachel Lindsay's Congo. I congo on. I rest my case, repeating that I am a hard worker.

Truly yours,
Eudora Welty*

---

*Available online at http://www.lettersofnote.com/2012/10/how-i-would-like-to-work-for-you.html. (Welty did not get the job at the *New Yorker* but she went on to become one of America's major writers who did often publish in that magazine.)

THE EMPEROR OF WRITING MALADIES

You fail as a writer if your writing is not concrete, if it is vague and abstract, and your reader is unable to see what you mean. In a textbook I have used in my journalism class, the author offers the following anecdote about Gene Roberts, former editor of the *New York Times*, whose first job was writing farm columns for a small newspaper in North Carolina: 'Roberts' editor was Henry Belk, who was blind. Roberts recalls that when he showed up for work in the morning, Belk would call him over and inform the young reporter that his writing was insufficiently descriptive. "Make me see," he would order.'*

I now tell this story to my writing students each semester. *Make me see, make me see!*

Siddhartha Mukherjee is a reputed oncologist at Columbia University and the author of the Pulitzer Prize-winning book on cancer, *The Emperor of All Maladies*.** Mukherjee is an admirer of Anton Chekhov's writing. Chekhov, of course, was also a doctor, and what Mukherjee particularly likes in him is that Chekhov, as a writer, when surrounded by misery during a visit to Sakhalin Island, 'neither turns away in disgust nor rushes forward to satisfy a sadistic curiosity'.*** There is a quality of professional attention

*Melvin Mencher, *News Reporting and Writing*, New York: McGraw Hill, 2011, p. 247.

**Siddhartha Mukherjee, *The Emperor of All Maladies: A Biography of Cancer*, New York: Scribner, 2010.

***Siddhartha Mukherjee, 'Love in the Time of Numbness; or, Doctor Chekhov, Writer', *New Yorker*, 11 April 2017. https://www.newyorker.com/culture/cultural-comment/love-in-the-time-of-numbness-or-doctor-chekhov-writer

that distinguishes this looking. Mukherjee's description is exact: 'He simply looks, and looks again. The gaze is unsparing and penetrating, clear-eyed, *clinical*—a word used often in association with Chekhov.' Chekhov does not sentimentalize. He is able to see everything because his eyes are not clouded with tears. At the same time, Mukherjee wants us to know that the Russian master's 'cool, unsparing, astringent gaze gives way to tenderness, to a sensitivity that is precisely the opposite of dispassion'. The word that Mukherjee clearly has in mind is compassion.

I have been quoting from Mukherjee's 2017 keynote address to the recipients of the Whiting Awards for emerging writers. The good doctor was speaking as an older, experienced writer; his words were meant to have pedagogical value. It was only right, therefore, that he provided examples of what he meant by Chekhov's ways of seeing. Mukherjee gave two examples. One was of an encounter that Chekhov had on the ferry across the Amur River:

> On the Amur steamer going to Sakhalin, there was a convict who had murdered his wife and wore fetters on his legs. His daughter, a little girl of six, was with him. I noticed wherever the convict moved the little girl scrambled after him, holding on to his fetters. At night the child slept with the convicts and soldiers all in a heap together.

The second described Chekhov's meeting with a woman on Sakhalin Island:

> An old woman called Miss Ulyana cohabits with a prosperous old peasant in exile. Once, a very long time ago, she had killed her baby and buried it in the ground; at the trial, she said that she had not killed the child but buried it alive—she thought that she would stand a better chance of being acquitted that way. The court sentenced her to twenty years. Telling me about this, Ulyana wept bitterly, but then she

> wiped her eyes and asked, 'Fancy buying a nice little bit o' pickled cabbage?'

Against the numbness of desensitization, and the professional hardening of the heart, against the *anaesthetic*, Mukherjee was positing Chekhov's *aesthetic*. He went on to tell the emerging writers about Chekhov's rules of writing that are, of course, as good as any I have encountered:

> 'Six principles that make for a good story,' Chekhov would later write, 'are: 1. Absence of lengthy verbiage of a political-social-economic nature; 2. total objectivity; 3. truthful descriptions of persons and objects; 4. extreme brevity; 5. audacity and originality . . . and; 6. compassion.' The first five principles cleanse and desensitize our wounds. But it is the last—compassion—that moves us beyond numbness toward healing.

I BLAME THE TOPIC SENTENCE

In recent years, I have heard Ira Glass, the host of the public radio show 'This American Life', tell audiences during interviews and speeches that the two basic building blocks of a story are the anecdote and a moment of reflection explaining what it all means. In other words, the most satisfying structure for a story has a simple pattern: action followed by summary, action followed by summary.... The purpose of the anecdote is to draw the listener into the action, and the point of the summary is to tell the listener why the story is being told in the first place. I find this insight as important as his crucial insistence that it takes a lot of time and volume of work to be good at what you are doing. Or that those who are doing creative work have good taste, and that it is this taste that tells the beginner that the work isn't satisfactory yet.* This is what I have learned from the best stories in 'This American Life': To keep the listener interested, the action ought to be surprising, but as much as the action or the event that is being narrated, the thought being communicated ought to be surprising too. Everything need not be stated or explained in the very first paragraph, the way academic writers are supposed to lay out when explaining the intent of their essays. Why are dull stories told, without a compelling plot or structure? Ira Glass believes he knows who is responsible. He says, 'I blame the topic sentence.'** The topic sentence is the

*Watch online the Daniel Sax video presenting Ira Glass's advice to beginners: https://www.brainpickings.org/2014/01/29/ira-glass-success-daniel-sax/

**Charles Bernstein, *Content's Dream: Essays 1975-1984*, Chicago: Northwestern

opening in the paragraph where we routinely set forth our purpose: 'In this paper I will assess the limits and possibilities of land revenue reforms introduced by Sher Shah Suri.' Let go of the topic sentence! Throw it away. Try to start in the middle of the action. Find a new form. Here is the poet Charles Bernstein mocking the old conventions of academic writing: 'Topic sentence. However; but; as a result. Blah, blah, blah. It follows from this. Concluding sentence.'

University Press, 2001, p. 25.

IN PRAISE OF NON-FICTION

If you want to avoid stale academic language or dull prose that has no qualities of voice or personality, you will need to develop the habit of wide reading. I encourage my students to read as well as write non-fiction. Good non-fiction does not make a fetish of difficulty.* I teach undergraduates at an American college and in my non-fiction courses over the past several years I have chosen my titles from a list like the one below. (If I were teaching a similar course in India I would include books by Romila Thapar, Ashis Nandy, Arundhati Roy, Ramachandra Guha, Sunil Khilnani, Nandini Sundar, Akshaya Mukul, Mukul Kesavan, Samanth Subramanian and Snigdha Poonam.)

Svetlana Alexievich's *Voices from Chernobyl* or *Secondhand Time*, to think about how to record human voices and shape them into indelible narratives; Sven Lindqvist's *A History of Bombing*, not only for its erudition, or its compressed histories, but its incredible structure; Eliot Weinberger's *What I Heard About Iraq*, for its

---

*In an old notebook from 2010, which I had kept while serving on a committee to judge a literary prize, I had copied down a quote by Martin Amis about other literary prizes: 'There was a great fashion in the last century, and it's still with us, of the unenjoyable novel… And these are novels which win prizes, because the committee thinks, "Well, it's not at all enjoyable, and it isn't funny, therefore it must be very serious."' Academics often behave in a way similar to the committees that Amis has in mind—if the book is serious, and the writing is difficult to read, it must be saying something good and meaningful. A banal statement worth repeating: I don't think difficult writing is necessarily good writing most of the time. I'm on the side of Amis when he tries to distinguish himself from writers of unenjoyable novels: 'I want to give the reader the best glass of wine I have, the best food in my kitchen.'

demonstration that rumour and reportage can be turned into criticism but also poetry; Janet Malcolm's *In the Freud Archives* or *The Journalist and the Murderer*, for their intelligent, lucid accounts of debates as well as conflicting narratives; John Berger's *The Success and Failure of Picasso*, for its insightful materialist reading of art; Stephen Greenblatt, *Will in the World*, for doing with Shakespeare what Berger had done with Picasso; Rebecca L. Skloot's *The Immortal Life of Henrietta Lacks* or Atul Gawande's *Being Mortal* as models for writing about science and pressing intersecting questions about social factors like racism or ageism; Katherine Boo's *Behind the Beautiful Forevers*, or Adrian Nicole LeBlanc's *Random Family*, or Suketu Mehta's *Maximum City*, for how to write about cities and families; Wayne Koestenbaum's *The Queen's Throat*, for its gorgeous language, yes, but also its candour, the ways in which it makes visible the author's passion and vulnerability; Heather Ann Thompson's *Blood in the Water*, for its comprehensive, compelling account of a fight for justice; Ibram X. Kendi's *Stamped from the Beginning*, for its rigorous, riveting intellectual history of racism in America; Kevin Young's *Bunk* for an examination of how hoaxes and counterfeits were long a part of American culture before the rise of Trump; any of the books by Elaine Scarry or Susan Stewart or Daniel Mendelsohn or Fred Moten for well-written, mobile, interdisciplinary studies of art, or poetry, or music.* And titles by Susan Sontag, Edward

*Svetlana Alexievich, translated by Keith Gessen, *Voices from Chernobyl: The Oral History of a Nuclear Disaster*, New York: Dalkey Press Archives, 2005.

———, translated by Bela Shayevich, *Secondhand Time: The Last of the Soviets*, New York: Random House, 2016.

Sven Lindqvist, *A History of Bombing*, New York: New Press, 2003.

Eliot Weinberger, *What I Heard About Iraq*, New York: Verso, 2005.

Janet Malcolm, *In the Freud Archives*, New York: NYRB Classics, 2002.

———, *The Journalist and the Murderer*, New York: Vintage, 1990.

John Berger, *The Success and Failure of Picasso* (first published in 1958), New York: Vintage, 1993.

Stephen Greenblatt, *Will in the World*, New York: W.W. Norton, 2004.

Rebecca L. Skloot, *The Immortal Life of Henrietta Lacks*, New York: Crown, 2010.

Said, Saidiya Hartman, Maggie Nelson, Matthew Desmond, David Shields and others, all mentioned elsewhere in this book.

Atul Gawande, *Being Mortal*, New York: Metropolitan Books, 2014.
Katherine Boo, *Behind the Beautiful Forevers*, New York: Random House, 2012.
Adrian Nicole LeBlanc, *Random Family: Love, Drugs, Trouble, and Coming of Age in the Bronx*, New York: Scribner, 2003.
Suketu Mehta, *Maximum City: Bombay Lost and Found;* New Delhi: Penguin Books India, 2004.
Wayne Keostenbaum, *The Queen's Throat: Opera, Homosexuality, and the Mystery of Desire*, New York: Vintage Books, 1994.
Heather Ann Thompson, *Blood in the Water: The Attica Prison Uprising of 1971 and Its Legacy*, New York: Pantheon, 2016.
Ibram X. Kendi, *Stamped from the Beginning: The Definitive History of Racist Ideas in America*, New York: Nation Books, 2016.
Kevin Young, *Bunk*, Minneapolis: Graywolf Press, 2017.

THE SCENE OF WRITING

Annie Dillard's *The Writing Life*; Ursula Le Guin's *Steering the Craft*; Anne Lamott's *Bird by Bird*; Stephen King's *On Writing*; Rainer Marie Rilke's *Letters to a Young Poet*. These are just some of the books I have used in my classes, or have relied upon to find help for my own writing—but I know of no books like these for *academic writers*. (I'm not comfortable with that phrase. We are all writers. My point is that all of us in academia, especially those in the humanities, ought to think of ourselves as writers and of our writing as creative and imaginatively structured or patterned.)* Distinguished academics don't usually write rich accounts of their writing life. You might get assorted guide-books on how to publish your dissertation, or even manuals about how to write more, but I cannot think of a single title by an academic scholar that, like the books I mention above, is at once a memoir of a writing practice, an artistic manifesto, and a letter on methodology and form addressed to younger scholars. Even in the case of an academic like Edward Said, author of *Orientalism* and several other classic works of scholarship, most of what we know about his judgements on style is extrapolated from what he writes about others. Said was someone who probably wrote hundreds of thousands of words in the mainstream press and gave countless interviews to journalists. And yet, why is it rare to find accounts where Said is explaining

*Which is to say, this isn't a book narrowly about creative writing. As Junot Diaz said during a reading at Vassar College, 'There is more advice for creative writers than there is porn.'

how he came to write *Orientalism*, or how he found the structure for *After the Last Sky*, and why there is so little about his growth as a writer in his memoir, *Out of Place*?*

Maggie Nelson's *The Argonauts*, published in 2015, is emblematic of a shift that has long been underway in academic writing.** Winner of the National Book Critics Circle Award for criticism, *The Argonauts* represents the triumphant, even celebratory, search for an adequate form to mix critical theory with personal experience. Endlessly self-reflexive, Nelson returns the reader again and again to the scene of writing, and in doing this, she achieves a hybrid form that makes nearly transparent how language, and mind, and bodies, not to mention, bodies in transition, are linked.*** I had begun writing this book long before *The Argonauts* was published; in my book, I knew I was calling for a particular kind of writing, a writing that felt out of place in academia but was so compelling that it created a new space for its kind inside academia; the experience of reading *The Argonauts* was to find not only that possibility realized but *expanded*.****

---

* Edward Said, *Orientalism*, New York: Pantheon, 1978. (I recommend the documentary *Edward Said: On Orientalism*, directed by Sut Jhally, produced by Media Education Foundation, 1998, 40 mins. ISBN: 1-893521-46-X.)

——, *After the Last Sky: Palestinian Lives*. With photographs by Jean Mohr. New York: Pantheon, 1985, 1986.

——, *Out of Place: A Memoir*, New York: Knopf, 2000. (Said was enormously engaged, of course, with the question of a writer's fashioning of both a craft and a writing self. He was also alert to the relation that the individual has to larger social and historical forces, the latter providing a more powerful explanation for the drift of small destinies. Said's very first book attests this understanding. See Said, *Joseph Conrad and the Fiction of Autobiography*, Cambridge: Harvard University Press, 1966.)

**Maggie Nelson, *The Argonauts*, Minneapolis: Graywolf Press, 2015.

***At one point, Nelson writes in *The Argonauts*: 'I have never really thought of myself as a "creative person"—writing is my only talent, and writing has always felt more clarifying than creative to me. But in contemplating this definition, I wonder if one might be creative (or queer, or happy, or held) *in spite of* oneself.'

****In an interview, Nelson admitted that she has yet to come to terms with the great success of *The Argonauts*: 'Like so many of my books, it was turned down initially by people [i.e.

Maggie Nelson's word for *The Argonauts* is 'autotheory', a mix of autobiography and critical theory.* Often, writers fail at autobiography because experience is presented as complete fact; in Nelson's case, there is a great deal of instability in the experience of experience. And uncertainty. The theory that enters the conversation isn't at all a parade of arid abstractions. Instead, the thinking that takes place is a struggle to make sense of bodies and our social selves. Every intimate detail that is offered is never *not* an item for thoughtful parsing. I found this as remarkable as the fact that Nelson brings a great deal of clarity and passion to the page, her sentences swerving from the colloquial to philosophical in dazzling turns. In a context where she is discussing 'transitioning', Nelson writes: 'How to explain, in a culture frantic for resolution, that sometimes the shit stays messy?'** One of the great appeals of Nelson's brand of 'autotheory' is how this commitment to keeping it messy makes for the most open and generous, and also honest, articulation of what it means to perform critical labour.

~

publishers] saying it was too academic. It certainly wasn't intended as what people call a "crossover". But I've always believed that, in a way, you invent your own readers—and that people can read more complicated books than they're given credit for.' See Rachel Cooke, 'Maggie Nelson: There Is No Catharsis… The Stories We Tell Ourselves Don't Heal Us', *The Guardian*, 21 May 2017.

*In an earlier interview, Nelson had said that the term comes from her reading of Paul Preciado's *Testo Junkie*. See 'Riding the Blinds: Micah McCrary interviews Maggie Nelson', *Los Angeles Review of Books*, 26 April 2015. My favourite part of the interview is Maggie Nelson's response to a question about her audience. The interviewer remarks that her work reaches out 'to a demographic that is neither strictly mainstream nor academic', and Nelson says: 'I don't aim to bridge any gap, but if the writing does so, that's cool. I write in the idioms that are most native and compelling to me. Probably my writing is too mainstream for some and too academic for others; that doesn't bother me. I would be more bothered if I thought I fell prey to *the most deadening aspects of either or both…*' (Emphasis added)

***The Argonauts*. See p. 53.

THE END OF THE LINE

In the opening pages of *The Writing Life*, Annie Dillard urges the writer to discard what doesn't belong in a book.* Cut it. Is it only the beginning that you must cut? No, Dillard is saying, you begin with the beginning. But anything else can also go, including what had appeared to be the best, the very reason for your thinking about writing the book. Why does Dillard deliver this harsh lesson on detachment in her opening pages? I think she is trying to say that the writer is not important, what is important is the work, the book in progress.

The Writing Life is a slim book that mixes observations on writing with lyrical, evocative descriptions of places where Dillard has done her writing. The exhortations to subscribe to a schedule or to deal with the problem of structure are tied to startling anecdotes of encounters with nature. The book ends with a truly lovely elegy to a stunt pilot and the transcendence of his improvised art in the air. The pilot, a few months before the tragic accident that killed him, had told Dillard that he thought of air as a line. 'This end of the line, that end of the line—like a rope.... I get a rhythm going and stick with it.' The lesson that the pilot, Dave Rahm, offered Dillard was a new idea of beauty. So, all of this is to say that the way I see Dillard has organized *The Writing Life* is to begin with anecdotes on routine and craft but end with an intense, if elegiac, tribute to a daredevil artist who forced her to imagine a new art.

---

*Annie Dillard, *The Writing Life*, New York: HarperPerennial, 1989, 1990.

CREATIVE CRITICISM

I want to begin where Annie Dillard ended, with an example of an unnerving improvisatory performer.

Geoff Dyer's *Out of Sheer Rage* is an exhilarating book because it is so full of despair. Academics ought to like it. At least I did. Here was a book that started by declaring the writer's desire to begin 'a sober, academic study of D.H. Lawrence' and, in the same breath, expressed astonishment at such an ambition as well as its misrecognition of the 'psychological disarray' that lay beneath it.* *Out of Sheer Rage* is a book whose winning conceit is that it is about the inability to write a book. It enacts an artful, not to mention very funny, deferral. However, as we follow in Dyer's footsteps as he journeys distractedly to all the different countries where Lawrence the writer had lived, we acquire knowledge about Lawrence and his writings, his views on money, the search for inner peace (Lawrence was opposed to it—'I prefer my strife infinitely, to other people's peace, haven, and heavens'), the crimes of nineteenth-century industrialism, his knowledge of the names of trees, and even his love for giving directions. We see in this Dyer's cunning: even in seemingly avoiding Lawrence, he gives us Lawrence. He writes at one point that Lawrence took 'the imaginative line in all his criticism' and as his readers we recognize that this judgement holds true also for the book in our hands.

At first, I thought Dyer was only procrastinating. It is an

*Geoff Dyer, *Out of Sheer Rage: Wrestling with D. H. Lawrence*, New York: North Point, 1998.

impulse I can easily identify with. There are pages in *Out of Sheer Rage* where he goes on and on about whatever he is doing with his girlfriend. On a gorgeous Greek island, for example. It was all so beautiful on the island that Dyer was actually finding things hellish. We also learn that 'Lawrence wasn't too keen on islands either'. Dyer's account of his days on the island, where he was *not* working on his study of Lawrence, was given over to a detailed description of an accident he suffered while riding on a moped. In fact, there were several such passages, digressive, dilatory, going on at length about the conditions under which writing got accomplished, or, more accurately, avoided. Why was Dyer doing this? It seems counterintuitive to say this but we got so much of him rather than Lawrence because he wanted Lawrence *whole*. Or he wanted him in a particular way. He wanted Lawrence 'in the original, as it were, without quotation marks'. He had no taste for a version of Lawrence that could be found in 'one of the hundreds of critical studies of him'. There we have it! Dyer's extraordinary, even extreme, reaction against a common kind of academic criticism—the 'stacks and stacks of books on Lawrence by academics' that 'form the basis of literary study in universities and none of them has anything to do with literature'.

Pages given over to kvetching about the placid beauty of the sea or the traffic near the Ikea in Lawrence country have given way to pages of irascible, impatient ranting against academe. Dyer rails against the language of theory that has 'become more of an orthodoxy than the style of study it sought to overthrow'. His complaint against what he calls the 'state-of-the-fart theorists' and other academics is a blend of hysteria and hilarity: 'That is the hallmark of academic criticism: it kills everything it touches. Walk around a university campus and there is an almost palpable sense of death about the place because hundreds of academics are busy killing everything they touch.' Instead of academic criticism, what Dyer wants is prose wherein 'the distinction between imaginative and critical writing disappears'. His examples are poets writing about other poets (Auden's elegy for Yeats, Brodsky's elegy for Auden, Heaney's elegy for Brodsky). Once, I heard Dyer say that when he was in his third year at Oxford, he was in a class studying Shakespeare's *Julius Caesar*. Dyer and his classmates were reading critical essays on the play—'sometimes interesting, sometimes quite dull'—and quite by chance he happened upon Roy Fuller's poem, 'The Ides of March'. The poem takes the form of a monologue spoken by Brutus. It is a commentary on the play but it is also imbued with its atmosphere. Dyer recited from memory several lines in the voice of Brutus—'...about / To select from several complex panaceas, / Like a shy man confronted with a box / Of chocolates, the plainest after all'—and added that the poem had offered him 'the first glimpse' of creative criticism. Till then, conscious only of the gap between criticism and literature, he felt the gap shrinking and realized that one could construct something that was a commentary as well as a work of art in itself.

So much for Dyer's examples; my own example of course is Dyer himself. And *Out of Sheer Rage* is—well, I hesitate to say exemplary because Dyer's books are quite unlike each other—a fine instance of what I see as his effort to close the gap between the pleasure of reading Lawrence and the pleasure of reading critical commentary on his work. Dyer's success at merging the idea of the critical and creative, or the imaginative and the commentary, following in the footsteps of idols like John Berger, is partly the function of writing as a fan.

An essay by Dyer on Nietzsche, written for *The Guardian* newspaper in 2011, and only a little over three hundred words long, is among the finest 'My hero' essays I've come across. The essay is pleasurable not least because of its immediacy—Dyer's language giving the sensation of directly encountering Nietzsche's thought and even his life. The writer isn't too anxious about displaying his learning, but he doesn't hide it either. His passion is evident on the page.* (One evening, after a meeting with Annie Dillard at a literary festival, Dyer told me that he had 'one of the biggest literary crushes on Dillard…in a lifetime dominated by literary crushes'. He went on to say that, as with Berger, there was in Dillard 'an easy traffic between the sensual and the cerebral'. Wasn't this true of Dyer too?) But this feeling of being a fan, celebrating a love of literature or art or cinema, isn't necessarily reverential. Dyer's book on Tarkovsky's *Stalker* has as its epigraph a line from Albert Camus: 'After all, the best way of talking about what you love is to speak of it lightly.'** Which is to say that there is no contradiction between a piece of writing having a lightness and also, at the same time, a depth to it. This lightness, even irreverence, the move away from solemnity while achieving insight, is a part of Dyer's charm. His candour is striking, and so is his consistent crankiness: those are the qualities that, in Dyer at least, tell you that something more profound, and perverse, is at play. It is an added bonus that his crankiness is brought out by the absurd practices of academics. Here, as an example, are the opening lines of his inaugural column in the *New York Times Book Review*:

> In this column I want to look at a not uncommon way of writing and structuring books. This approach, I will argue, involves the writer announcing at the outset what he or she will be doing in the pages that follow. The default format of academic research papers and textbooks, it serves the dual purpose of enabling the reader to skip to the bits that are of particular interest and—in keeping with the prerogatives of scholarship—preventing an authorial personality from intruding on the material being presented.***

---

*Geoff Dyer, 'My Hero: Friedrich Nietzsche', *The Guardian*, 4 February 2011.

**———, *Zona: A Book About a Film About a Journey to a Room*, New York: Vintage, 2012.

***———, 'An Academic Author's Unintentional Masterpiece', *New York Times Book Review*, 22 July 2012.

No lengthy introductory paragraphs, then, explaining what this book is about.* Instead, a fan letter to Geoff Dyer, and to many others, in the pages that follow. One more thing. I've long admired and taught in my classes the work of Susan Sontag. She is another writer who blurred the lines between the critical and the creative. Sontag had many qualities that made her a special kind of intellectual: a broad reach, a sense of aesthetics to match the avowed politics, a distrust of received opinion, the precision of language, and the ability, or need, to cultivate inwardness. I am a fan. I keep a photo of her in my study. Here is Terry Castle's description of this image which apparently also serves as her screensaver: 'The most beautiful photo I downloaded was one that Peter Hujar took of her in the 1970s, around the time of *I, Et Cetera*. She's wearing a thin grey turtleneck and lies on her back—arms up, head resting on her clasped hands and her gaze fixed impassively on something to the right of the frame. There's a slightly pedantic quality to the whole thing which I like: very true to life. Every few hours now she floats up onscreen in this digitized format, supine, sleek and flat-chested.'** I don't have the picture in the original print form either. I had found the picture some years ago spread across a page of the *New York Times*, in a review of an exhibition at the Guggenheim, if memory serves. I was reading the paper when my daughter, who must have been three then, came up to my study and demanded that I buy her a tank top. A tank top? The photograph of Sontag's that I have kept in my study is from that same page in the *Times*, which I cut and turned into a paper tank top for my daughter.

---

*I want to insert here a line credited to philosopher Jonathan Wolff: 'A detective novel written by an academic would begin: "In this novel I shall show that the butler did it."' Cited in Helen Sword, *Stylish Academic Writing*, Cambridge: Harvard University Press, 2012. See pp. 79-80.

**Terry Castle, 'Desperately Seeking Susan', *London Review of Books*, 17 March 2005, Vol. 27 No. 6. 17-20.

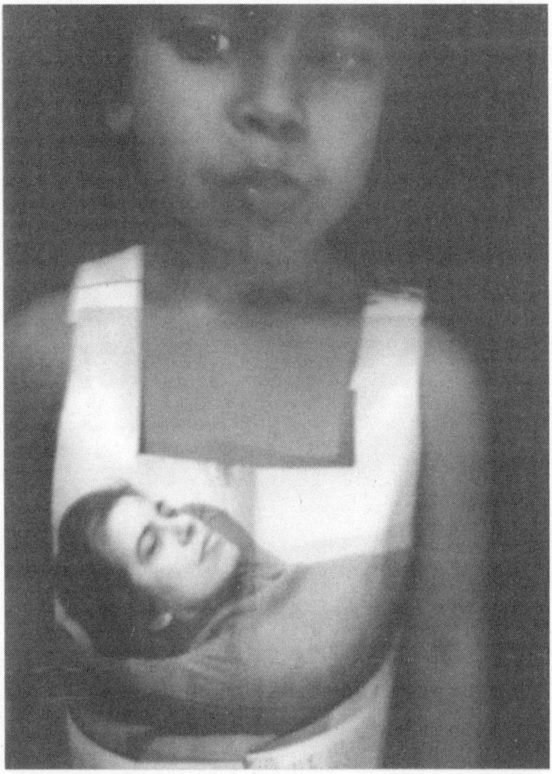

II

Credos

EYES ON THE GROUND

A friend, who might well be the most prolific academic writer I know, sent a note saying he was looking for a new job. He found his commute to and from work exhausting. Would I be one of his referees? I wrote back saying yes and added that I'd have to admit in my letter that I hadn't—and not that anyone else had either, not even my friend himself—read everything he had written.

A few hours later, my friend sent me a link to a video on YouTube in which the Japanese auteur Akira Kurosawa had been asked to give advice to young, aspiring filmmakers.* (In the video, the interviewer looked old. Kurosawa looked even older. The words came out of him in a flow, rubbed smooth by the experience of a lifetime of making art.) If you genuinely want to make films, he said, you ought to write screenplays. *Writing is key*. Then he quoted Balzac who said that for writers the most essential thing was 'the forbearance to face the dull task of writing one word at a time'.** And here Kurosawa slipped into a story. He said that Balzac's output was 'staggering' and we would be unable to finish reading it in a lifetime. Do you know how he wrote, Kurosawa asked the interviewer. Balzac would 'scribble along and then send it off to the printer right away'; once the printed pages were returned to him, Balzac made changes, revising 'until very little of the original writing remained'. The revised pages were then sent back to the printer. This method allowed Balzac to produce so much, Kurosawa

---

*https://www.youtube.com/watch?v=r-McmgQbee0 Accessed on 22 March 2017.

**Needless to say, I'm reminding myself of this advice as I work on this book.

was saying, and this might be what my friend was trying to tell me about his prolific writing. Kurosawa goes on to offer the example also of the great Japanese filmmaker Mikio Naruse whose writing was partial, quick, improvisatory. Once again, the point of the story is to experience a kind of liberation, if not also joy, in the act of writing that has been made nearly effortless by habit.*

Later in the video, Kurosawa laments, as he is no doubt entitled to do, that young people these days do not have the patience for the slog, the tedium of slow labour, the long wait for the end to come. He offers this useful advice: 'When you go mountain climbing, the first thing you're told is not to look at the peak but to keep your eyes on the ground as you climb. You just keep climbing patiently one step at a time. If you keep looking at the top you'll get frustrated. I think writing is similar. You need to get used to the task of writing.'

*The writer Jennifer Egan, author of *A Visit from the Goon Squad*, offered the following mantra during a visit to Vassar College: 'Write often. Write badly. Fix it.' During an interview, she told me: 'To me I think the biggest thing is to make writing enough of a habit that it feels like second nature to do it, rather than second nature *not* to do it. And so what I'll often advise is that people start with a very small amount of time or number of pages or words that they're requiring of themselves so it's not overwhelming, but enough to work it into part of a daily rhythm, and then to try to slowly expand it. I think that's the most important thing and then the corollary of that is that you have to be willing not to judge yourself as you do it, because it's just not fair or possible to require regularity and top quality. It doesn't happen in reality.' It isn't terribly relevant here but I just want to slip in the additional detail that Egan said that 'there's no better major you can have' than an English major. Egan majored in English at the University of Pennsylvania.

DECLARATIONS OF INDEPENDENCE

My friend Jeff Williams, then editor of *minnesota review*, asked several critics for essays that explained their 'critical credo'. The piece I wrote was called 'Declarations of Independence' and it described my attraction to academic writing and my rebellion against it.* I was also painting myself as a figure in outline against the backdrop of a stifling academic culture. More importantly, the essay identified the different kinds of unconventional, often inventive, scholarly writing that I admired. I had put a photocopy of this essay on the bar counter one evening at an MLA convention in San Francisco. This was during a meeting with my editor, Ken Wissoker, who, after one or two sips of his Campari and soda, suggested that I write a short book on academic style. You are holding that book in your hand—and this is my critical credo:

I'm in an overheated hotel room in Beijing, reading a *New Yorker* travel piece about China by Jonathan Franzen.** The essay is describing the ecological devastation caused by rapid development, but what stops me is a remark that Franzen makes about his Chinese guide. David Xu has 'the fashionably angular eyeglasses and ingratiating eagerness of an untenured literature professor'. In that throwaway phrase, in its quick malice and wit, I come home. Whether this is revealing of the traveller's loneliness abroad or not, I find myself thinking that I belong not to India or to the United

---

*Amitava Kumar, 'Declarations of Independence', *minnesota review* 71 (2008).

**Jonathan Franzen, 'The Way of the Puffin', *New Yorker*, 21 April 2008, 90-105. The quote appears on p. 92.

States but to the academy. I realize that I'm a sad provincial; for years, I've been living in a place called the English Department.*

Our relationship, as the cliché would have it, is complicated. The most significant turns in my scholarship, and in my writing, have been attempts to first fit into, and then violently move away from, the existing codes of naturalization for gaining citizenship in the English Department. Of late, this movement of mine has appeared very much like a person lurching away from an accident—for anyone who has just arrived at the scene it is impossible to judge exactly where the screams are coming from, but what is undeniable is the fact of the twisted wreckage and the smoke and the shock.

'Haven't you noticed how we all specialize in what we hate most?' This is the question posed by James Dixon, the protagonist of *Lucky Jim* by Kingsley Amis. If there is abjection and fine defeatist humour there, it gets even better towards the end of the novel when Dixon is getting ready for his public lecture and quickly getting incapacitated with drink. In the course of his climactic, doomed lecture, our anti-hero will have proven himself unfit for the teaching profession and, more happily, drawn the approval of a rich patron who will offer him suitable employment in faraway London. But before this happens, while in conversation with said patron, Dixon declares:

> I'm the boredom-detector. I'm a finely-tuned instrument. If only I could get hold of a millionaire I'd be worth a bag of money to him. He could send me on ahead into dinners and cocktail-parties and night-clubs, just for five minutes, and then by looking at me he'd be able to read off the boredom-coefficient of any gathering. Like a canary

*But you, dear reader, it is quite possible, do not carry the same passport. You left the shores of academe long ago. You should skip reading the rest of this chapter. For those in your position, I have supplied a different set of credos articulated in a brief interview with PEN. Please see Appendix B.

> down a mine; same idea. Then he'd know whether it was worth going in himself or not. He could send me in among the Rotarians and the stage crowd and the golfers and the arty types talking about statements of profiles rather than volumes and the musical...*

We know from Dixon's experience—and sadly, our own—how this talent for discerning boredom is the result only of a long intimacy with it. An intimacy nurtured over countless departmental meetings, lectures, corridor conversations, numbing conferences, not to mention attendance at academic parties, where neurotics are nearly as numerous as blowhards.

You'd think there would be regular revolts against this culture of oppression. But we hardly witness any institutional uprisings. A few novels written about poisonous campus life, sure, but no prison breaks. In fact, going by what I have seen at the places where I have worked, it is more common to see the formerly oppressed slip easily into the role of the new, coercive jailers. The behaviour of some of my coercive colleagues in a department where I worked was regularly explained away as only the result of 'past wounds' inflicted during the process of acquiring tenure.

But I digress. I was talking about boredom. One of the things that can be said about much of postcolonial criticism is that it is boring, although it'd be more accurate to say that it is often unintelligible *and* boring. However, when I arrived in this country, in the late eighties, and read postcolonial critics for the first time, I was intrigued. They seemed such a welcome change from my teachers in Delhi. As an undergraduate at Hindu College, I would take a bus to the university. I'd look out of the window, and when we were crossing the gates of Nigambodh Ghat, I'd sometimes see men carrying in their arms little bundles wrapped in white. Each bundle was a child whose corpse was being taken to the river by

*Kingsley Amis, *Lucky Jim*, New York: Penguin, 1992, p. 215. (First published in 1953.)

the father. A small mute procession would follow some men, but often a man would be alone with his enormous burden. I would watch for a few moments from the bus—and then I'd arrive in class. My professors would be delivering lectures on Locke or Rousseau from notes held together with tape—the yellowing paper would flake off in little pieces when shaken in the air.

The pedagogical climate appeared dramatically different when I came to the US. In this country, I suddenly felt that criticism was something that was both fresh and live. My teachers were the critics whose writings one read in academic journals. What I was being taught was original work. In some classes, such work also felt urgent. I had never read Edward Said before, or others whose names brought them somehow closer to me in my imagination, critics like Homi Bhabha and Gayatri Chakravorty Spivak. But I didn't share the belief, seemingly dear to the editors of special issues devoted to postcolonial theory, that the 3.2 million poor in Chiapas or the half-million beggars in Calcutta hungered to read debates between the elite of New York and New Delhi in the pages of scholarly journals. My indifferent education in Delhi meant that I hadn't received any real training in writing, academic or otherwise. But it became clear to me, as the years passed, that I wanted the words I wrote on the page to be worldly, sensual, even personal. I was trying to make postcolonial theory look more like what the larger world associated with postcolonials like Salman Rushdie. Couldn't our analyses become more exuberant, imaginative, and even playful? I wanted very badly to be a writer, and any writer needs readers, but it seemed impossible that postcolonial theorists would ever acquire a real audience.

A part of the search for readers is a search for venues that will publish you. I was fortunate to receive valuable support from small journals like the *minnesota review*. As a beginning assistant professor, I published in its pages one or two critical pieces but also poems, photographs, and even a bit of doggerel verse written on the evening of Princess Di's death. And during those years, the journal's editors, Jeff Williams and also Mike Hill, collaborated with me in several discussions about academics and intellectuals who wrote for a wider public. While this was an often repetitive, and even self-congratulatory, exercise on our part, it also represented a demand for legitimation, and a search for a broader argument on behalf of a brand of writing that would earn us, if not hordes of readers, then at least tenure.

I'm talking of events that occurred two decades ago. The book that earned me tenure was *Passport Photos*, a multi-genre report on what has been called immigritude.* The book was published at a time when not only postcolonial theory but the entire enterprise of pure theory was beginning to lose its hegemony. I was very much aware that there were no *people* in postcolonial theory, and I tried to put in my book details of ordinary lives, including photographs and poetry about migrants. Tenure should have freed me to pursue more unconventional writing, but I have never again attempted the formal experimentation of *Passport Photos*. What tenure really allowed me to do was to quietly settle into the habit of writing what, till recently, I would have considered unexciting because it wasn't fragmentary or hybrid and relied on narrative, the style more associated with memoirs and long-form journalism.

In this turn toward more old-fashioned writing, I was helped by the emergence of a new, younger body of Indian writers who were just then making their mark in India as well as abroad. I'm talking now of the latter part of the nineties and names like Arundhati Roy, Pankaj Mishra, Amit Chaudhuri, Raj Kamal Jha, and Jhumpa Lahiri. I remember reading these writers and experiencing a great deal of excitement; I made an effort to get in touch with them, and some of these writers also became my friends. It couldn't have happened overnight, but in those days it seemed as if this single fact had

*Amitava Kumar, *Passport Photos*, Berkeley: University of California Press, 2000.

allowed me to escape the small world of the English Department. For years, I had not read a single novel; now I began to read fiction written by both well-known and emerging Indian writers. This was also the time when the Internet arrived and, suddenly, the Indian newspapers I was reading were no longer two weeks old. This meant that the new fiction I was devouring no longer seemed to be reporting on an impossibly distant country. Cricket matches, riots, the deaths of politicians, murders as well as mergers, the release of Bollywood films, literary gossip, everything that was happening in India acquired an immediacy again. It became easy for me to write for the Indian newspapers and magazines that I was regularly reading on the Web. 'Location, location, location' sounds very much like a postcolonial mantra, but it has amazed me how profoundly a writer's sense of the world, and also of fellowship, has been transformed by the emergence of the World Wide Web. You can be working at a disgustingly badly-paid job in an acrimonious English Department at the University of Florida, but when you sit down at the computer and are able to file a story for a newspaper in India, a story that will appear in its published form on your screen only a few hours later, it becomes easy to imagine that you have escaped your immediate setting.

A few years prior to the period I've been just describing, I had read an article by Frank Lentricchia that had been published in the now-defunct journal *Lingua Franca*. Lentricchia's essay, which was entitled 'Last Will and Testament of an Ex-Literary Critic', was an odd, slippery text.* One moment it seemed to be arguing against overly political literary criticism, but just when you were expecting an elaboration of an alternative literary approach, Lentricchia slipped into a more vociferous railing against the incompetence of all literary critics. In the end, you could forgive the essay's incoherence because

*Frank Lentricchia, 'Last Will and Testament of an Ex-Literary Critic', *Lingua Franca*, September/October 1996.

the argument Lentricchia was putting forward was against any system or method of literary appreciation. All one could hope to do, and all that Lentricchia himself wanted to do, was become a worshipper of great literature.

But this was not my aim. Unlike Lentricchia, I still had much to learn. About theory and criticism, and also about literature and the world. I didn't see myself reading the Indian writers I liked without exercising my judgement, and I certainly didn't want to write while pretending that I was in some kind of a trance. For good or bad, I was still very much a part of the academy.

The best allies I found in developing a language of reading—not only texts but also people and places—were academics from my field, or fields close to mine, who were writing long narrative pieces as well as books that mixed memoir and analysis.

One of my earliest models was Manthia Diawara's *In Search of Africa*.* It was an inventive book and yet it performed the old task of storytelling. In the book, Diawara goes back to Guinea looking for his childhood friend, and this search, spanning over the course of the entire book, becomes a way of introducing the reader to everything from the legacy of the dictator Sekou Touré to the traditional arts of the griots and mask-makers. Diawara also exercised an additional fascination over me because I had tried my hand at documentary photography for several years, and Diawara was making documentaries about Africa. In a wonderful example of counter-anthropology, he had made a film called *Rouch in Reverse* about the classic French filmmaker Jean Rouch. Even *In Search of Africa* was actually the result of a documentary project of the same name. In elegant essays on photography, particularly in his studies of West African photographers like Seydou Keita and Malick Sidibé, Diawara would offer a language that I had wanted to use for so long. He wrote simply and yet with sensuous precision. Equally

*Manthia Diawara, *In Search of Africa*, Cambridge, MA: Harvard University Press, 1998.

important, departing from the kind of sour, astringent critique that quickly becomes second nature to academic critics, Diawara celebrated the practice of art. He found joy in the work of street photographers, and his writing eloquently communicated that joy to the reader. After a decade of metacritical discourse about 'the constructedness of culture', it was refreshing to find in Diawara a sophisticated but honest search for authenticity and the good life. When I finished reading *In Search of Africa*, I couldn't wait to begin writing about Hindi poets struggling in obscurity, or the Indian novelists that I admired, and even the Bollywood filmmakers I had adored since childhood.

There were also other writers from inside academia who helped me give shape to a narrative voice. The names that readily come to mind are Amitav Ghosh (*In An Antique Land*),* Michael Taussig (*The Nervous System*),** and Edward Said (*Out of Place*). But perhaps the example that meant the most, and which I also offered to my students as a model, was *Dreambirds* by Rob Nixon.*** As a graduate student, I had read Nixon in the pages of the *Village Voice* and *The Nation*, and later still I pored over his magisterial book on V.S. Naipaul. But in *Dreambirds*, which came out in 1999, Nixon successfully enacted the turn I had been practising in the privacy of my room, the transformation of the critic into a memoirist and travel-writer. Brilliantly using the ostrich and its migration across history and continents, Nixon had produced a book that was as much a rich cultural history of capitalism as it was a deeply affecting memoir about his own South African childhood.

Later, when offering a course for graduate students that I had entitled 'Top Ten Reasons for Doing Cultural Studies', I used Nixon's *Dreambirds* as a prime example. Apart from some of the books

*Amitav Ghosh, *In An Antique Land*, New York: Vintage, 1994.

**Michael Taussig, *The Nervous System*, New York: Routledge, 1991.

***Rob Nixon, *Dreambirds: The Strange History of the Ostrich in Fashion, Food, and Fortune*, New York: Picador, 2000.

mentioned above, on the course list that semester were Michael Bérubé's *Life As We Know It*, Barbara Ehrenreich's *Nickle and Dimed*,* Susan Sontag's *Illness as Metaphor*,** and Alain de Botton's *How Proust Can Change Your Life*.*** These weren't all books by academics, nor were these the only books used in that course; but these titles most clearly represented what I wanted my students to attempt in their writing. Not simply the range from the journalistic to the philosophical, or from the overtly political to the very playful, but also the right mix of the personal and the public. God knows, I was trying my best to do the same. I had long complained that ideological certainties arrived at in seminar rooms needed to be replaced by the real, often contradictory, complexity of people's lives, and now I wrote narratives that relied a great deal on reportage. This turn towards journalism, in some instances resembling what Andrew Ross calls 'scholarly reporting', seemed to be the right response to the dead end of postcolonial theorizing.

In the face of a dead critical vocabulary, what was needed were works of imagination. I wanted writing that said clearly that there *is* no clean independence from anything. That, too, would be a sort of declaration of independence, I think.

That there is no escape into pure certainty or into some antiseptic haven of academic political correctness. That radical statements made at venues like the MLA Delegate Assembly falsely assume that bold posturing will change the profession and indeed the wider world. That, if we were more honest, there would be in what we say or do more self-questioning and doubt. And that our writing should express that condition. I'm putting this down, somewhat crudely and yet I realize that I should perhaps be doing a better job of it

---

*Barbara Ehrenreich, *Nickel and Dimed: On (Not) Getting by in America*. New York: Picador, 2011. First published in 2001.

**Susan Sontag, *Illness as Metaphor*, New York: Farrar, Straus and Giroux, 1978.

***Alain de Botton, *How Proust Can Change Your Life: Not a Novel*, New York: Pantheon, 1997.

because for some years now I've adopted this position as a credo.

This viewpoint is far better described in a passage in V. S. Naipaul's *A Bend in the River*. The narrator is an African of Indian origin; he is named Salim and runs a shop in a turbulent republic that resembles Zaire. One night Salim is attending a party at the home of a Western intellectual favoured by the country's dictator. Two or three couples are dancing in the tastefully darkened room. There is music playing, Joan Baez is singing 'Barbara Allen'. And then other songs. Here's how Naipaul describes the scene:

> Not all songs were like 'Barbara Allen'. Some were modern, about war and injustice and oppression and nuclear destruction. But always in between were the older, sweeter melodies. These were the ones I waited for, but in the end the voice linked the two kinds of song, linked the maidens and lovers and sad deaths of bygone times with the people of today who were oppressed and about to die.
>
> It was make believe—I never doubted that. You couldn't listen to sweet songs about injustice unless you expected justice and received it much of the time. You couldn't sing songs about the end of the world unless—like the other people in that room, so beautiful with such things: African mats on the floor and African hangings on the wall and spears and masks—you felt that the world was going on and you were safe in it. How easy it was, in that room, to make those assumptions!*

*V.S. Naipaul, *A Bend in the River*, New York: Vintage, 1989, pp. 128-29. First published in 1979.

NEITHER/NOR

One of the earliest clippings pasted in a notebook I kept while writing this book:

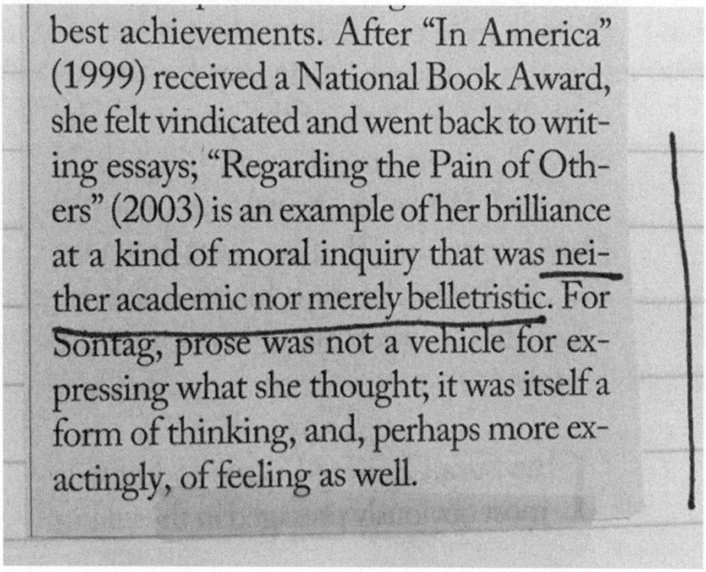

best achievements. After "In America" (1999) received a National Book Award, she felt vindicated and went back to writing essays; "Regarding the Pain of Others" (2003) is an example of her brilliance at a kind of moral inquiry that was neither academic nor merely belletristic. For Sontag, prose was not a vehicle for expressing what she thought; it was itself a form of thinking, and, perhaps more exactingly, of feeling as well.

So is that the ideal—to steer clear of the offending shores? The meagre choice between, on the one hand, what is stereotypically regarded as opaque, limited, and jargon-ridden, and, on the other, the seductions of narrow, overly formal, aesthetic concerns. I cannot now recall what I was thinking when I cut the above lines out of the magazine that I had been reading. It is possible I thought I'd present Sontag as a model; I've often taught *Regarding* *the Pain of Others* in my class on war. But reading those lines now I want to suggest, as an opening gesture, that one not think of either possibility as *fatal*. The rigid binarism of merely academic and merely belletristic is the condition of paralysis. Welcome to the zone of occult instability!*

Viet Thanh Nguyen's debut novel, *The Sympathizer*, won the Pulitzer Prize for fiction.** Nguyen is a writer and also a professor of ethnic studies. In an interview in *The Guardian*, Nguyen said that he had spent twenty years 'trying to bring together his academic scholarship and literary ambitions'.*** This interested me as much as his later remark during the same interview that the novel brought him closer to 'his ideal of writing criticism as fiction and fiction as criticism'. Around the same time as his Pulitzer win, Nguyen also published his non-fiction book, *Nothing Ever Dies: Vietnam and the Memory of War*, a finalist for the National Book Award.**** I asked Nguyen if the non-fiction book, too, published by a university press, was written in a style that was a departure from standard academic writing. Nguyen said:

I worked out many of the ideas for *Nothing Ever Dies* in

*A phrase I came across in a review I was reading decades ago and can't find anymore: 'blood on the bandage'. This was meant as a description of a writing that was fresh and newsy (in a good way). Immediacy, urgency, these have always appealed to me as qualities of good writing. The phrase also evokes for me the feeling of a provisional act. After all, the bandage that has blood seeping through it will soon have to be replaced. I think of clippings in my notebook as that kind of bandage. They hide—and reveal—wounds. They show that writing is both contingent (dependent on a chance encounter in a magazine's pages) and deliberative (rooted in an obsession or a considered idea).

**Viet Thanh Nguyen, *The Sympathizer*, New York: Grove Press, 2015.

***'Pulitzer winner Viet Thanh Nguyen: My book has something to offend everyone', *The Guardian*, 22 April 2016.

****Viet Thanh Nguyen, *Nothing Ever Dies: Vietnam and the Memory of War*, Cambridge, MA: Harvard University Press, 2016.

> academic articles, but when it came time to writing the book, I began from scratch. I wanted the book to have a narrative feeling, to tell a story, about the history and memory of this war and about my own personal story as a refugee, an American, and a scholar. So I incorporated flashes of my own autobiography as a refugee who became an American, a journey that is inseparable from the history and memory of war, and I charted my own evolving reactions to the texts and sites of memory that I read or visited. I hadn't deliberately set out to write a travel narrative while I visited these sites, but in writing the book, I did see that the experiences of my visits and the physical and emotional experiences of travelling to difficult places would be valuable in telling the story. Finally, I did also deploy a writerly care to rhythm, word choice, style, characterization (of myself and the people I met), emotion, and revelation. Hence the final story is one drawn from my own family history, as the ultimate expression of the emotion and revelation that I experienced in writing this book.

And what about the novel itself, *The Sympathizer*, in whose pages academic debates find dramatic expression? There is mention of Marx and the struggle over representation. In fact, there's even a reworking of Gayatri Spivak's reworking of Derrida when we read about white men saving good yellow people from bad yellow people. My question to Nguyen was whether he had followed a deliberate strategy to cleverly embed not just political but political-understood-as-theoretical issues into the novel. How hard was it to make this work? Here is his response:

> The political novel has a bad reputation in American literature. The ones that are about empirical politics—election campaigns, for example—aren't that interesting (to me) and may seem too topical in general. The ones that are explicitly theoretical, dealing, for example, with Marxism and labour,

can seem clunky and determined by the author's agenda. I wanted to write a political novel that was also exciting and fluid, and one that would foreground theory and find a way to express formally a concern with dialectics. Carlos Bulosan was a writer who tried to do the same thing in books like *America Is in the Heart* and *The Cry and the Dedication*, and while I found those works inspiring, I found them also to be a bit awkward formally. Do his books succeed? It depends on the definition of success. I wanted my book to succeed both in terms of putting these theoretical and political ideas out there and also to entertain the reader. How I did that was to devise a first person narrator who could be a believable spy and a believable critic. The success of the novel depends on whether the reader believes this one person can naturally say the things that he does.

CRITICISM BY OTHER MEANS

On the Acknowledgements page of *10:04*, Ben Lerner writes the following: 'The "Institute for Totaled Art" is modeled on Elka Krajewska's Salvage Art Institute; my description of the fictional version overlaps with my account of Krajewska's actual work in "Damage Control," an essay that appeared in *Harper's Magazine*.'* The main story here is not that a piece of text that had been published as non-fiction is reborn in the novel as fiction; instead, in Lerner's hand the novel is the capacious form that can assimilate diverse kinds of writing, in particular critical forms.

Lerner told me, 'Sometimes people say, Oh, that novel is an essay or it is very essayistic, and they mean it as a criticism, and I know what they mean, that it doesn't feel motivated in the life of a novel, but the novel for me has always been about a kind of frame for a series of essayistic investigations and digressions. I wrote my novels as ways of trying to imagine a nonprofessional criticism.' The novel for him had quite literally begun 'as a way of thinking through issues in poetics, poetry criticism in particular, and dramatizing encounters with poems and seeing how aesthetic ideas spread out in other domains of experience'.

Lerner also gave the example of art criticism. He said that that one of the great fictions about most art criticism is that it decontextualizes acts of viewing. And the remarkable thing about a novel is that you get to 'describe an encounter with a work of art after you've eaten a certain thing, or had your heart broken,

*Ben Lerner, *10:04*, New York: Faber and Faber, 2014. See pp. 243-44.

or passed a protest on the street or whatever'. Everything that a professional art discourse would tend to bracket becomes, in a novel, a part of a more robust description of what it means to deal with art. Also, as a novelist you have the freedom to manufacture your art object, you are not bound by art that already exists. This kind of invention is at play in *10:04*—some of the art works are real, but some others aren't, and the protagonist's discovery of them didn't always happen as described. The name Lerner gave to this mode of writing was 'science-fiction criticism'.

A few months before this conversation from which I'm quoting I spent a month in Marfa, Texas, on a Lannan Foundation writing residency. The house in which I was living makes an appearance in *10:04*. Lerner had also been a resident there. I was exhilarated by the address I saw on p. 163 and the description of people and landmarks, but I also found the passages challenging because the writing was so precise and evocative. Out of the chaos of the days I myself was leading, and out of the endless traffic of sights and sensations, what was I to choose to put in the story I was writing?

Lerner's alertness to the language he was using on the page served as an incitement to hold up to scrutiny our experience of life in the here and now, the relation of our self, or selves, with larger systems that are in place or just evolving. As I went about my days in Marfa, walking in the summer heat from the house on North Plateau Street to galleries or burrito places around town, I'd think of the passages I had read in *10:04* earlier in the day. I was struck by how accurate Lerner's writing was, accurate even in its provisionality, how his investment in a humble, or faltering, or flawed writing persona delivers a world lit up by a critical, often witty, and unfailingly incisive energy. A heady mix of intellectual ambition and an openness to the possibility of its utter ridiculousness. In other words, a conflation not only of fact and fiction but also of seriousness and play. I saw in it a model of criticism, whether professional or non-.

THERE IS NO SINGLE WAY

There is a passage in Zadie Smith's essay collection, *Changing My Mind*, where she writes that what is universal or timeless in literature is *need*—the need we experience, as readers, for writers 'who seem to know and to feel'.* She goes on: 'What is not universal or timeless, though, is form. Forms, styles, structures—whatever word you prefer—should change like skirt lengths. They have to; otherwise we make a rule, a religion, of one form....' Smith's astonishing debut novel, *White Teeth*, has been followed by other, also successful, novels—each formally innovative and moving, in particular, *NW*. During a visit to Vassar, where I was engaged in a public conversation with Smith, she said that there was no single way to write. And when I asked her to talk about her formal inventiveness, she explained her restlessness in terms of trying to fill a gap in the English tradition. To discover that a tradition has had no place for someone like you gives a lot of energy to your writing. Smith mentioned the example of others in Britain who were writing when she was coming up—Jeanette Winterson, Salman Rushdie, and Hanif Kureishi. They were all filling a gap. Thus, a novel like *On Beauty*, while 'formally conservative or familiar' still offered the pleasure to its writer of imagining 'what if the nineteenth-century novels had had brown people in them'. So, two credos: 1. There is no single way, and 2. Write yourself into the tradition—fill a gap.

---

*Zadie Smith, *Changing My Mind: Occasional Essays*, New York: Penguin Books, 2009. See p. 40.

HOW TO THROW YOUR BODY

The advice about writing that I have been puzzling over and would like to adopt as a motto comes from Ralph Waldo Emerson by way of David Shields in *Reality Hunger*: 'The way to write is to throw your body at the mark when all your arrows are spent.'*

Shields likes the quote from Emerson for what it says about writing in general but it might also apply more narrowly to critical writing at its creative best. Shields has a beautiful formulation for it: 'the critical intelligence in the imaginative position'.** His examples are: 'D. H. Lawrence, *Studies in Classic American Literature*; Wayne Koestenbaum, *The Queen's Throat*; Nicholson Baker, *U & I*; Geoff Dyer, *Out of Sheer Rage*; Terry Castle, 'My Heroin Christmas'; Anne Carson, *Eros the Bittersweet*; Roland Barthes, *S/Z*; Nabokov, *Gogol*; Beckett, *Proust*; Proust, all; William James, *Varieties of Religious Experience*. Sister Mary Ignatius, in other words, explaining it all for you—*les belles dames sans merci*: Joan Didion, all the essays; Pauline Kael, pretty much everything; Elizabeth Hardwick, *Sleepless Nights*.'

'I think the key,' Shields told me, 'is understanding one's reading of a text as revelatory of one's own psyche—an understanding that the critical gesture is mainly or substantially projection.' I offered two, somewhat dated, titles—*Anatomy of Criticism* by Northrop Frye and *Mimesis* by Erich Auerbach—and Shields was enthusiastic. He described their appeal: 'incorrigibly and unapologetically personal, passionate, wayward and subjective works.'

---

*David Shields, *Reality Hunger*, New York: Alfred A. Knopf, 2010. See p. 186.

**Ibid, p. 146-47.

The point about Emerson's aphorism, it seems to me, is to write from a position of acute vulnerability.* Books that have a distinct authorial presence, especially a presence that reveals its author's humanity or weakness, leave a greater impression on the reader's mind. I remember a young academic telling me that she had assisted the eminent African-American scholar Saidiya Hartman during the research for her book *Scenes of Subjection: Terror, Slavery, and Self-Making in Nineteenth-Century America*; this young professor then went on to say that it wasn't until she was reading Hartman's second book, *Lose Your Mother: A Journey Along the Atlantic Slave Route*, that Hartman as a writer came alive for her.** What was it about the writing of *Lose Your Mother* that was different? The book describes Hartman's entry into the slave archive to search for the memory of her ancestors. In the book's opening pages she recounts her journey to Ghana, a journey undertaken to get closer to the past. We are with the author in a rundown room in the Marcus Garvey Guest House; the bathroom is far away from her, somewhere down the hall; it is night and suddenly, amidst shouts, she is asked to turn off the lights. Outside, shots are being fired. There are soldiers and armoured tanks on the street. A coup is underway. Hartman writes that her knees began to tremble and then urine rushed down her legs. And years later, what a young scholar remembered most of her mentor's writing was the description of the need to go to the bathroom and her effort to pee in an empty water bottle. The writer, her estrangement from her surroundings, her bodily fear marking her presence on the page.

There is a lesson here both for readers and writers. I once asked

*'In much academic writing, clarity runs a poor second to invulnerability.' I found this quote, attributed to the poet Richard Hugo, in Rachel Toor, 'Becoming a "Stylish" Writer', *The Chronicle of Higher Education*, 2 July 2012. https://www.chronicle.com/article/Becoming-a-Stylish-Writer/132677

**Saidiya V. Hartman, *Scenes of Subjection: Terror, Slavery, and Self-Making in Nineteenth-Century America*, New York: Oxford University Press, 1997. Hartman, *Lose Your Mother: A Journey Along the Atlantic Slave Route*, New York: Farrar, Straus and Giroux, 2007.

the critic James Wood how he taught his students to read literature. He said, 'I get the distinct sense that my Harvard undergraduates enjoy being asked to think about, say, Naipaul, as an uncertain and anxious but very confident and imperious twenty-five-year-old, somewhere in South London, full of sadness and rage, wearing out the nib of a pen as he covered page after page with *Biswas*. I remember Edmund Wilson writing about his old teacher Christian Gauss at Princeton, and how Gauss tried to bring alive the scene of creation itself: can we imagine Rousseau at his desk, shivering and neurotic? Etc. This made an impact on me. I try to paint a picture of creation; or to put it differently, I tell a story about stories.'*

---

*In the Preface to his book, *How Fiction Works*, James Wood tells us about John Ruskin writing in 1857 a little book called *The Elements of Drawing*. Ruskin was 'casting a critic's eye over the business of creation', urging his reader to look at what the artist is looking at and how the steps lead to the final work of art. Wood, *How Fiction Works*, New York: Farrar, Straus and Giroux, 2008. See p. xi.

RAGE ON THE PAGE*

I am trying to remember when it was that I stopped thinking of myself as a new immigrant.

Was it after three years? Five? Fifteen?

I have a narrative in my mind that is teleological—I think the word for this, from my graduate-student days, is 'Hegelian'—and it culminates in my becoming a writer. A writer of immigritude. I cannot put a date to it, but I suspect that the rawness of always feeling out of place, of not belonging—that fighting sense I had of forever being on edge—diminished or even disappeared once I reached the understanding that I no longer had a home to which I could return. This went hand in hand (and this is part of the Hegelian schema I'm inhabiting here) with my finding a home in literature.

I arrived in the US, for graduate study, in literature, in the fall of 1986. I was twenty-three. After a year, I began to paint, even though I had come to the US intending to become a writer. I painted small canvases, abstract forms that sometimes had words, often in Hindi, written on them. Why did this happen? Maybe because one day, in the college bookstore, I had seen a coffee-table book that had the word 'India' printed on it in large letters. It was an expensive book, but it was marked with a discount sticker, and I bought it. Inside were the expected photographs of the Taj Mahal, busy streets, people playing Holi, a Rajasthani shepherd

---

*Published as 'Love Poems for the Border Patrol', *New Yorker*, 25 February 2018. Adapted from a longer piece with the same title in Rowan Hisayo Buchanan (ed.), *Go Home!*, New York: Feminist Press, 2018. See pp. 197-204.

wearing a bright turban. There was also a section on art. I saw the reproduction of a painting by S. H. Raza. On the left side of the canvas, at the bottom, were words in Hindi: 'Ma, laut kar jab aaonga kyaa laoonga?' ('Ma, when I return, what will I bring with me?') Abstract art had never pierced me like that.

The real change, which happened soon after that time, was that I began writing poems. My poems were about India; they were political and of little aesthetic value. But they allowed me to imagine scenes from the life and the landscape I had left behind. The moon, voices in the dark, a village path, a fire. Which is to say, I had carried my memories with me when I left home, and after a while they found expression on the page. I haven't looked at these poems for a long time. They speak to me now of a missing wholeness. 'I brought two bags from home, but I left a third behind. / Bags, passport, my shoes crossed the yellow lines, something was left behind. / Here I am, a sum of different parts. Travel agents sell ads for the parts left behind.'

In the poetry of immigrants, nostalgia is as common as confetti at parades or platitudes at political conventions. My nostalgia was simply the clear bottle in which I stored my explosive rage. This was a rage directed against the figure of the immigration official.

Other people, unluckier than me, have suffered definite traumas: famines, dictatorships, bombed cities, families wiped out. All I had experienced was ritual humiliation, at the American Embassy in Delhi, the immigration counters in several airports, and land crossings in the US. The poems I started writing after a few years in this country were accounts of such encounters. I wrote a series, 'Poems for the I.N.S.'—the acronym stands for Immigration and Naturalization Service, a name that changed, in 2003, when the agency was subsumed by the newly created Department of Homeland Security—offering vignettes that staged imaginary conversations between the narrator and the official at the visa counter.

'You can't trust them,' one officer says.
I'm prepared to bet he is from Brooklyn.
There is no response from the other one. He is not angry,
just sad that I now work in his country.
This quiet American has pasted a sheet with Hindi alphabets
on his left, on his right there is a proverb from Punjab.
'You just can't trust them,' the first one repeats,
shaking his wrist to loosen his heavy watch.
The one sitting down now raises his weary eyes.
'Did you, the first time you went there,
intend to come back?'
'Wait a minute,' I say, 'did you get a visa
when you first went to the moon? Fuck the moon,
tell me about Vietnam. Just how precise
were your plans there, you asshole?'

It was writing as revenge, fantasy in the purest form: fantasy tethered to the hurt of the real. Now, more than two decades later, I feel a distance from that rage. And I also feel some tenderness for the person who was trying so very hard to inscribe an idea of himself against nullity. How else to understand this desperate stance?

The cigarette smoke lingered
in the blue Minnesota chill
as my friend said, 'I'd like to talk
to you of other things.
Not politics again but things like
whether you are lonely.'

'What could be more political
than the fact that I'm lonely,
that I am so far away
from everything I've known?'

I feel tenderness, also, for the humble inventory provided to the immigration official after the applicant is asked if he has any property in India, or relatives, anything. The list included the yellow of mustard blossoms stretching to the horizon, the old house with its damp walls and his sister's laughter, the smell of spices over a naked fire. But here's the crucial thing: in drawing up this inventory, I was already moving away from who I was when I had arrived in the US. In remembering what I had lost, I was filling my mind with memories. These poems became the screen behind which my past receded.

After ten or fifteen years, the confusion and loss had been replaced by a self-conscious construction of an immigrant self. I'm calling it a construction because it was an aesthetic and a textual idea. I was taking pictures of immigrant life; I was reporting on novels and non-fiction about immigrants; my own words were an edited record of what I was reading. An eclectic mix of writers: Frantz Fanon, Aimé Césaire, June Jordan, Jamaica Kincaid, Hanif Kureishi, Salman Rushdie, Marguerite Duras, Guillermo Gómez-Peña. Reagan was still president when I came to the US. The Iran-Contra hearings were my introduction to televised spectacle. Gap-toothed Ollie North and his proclamations of innocence, the volume of hair on his secretary Fawn Hall, reports I read of Reagan declaring, 'I am a Contra.' I had consumed all of this as an innocent—and by writing poems I began issuing my declarations of independence.

Recently, I was reading the lectures that the novelist James Salter delivered at age ninety, at the University of Virginia, shortly before his death. In one of them, he quoted the French writer and critic Paul Léautaud, who wrote, 'Your language is your country.' Salter added, 'I've thought about it a great deal, and I may have it backwards—your country is your language. In either case it has a simple meaning. Either that your true country is not geographical but lingual, or that you are really living in a language, presumably your mother tongue.' When I read those words, I thought of my grandmother, who died a few years after I came to America. She was the only person to whom I wrote letters in my mother tongue, Hindi. On pale blue aerogrammes, I sent her reports of my new life in an alien land. Although she could sign her own name, my grandmother was otherwise illiterate and would ask the man who brought her the mail in the village or a passing schoolchild to read her the words I had written. And when my grandmother died, I had no reason to write in Hindi again. Now it is a language that I use only in conversations, either on the phone, with my friends and relatives in India, or, on occasion, when I get into cabs in New York City.

At another point in his lectures, Salter told his audience that 'style is the entire writer'. He said, 'You can be said to have a style when a reader, after reading several lines or part of a page, can recognize who the writer is.' There you have it, another definition of home. In novels such as *A Sport and a Pastime* and *Light Years*, the sentences have a particular air, and the light slants through them in a way that announces Salter's presence. All the writers I admire, each different from the other, erect structures that offer refuge. Consider Claudia Rankine. You are reading her description of a woman's visit to a new therapist. The woman has arrived at the door, which is locked. She rings the bell. The therapist opens the door and yells, 'Get away from my house. What are you doing in my yard?' The woman replies that she has an appointment. A pause. Then an apology that confirms that what just happened actually happened. If you have been left trembling by someone yelling racist epithets at you, Rankine's detached, near-forensic writing provides you the comfort of clarity that the confusion of the therapist in the poem does not.

Thirty years have passed since I left India. I have continued to write about the country of my birth. This has allowed me to cure, to some degree, the malady of distance. I've reflected a great deal on the literature that is suited to describing the conditions in the country of my birth. But I have also known for long that I no longer belonged there.

I haven't reported in grand detail on rituals of American life, road journeys or malls or the death of steel-manufacturing towns. I think this is because I feel a degree of alienation that I cannot combat. I've immersed myself in reading more and more of American literature, but no editor has asked me to comment on Jonathan Franzen or Jennifer Egan. It is assumed I'm an expert on writers who need a little less suntan lotion at the beach. I don't care. Removed from any intimate connection to a community or the long association with a single locale, my engagement with literature is now focussed on style. Do my sentences reveal once again the voice of the outsider, a mere observer?

In a cemetery that is only a few miles away from my home, in the Hudson Valley, is the gravestone of an Indian woman. The inscription reads: 'Anandabai Joshee M.D. 1865-1887 First Brahmin Woman to Leave India to Obtain an Education.' Joshee was nine when she was married to a twenty-nine-year-old postal clerk in Maharashtra, and twenty-one when she received a medical degree in Pennsylvania. A few months later, following her return to India, she died, of tuberculosis, at the age of twenty-two. Joshee's ashes were sent to the woman who had been her benefactor in the US, and that is how she found a place in Poughkeepsie. I'm aware that, when she died, Joshee was younger than I was when I left India for America. Involved in medical studies, and living in a world that must have felt immeasurably more distant than it does now, she probably didn't have time to write poems or worry about style. I recently read that last year a crater on the planet Venus was named after her. It made me think that brave Anandabai Joshee now has a home that none of us will ever reach.

ON TRAINING

Credos remain meaningless abstractions unless put to use. Daily practice is an ideal. On a friend's website, a quote from Susan Sontag: 'A writer, like an athlete, must "train" every day. What did I do today to keep in "form"?'

III

Style

IN MEMORY OF

As I have already revealed, this book was a long time coming. I started it on the day of Barack Obama's inauguration as president in 2009. Earlier in the day, watching the ceremony in Washington, DC, I told the friends in the house where we were gathered about this book I was going to write. (Another friend, Elizabeth Alexander, appeared on the TV screen. She read out her inaugural poem. One line was: 'A teacher says, *Take out your pencils. Begin.*' Another: 'In today's sharp sparkle, this winter air / anything can be made, any sentence begun.' There was so much hope then, and not just about words.) Because of the years I have worked on and off on this project, I have had reason to look at books in relation to their surrounding history. Let me explain. I had decided I was going to write a book about style—*writing style*—and during this process I was always attentive to the historical circumstance in which any new book found its significance. One of the crucial, critical books to be published during the Obama years was Claudia Rankine's *Citizen*.* So many of the brief prose-poems that make up *Citizen* are tight narratives that deliver reports on both the public and private violence of racism in America; the longer pieces, like those that examine the treatment of Serena Williams at the hands of the media and sports officials or the one about the famous head-butting

*Claudia Rankine, *Citizen: An American Lyric*, Minneapolis: Graywolf Press, 2014. Other titles would include *Between the World and Me* by Ta-Nehisi Coates and *The Underground Railroad* by Colson Whitehead. It seemed very appropriate that in what was widely seen as an act of civil disobedience a young black woman named Johari Osayi Idusuyi was spotted reading *Citizen* at a Trump campaign rally in November 2015.

by Zinedine Zidane in a World Cup soccer final, are also rendered at a perfect rhetorical pitch, catching at once both the anguish and rage of witnessing, if not also experiencing, racist behaviour. The language Rankine uses makes its own sound, in an in-between space between poetry and prose, theory and experience, even between writing and the art of multimedia artists like Kate Clark, Glenn Ligon, Carrie Mae Weems and John Lucas. I especially appreciate the fact that *Citizen* was a finalist for the National Book Critics Circle Awards in *two* categories: Poetry as well as Criticism. (It was the eventual winner for Poetry.)

Such is the imprint of the current times on *Citizen*, and so fresh and vivid and immediate is the poet's response to the kind of country we are living in, that the pages that precede the lines

> because white men can't
> police their imagination
> black men are dying

commemorate the black people recently killed in the US in acts of police violence. On page 134, my edition of the book says the following:

> In Memory of Jordan Russell Davis
> In Memory of Eric Garner
> In Memory of John Crawford
> In Memory of Michael Brown

Later, in a class I was teaching, my students were using a more recent edition of *Citizen* and they pointed out that the list of names had grown longer.

HOW PROUST CAN RUIN YOUR LIFE

In his excellent guidebook, still meaningful as a guide to thesis-writing despite its initial publication in Italy in the 1970s, Umberto Eco makes the recommendation that the student should have as her audience the whole of humanity and not just her adviser. That advice is followed by this admonition: '*You are not Proust.* Do not write long sentences.'* Two pages later, another paragraph begins, the words again in italics, '*You are not e.e. cummings.*' You can guess the rest. And it is difficult to disagree. Eco writes, 'You are not an avant-garde poet. Not even if your thesis is on avant-garde poetry. If you write a thesis on Caravaggio, are you then a painter?' I have been part of dissertation committees supervising what Eco scornfully calls '"alternative" theses', and, truth be told, the results were uneven and also, occasionally, disastrous. It can be easier, and maybe also effective, to write pages of straightforward academic prose, but part of my mission here is to disabuse ourselves of the notion that it is the only way to write. For instance, you are writing a thesis on Caravaggio. You are not a great painter, you know that well, but what fascinates you about Caravaggio is that he seems to know a lot about the dark corners in the spaces he paints, and also, of course, the darkness of the human soul, and to enter into a dialogue with that artistic practice you feel it necessary to employ a new language, a language that is different from the uniform and detached meta-language you learned in the classroom. You would

---

*Umberto Eco, *How to Write a Thesis*, translated by Caterina Mongiat Farina and Geoff Farina, Cambridge, MA: MIT Press, 2015. See pp. 146-50.

like very much to write long sentences. On an index card you copy down the following sentence by John Berger on Caravaggio's art and pin it on the wall above your desk: 'His darkness smells of candles, over-ripe melons, damp washing waiting to be hung out the next day: it is the darkness of stairwells, gambling corners, cheap lodgings, sudden encounters.'*

*John Berger, 'Caravaggio: A Contemporary View', *Studio International*, 1983, Volume 196, Number 998. Accessed online http://timothyquigley.net/vcs/berger-caravaggio.pdf on 26 March 2017.

REALITY HUNGER

From time to time, you will read arguments about how the days of the traditional book-length dissertation are numbered. You might be asked to focus on writing articles instead. Or perhaps a digital document, preferably multimedia.* I don't disagree with the call to take note of the conditions of our changed world; but how might one understand the excitement or the challenge of new writing using new media?** Allow me to present Josh Begley, data

*See, for instance, Stacey Patton, 'The Dissertation Can No Longer Be Defended', *Chronicle of Higher Education*, 11 February 2013. http://www.chronicle.com/article/The-Dissertation-Can-No-Longer/137215 Last accessed on 20 May 2017.

**But before we go further, what about older forms of writing about *older* media? Here are my models for writing about photographs, not just because these writers are insightful about images or, for that matter, about politics or society, but because in their work, in the space between word and image, their language takes flight. Criticism becomes a creative act, more open-ended, certainly more sensual; often, like the eye, darting in different directions; and at other times, finding focus, dwelling at length on a detail or two. In some cases, these writers achieve a clarity—and make connections—that is more akin to what we find in dreams. Here is my brief list: Roland Barthes, *Camera Lucida: Reflections on Photography*, New York: Hill & Wang, 1981; Susan Sontag, *On Photography*, New York: Farrar, Straus and Giroux, 1977; Malek Alloula, *The Colonial Harem*, Minneapolis: University of Minnesota Press, 1986; John Berger, *About Looking*, London: Vintage, 1992, and *Another Way of Telling*; John Berger and Jean Mohr, *A Seventh Man*, New York: Verso, 2010; Edward Said and Jean Mohr, *After the Last Sky: Palestinian Lives*, New York: Columbia University Press, 1998; essays by Eudora Welty and Tina Modotti; Carol Mavor, *Becoming* and Carol Mavor, *Black and Blue: The Bruising Passion of Camera Lucida, La Jetée, Sans soleil, and Hiroshima Mon Amour*, Durham: Duke University Press, 2012; Teju Cole, *Blind Spot*, New York: Random House, 2017; Geoff Dyer, *The Ongoing Moment*, London: Vintage, 2007; Christopher Pinney, *Camera Indica: The Social Life of Indian Photographs*, Chicago: University of Chicago Press, 1998.

artist. Begley's work is archival—both in the sense that it relies on historical archives and in the sense that it attempts to excavate new ones. In fact, he told me, the bulk of what he does is collect and catalogue information that already exists—ideally making it more accessible or digestible to new audiences along the way. The other part of his work could be described as an attempt to visualize archives. So, for instance, in a project called 'Officer Involved', Begley presents aerial images from Google Maps of sites (streets, crossroads, blocks of cityscape) where people have died at the hands of the police. These sites are based on recent archival data collected by non-governmental and news organizations.

Back in 2012, Begley was in the news because Apple rejected an app that would send phone users a notification every time a US drone killed someone anywhere in the world.* At that time, Begley was a graduate student in NYU's Tisch School of the Arts studying Interactive Telecommunications. I follow Dronestream, the Twitter account that Begley created to chronicle every drone-strike by the US, starting with the first one in 2002. I was interested in talking to Begley not only to speak to him about his brand of academic activism but also to report on a new form of writing that fulfilled his degree requirements—a narrative about the world produced by writing code. I believe that Begley is asking us to think about new narrative structures being employed by users of social-media platforms. When I asked Begley to talk about his experience working on his own apps, he told me:

'To be real, I'm just learning how to make apps. Every piece of code I've ever written has been in whole or in part lifted from somewhere else, tweaked, and cobbled together to fit my own objectives. I think a lot of programmers do this. (Writers too, perhaps.) A lot of times there are citations and thank yous written

*Christina Bonnington and Spencer Ackerman, 'Apple Rejects App That Tracks U.S. Drone Strikes', *Wired*, 30 August 2012.

into this code. It can feel a bit like reading the Acknowledgements section of a book.

If I'm honest with myself, the only reason I make apps now is because that's where people's attention spans are. An app is a container. Wrapping paper. An interesting one, no doubt, as it allows you to reach into someone else's pocket and interrupt them with a vibration—but the app itself is mostly packaging. What's exciting to me is learning how to speak the language of technology and make it stretch. Take advantage of the tech press, which loves to report on itself, and present a piece of content that either feels new or provocative or both. I think the lie I tell myself is that this is somehow a new form of scholarship. At its best, my work seeks to uncover an old story and tell it in a new way. At its worst, my work is simply repackaged techno-utopianism.'

DETECTING STYLE

Style is of interest to the FBI.

At Vassar, I had a colleague named Don Foster who is a Shakespeare scholar but most of his time off-campus, he once said, was taken up by 'police detectives, FBI agents, and district attorneys'.* At the beginning of his career, Foster had used close reading and textual analysis to assign authorship to ancient poems and anonymous plays, but in 1996 he was asked to ascribe authorship to the anonymously published book *Primary Colors*. The writer that Foster fingered as the author of *Primary Colors* was Joe Klein. Foster's conclusion had been based on text-based analysis. For instance, both Anonymous and Klein used unusual adjectives ending in '-y' ('cartoony', 'fluttery'), or adverbs constructed from those adjectives ('goofily', 'huffily); both were fond of words ending in 'ish' ('radicalish', 'wonkish') and also words like 'mode', 'gazillion', and common words like 'comfortable', 'uncomfortable', 'embarrassing', and 'explosive'. (In his article for *New York* magazine announcing the conclusion of his search, Foster explained his understanding of style: 'All writers have at their disposal thousands of words that they simply do not use. Words drift in and out of an author's active lexicon. But at a given point in a writer's career, he or she tends to use many of the same words repeatedly, even when moving from one kind of text to another. This is precisely what we see happening with Anonymous and Joe Klein.'**) Five months later,

---

*Donald Foster, 'The Message in the Anthrax', *Vanity Fair*, October 2003.

**———, 'Primary Culprit', *New York*, 26 February 1996.

after first refuting the evidence, Klein accepted that he was indeed 'Anonymous'. After this success, Foster became a resource for law enforcement who wanted him to use his skills to help locate the authors of notes and threats that came in the mail. Hence, Foster's remark: 'On the shelves of my office, the Great Books have been displaced by the writings of hoaxers, terrorists, kidnappers, the D.C. sniper, the anthrax killer.'*

I had once heard that as a graduate student Foster had found an anonymous poem that he believed to have been written by Shakespeare.** When his manuscript on the subject was rejected by a university press, he had used the same textual tools to establish the identity of the two anonymous reviewers for the press—who had been doubtful about the efficacy of his method—and then sent them letters to prove his point (and also perhaps to mock).

One distant afternoon, soon after beginning work on this book, I invited Foster out for lunch. When we were seated at our table, after engaging in some small talk about departmental politics, I told Foster that I had a proposal for him. I wanted to hire him to do a bit of textual sleuthing. It had often seemed to me, especially when sitting in the audience at academic conferences, that everyone spoke an identical language, and often, in the first few lines that were delivered, the same authoritative names would be invoked. I told Foster that I would show him four or five essays by postcolonial scholars—one or two of the authors would be recognizable stars but the others would be less well-known academics—and his job would be to prove conclusively that all the pieces had been written by a single author. Foster smiled and said that I had misunderstood the amount of time it took for the kind of work he did. I didn't belabour my point but you understand what I'm getting at, don't you, dear reader?

---

*Ibid.

**Adam Liptak, 'Paper Chase', *New York Times*, 26 November 2000.

STRUNK AND WHITE

Let's look at Rule Number 8 of Strunk and White's 'Rules of Elementary Usage'. There are twenty-two basic rules in that section of the book and Number 8 states: 'Use a dash to set off an abrupt break or interruption and to announce a long oppositive or summary.' I have a fairly good grasp of that rule but what matters really is the sentence that follows: 'A dash is a mark of separation stronger than a comma, less formal than a colon, and more relaxed than parentheses.' Why do I like this sentence so much? Unlike the rule itself, to which it is merely appended, the second sentence has rhythm. Its style is equal parts elegance and explanatory power.

I came to Strunk and White's *The Elements of Style* very late in life. The book's gift to me, which hasn't lessened over time, is that it encourages me to write clearer, more forceful, declarative sentences. Rule Number 17 is 'Omit needless words.' Yes, it instructs me to be more austere. (I wrote the last sentence and thought about that rule and realized that I could easily get rid of the word *more*.) But what the *form* of the sentence teaches me to do is make a strong statement. Where I've been unduly cautious in articulating a thought, or appeared mealy-mouthed, a book like Strunk and White demands the kind of simplification that is actually a refinement.

Style isn't universal. The best reading of Strunk and White I've come across is in an otherwise hagiographic account by a writer who quotes the following remark by Ian Frazier: 'I always thought of *The Elements of Style* as weirdly kind of related to Cornell's being an ag school. It had a plainspokenness about it that you would expect in some kind of farm manual.'* The analysis was startling but also struck me as true, not least because Frazier had quite colourfully conjured an image of Strunk as a 'well-dressed, kind of dusty guy who had just come in from the calving barn or something and was going to tell you something very practical'. And for Frazier, White also drew on that 'more homespun quality of Cornell' so that the book that resulted from their collaboration 'was of a piece with Robert Frost—a New England, laconic, get-to-the-point kind of book'. More than two decades ago, when a visiting friend gave me a copy of Strunk and White, I was reading Marxist theory; Althusser in particular. If you believed you were dealing with deep, world-changing ideas, would you care about what appeared to be a grammar textbook? I didn't read more than two pages of the small book. My world at that time lacked even objects to describe; I was wrestling with vast, abstract, invisible forces; since everything around me lacked definition, the book's demand for plainness or precision was wasted on me. When I came back to Strunk and White, I was fleeing the radical world of postmodern thought. The simple certainties of the style-book harked back to another age, and were maybe even a bit conservative, but they offered an antidote to the excesses of academic theorizing. I now inevitably reach for Strunk and White when I find a student's writing wordy or needlessly obscure.

Strunk and White demand clarity in writing, but it is perhaps a better idea to translate it as a desire for visual writing, language that conjures a picture in the reader's mind.** A blurb that accompanies Marilynne Robinson's well-known novel, *Housekeeping,* is by Walker

*Mark Garvey, *Stylized: A Slightly Obsessive History of Strunk & White's The Elements of Style*, New York: Touchstone, 2009. The quote is on p. 21.

**Even the aforementioned Althusser had offered a description that I have never been able to put out of my head: 'For, as Mao puts it *in a phrase as clear as the dawn*, "Nothing in this world develops absolutely evenly."' Louis Althusser, *For Marx*, translated by Ben Brewster, New York: Verso, 1989. The quote appears on p. 201; emphasis added.

Percy and it reads: '*Housekeeping* is a haunting dream of a story told in a language as sharp and clear as light and air and water.'* Percy's praise had fastened my attention to light and air and water even before I had turned a page in the novel. Those elements glinted on nearly every page. 'If one pried up earth with a stick on those days, one found massed shafts of ice, slender as needles and pure as spring water.' 'The mountains, grayed and flattened by distance, looked like remnants of a broken dam, or like the broken lip of an iron pot, just at a simmer, endlessly distilling water into light.' 'Lucille and I stepped through the door from sheer night to sheer night.' To write of light or air or water is to stage clarity. They are metonymic invocations of the act of seeing. As a writer, Robinson uses them as metaphors. She is a visually attentive writer and employs the same eye when not dealing with landscape or nature. 'Appearance paints itself on bright and sliding surfaces, for example, memory and dream. Sylvie's head falls to the side and we see the blades of my mother's shoulders and the round bones at the top of her spine.'

---

*Marilynne Robinson, *Housekeeping*, New York: Farrar, Straus and Giroux, 1980.

EROTIC STYLE

When I was finishing graduate work, I read in a book review that while in his life Roland Barthes was fairly closeted, his subjects and his sentences were all about gayness.* The reviewer had quoted from one of the books under review and from that quote I understood immediately that there was a new way to read sentences: 'The (poignant, exasperating) hysteria of Barthes's most invidiously written texts lies in the activity of this contradiction—that while they phobically sacrifice homosexuality-as-signified, leaving the appeased deity of *general theory* as fixed as ever in its white-male heterosexual orientation, they happily cultivate homosexuality-as-signifier.'** A sentence could have divided, even opposed, aims. I bought the book: D. A. Miller's *Bringing Out Roland Barthes*. In reading it, I saw that style could be an elaboration of an erotics—in this case, a gay erotics and also a gay aesthetics. Did I try to write in a more expressive style, or a frank and embodied way, after reading that? I have kept for the past twenty years a photocopy of that *Voice* review. I have read often the following lines that the reviewer, Michael Warner, had written about Miller's book: '*Bringing Out Roland Barthes* stretches the academic style in its personal, anecdotal method, in its indecorous fondness for and resistance to Barthes, but also in so much writerly

*Michael Warner, 'The Song of Roland', *Voice Literary Supplement*, December 1992, pp. 25-26.

**The quote is from D. A. Miller, *Bringing Out Roland Barthes*, Berkeley: University of California Press, 1992, p. 28.

freedom, so much will-to-drop-trou. Miller's style scarcely avoids—scarcely seeks to avoid—being mannered. (All beautiful sentences, apparently, are long.)' Did the readers of the *Village Voice* find freedom to write long sentences after reading that review? Did other graduate students who read Miller's book on Barthes also want to take a turn towards the personal and the novelesque? I certainly felt pulled in that direction, yes, especially in the poetry I was writing, but also in the critical writing I published at that time.* How soon after reading that Warner piece did I place an ad in the *Village Voice* when the newspaper was bringing out its special Valentine's Day issue? 'Hey babe, let's snuggle in bed and read Spivak's Scattered Speculations on Value or even the missionary-position Marxist writing you so admire. xoxoxo'

*Amitava Kumar, 'Teaching in the Academy of Love Letters', in *Poetics/Politics*, Amitava Kumar (ed.), New York: St Martin's Press, 1999, pp. 261-72.

BLACKNESS (UNMITIGATED)

In Paul Beatty's *The Sell-Out* the narrator happily lists towards the end of the book examples of what he calls 'Unmitigated Blackness'.* Here's an excerpt from his long list, which I find varied and interesting, presenting a near-credo in its drive against narrow identity, but what excites me the most is that bit at the end: 'Unmitigated Blackness is simply not giving a fuck. Clarence Cooper, Charlie Parker, Richard Pryor, Maya Deren, Sun Ra, Mizoguchi, Frida Kahlo, black-and-white Godard, Céline, Gong Li, David Hammons, Björk, and the Wu-Tang Clan in any of their hooded permutations. Unmitigated Blackness is essays passing for fiction.' A shout-out to the likes of Elizabeth Hardwick and John Berger but inspiring also because that last bit I've quoted says to me that what thrills you about culture can be clever and improvisatory.

~

*Paul Beatty, *The Sell-Out*, New York: Farrar, Strauss and Giroux, 2015. See p. 277.

CREATIVE WRITING

Toni Morrison's Nobel lecture in 1993 was a profound meditation on language. What sticks in my memory is that after her criticism of what she calls 'obscuring state language' and 'the faux-language of mindless media', she also ticks off another box which Morrison describes, in her own beautiful way, as: 'the proud but calcified language of the academy.'*

During the time that I worked on this book I would ask creative writers what they had to say about academic language. One of the first writers I queried was Marilynne Robinson, not least because Obama had revealed that she was one of the writers who had shaped him. When I reached her, Robinson said that she had been reading books by anthropologists, sociologists and even philosophers. 'There is a dreadful sameness in the vocabulary of all of them. And a sameness of voice from book to book, writer to writer. Thinking seems to be governed by this very laden—and severely limited—vocabulary. If I come across "hermeneuticization" one more time—'

A dozen other well-known novelists had more or less the same thing to say, so much so that when this manuscript was sent out to the first group of anonymous readers, it was pointed out to me

---

*Toni Morrison, 1993 Nobel lecture. https://www.nobelprize.org/nobel_prizes/literature/laureates/1993/morrison-lecture.html. Accessed on 17 May 2018.

by one of them that 'badmouthing academic writing is as much a badge of belonging to the profession of "creative writer" as "jargon" is a way to affiliate oneself with a discipline.' That is a fair point. Nevertheless, I found useful the specific bits of advice offered by different writers.

Vivian Gornick: 'My mantra for a writing student? "What exactly is this piece of writing about? Please tell me that as clearly and as simply as you can."'

George Saunders: 'In my view, all writing should be "gonzo", in the sense that we should concede that the writer's pre-existing prejudices and assumptions cannot be filtered out or quieted—better they should be admitted. I think we pick up a trace of this in earlier philosophical writers. The other thing that seems to be sometimes missing from academic writing is the sense that the writer might be wrong...that the method of enquiry is limiting etc.'

Lis Harris: 'I tell them all to be clear, to avoid clichés and tired language, to think about oblique angles and fresh approaches to a subject and to try for as much breadth and depth as possible. I try help them to clear away the brush that often obscures their strong, individual voices and am moved by their boldness. I think my academic colleagues should be telling the students the same things, often.'

David Means: 'As a fiction writer, so much academic writing seems sealed up and hermetic and uninspired, shorn away from a love of subject. In the end, I guess I'd say, before you write an academic paper, go back to whatever you loved early on; go back to whatever gave you the impulse to delve into the depths of the subject in the first place…whatever it takes to reestablish the pure meaning of the subject in your mind as it once stood, at that edge of discovery, thrilling and meaningful in the deepest way to your own emotional life.'

Francine Prose: 'With my students, it's really simple, and it just works wonders. And, just in terms of teaching writing, it cuts through a lot of crap. I meet with them one by one and I pick the most convoluted sentence from their papers, the most unintelligible, let's say, and I say to them, "What were you trying to say?" and they tell me, and then I say "Well, why don't you just write that down, and just say that?"'

Elizabeth McCracken: 'In academic books, what I always want is exactly what Frank Conroy always insisted were the most important things in fiction writing: meaning, sense, and clarity. As it happens, I have a greater tolerance for nonsense and mystery on the linguistic level in fiction...'

Richard Powers: 'The best academic writing knows what many different disciplines converged on around the beginning of the twentieth century: the observer is an inseparable part of the system under observation. The yardstick and its wielder are part of the measurement; the speaker and what can be spoken are reciprocally joined. Great academic stylists embrace that fact, and they use it to turn the prison house of language into something more like a beachside cottage.'

Jeffrey Eugenides: 'My intention in *The Marriage Plot* was not entirely satirical when it came to semiotics. [In fact], my work has been influenced by the same writers whom I occasionally lampoon. I'm afraid I don't have a quotation that sums up my feelings about academic writing any better than a line from my own novel: "Since Derrida claimed that language, by its very nature, undermined any meaning it attempted to promote, Madeleine wondered how Derrida expected her to get his meaning." And the paragraph that follows.'*

*'Reading a novel after reading semiotic theory was like jogging empty-handed after jogging with hand weights. After getting out of Semiotics 211, Madeleine fled to the Rockefeller Library, down to the B Level, where the stacks exuded a vivifying smell of mold, and grabbed something—anything, *The House of Mirth*, *Daniel Deronda*—to restore herself to sanity. How wonderful it was when one sentence followed logically from the sentence before! What exquisite guilt she felt, wickedly enjoying narrative! Madeleine felt safe with a nineteenth-century novel. There were going to be people in it. Something

Karen Russell: 'Ah, well, I'm not sure I know why the poor folks in academia aren't being encouraged to think about style—I often find myself wishing, these days, that I had a more solid grounding in theory, and that I'd read much more criticism, there are so many Swiss-cheese holes in my scholarly knowledge that I wonder if we couldn't arrange for some kind of literary "Freaky Friday", where MFA kids and PhDs swap places for a year or more, and then carousel around again back into their original disciplines… Some of the best advice I myself received, as a student, was to look for "heat on the page"—places where my own temperature and interest spiked. If you are not invested in what you're writing, if nothing personal is at stake for you, it seems sort of unfair to expect your readers to be interested. And the obverse holds—if you are riveted to the page, writing forward, and writing for sheer pleasure, and discovery, instead of out of grim obligation or on some self-conscious quest to impress, then it's much more likely a reader will respond to that genuine curiosity, investment, and energy.'

Colson Whitehead: 'Well, just because you are a good critic, it doesn't mean you're a good writer. They are two different skills—and it is great when a good critic is also a good writer, but your average person might not be gifted in both areas.

'I don't know why academics aren't taught more about how to write an elegant sentence. It's not the point? A knowledgeable professor isn't necessarily a good writer, and necessarily able to pass that skill on?

'Advice for writers of every stripe: fail, and fail better next time. Keep going. I got my start in journalism, so when I started an article I always had to ask myself: is the diverse readership out there going to understand what I am saying? Are we on the same page in terms of outlook and vocabulary and references? If

---

was going to happen to them in a place resembling the world.' Jeffrey Eugenides, *The Marriage Plot,* New York: Farrar, Straus and Giroux, 2011, p. 47.

not, where do we find our common ground? Perhaps this is true for literary critics, too—am I speaking to a fellow academic who knows all the terms, or a lay reader? You have to be aware of your audience, and make adjustments.

'I was a good student in high school, but got progressively passive aggressive once I got to college—skipping class, sitting in the back row not saying anything. (I was a nerd finally rebelling against the system, albeit in a useless, self-defeating manner.) We didn't have a creative writing major. You had to audition for classes, and I was turned down both times. Which was crushing, because I really thought I was a writer, what with all the smoking and wearing black. But I learned an important lesson: no one cares about your writing, so you may as well resign yourself to that fact and soldier on and be stoic.'

I mentioned earlier the anonymous readers of the first draft of this book. One of the readers, or perhaps the same one I quoted from above, had an additional note about the interviews with creative writers. According to this reader, a different set of interviews was called for, particularly 'with scholars who have written what in some ways are conventional scholarly monographs that are models of lucid writing, solid research, and groundbreaking claims, but are *not* necessarily written in an experimental or stylish way'. Again, a good point, but almost a bit irrelevant to my goals. My aim here is to make a case for books that are formally interesting. Unlike most creative writers, I don't think lack of clarity is a deal-breaker, even though I'll readily admit that the use of rote theoretical language at conferences has often threatened my sanity. Instead of merely demanding clarity, I want to emphasize *creativity*. The question to ask is the following one: whether as academic scholars or as creative writers, are we being inventive in our use of language and in our search for form?

This is a call for making style a crucial element of any writing. I don't think a lot of *creative* writing is very creative either. The form, and certainly the feel, of a lot of novels as well as stories being published is often disturbingly limited and formulaic. The joy of picking up and reading a book that invents its own form is so radical that I have little doubt that we should hold them up as models.

One such book that I read recently is Max Porter's *Grief is the Thing With Feathers.** Porter's book is marketed as a novel—and it is that, but it is also a poem, a dream or hallucination, and an act of creative criticism. A man, who is identified as Dad because he has two small boys, has lost his wife. This man, or Dad, is a Ted Hughes scholar; the book he is writing is called *Ted Hughes' Crow on the Couch: A Wild Analysis*. His plan for writing is, understandably, stalled—and just one of the ways in which the reader encounters this character's grief, his overwhelming sense of loss, is by seeing how the outlined plan for his proposed book has changed:

DAD

Introduction: Crow's Bad Dream I miss my wife

Ch. 1. ~~Magical Dangers~~ I miss my wife

Ch. 2. ~~Reign of Silence~~ I miss my wife

Ch. 3. ~~Unkillable Trickster~~ I miss my wife

Ch. 4. ~~Aphrodisiac Disaster~~ I miss my wife

Ch. 5. ~~Tragic Comedy~~ I miss my wife

Ch. 6. ~~The Baby (God) in the Lake~~ I miss my wife

Ch. 7. ~~The Song~~ I miss my wife

Conclusion: Recovery and Growth I miss my wife

*Max Porter, *Grief is the Thing With Feathers: A Novel,* Minneapolis: Graywolf Press, 2015.

And yet, and yet. The subject of this writing project—Ted Hughes' Crow—is hardly under erasure. He emerges as the story's main agent—an unsentimental friend, a bully, a bodyguard, a therapist aiding recovery, etc. This is at once an act of creative appropriation and the best critical response to the work and, I daresay, the life of Ted Hughes. I loved Porter's book for the way in which it makes the scholar's academic obsession burst into his life, as a curse, and, more important, as redemption. Would I want to read another work of dull criticism that drones on and on about Ted Hughes? No. Will I want to read what Porter's Hughes scholar tells his publisher he would next like to write—'a complete works of Ted Hughes annotated by Crow'? Yes, yes.

IV

Reading Comes Before Writing

GULZAR BAND AND COMPANY

I am a writer, and I teach literature, but I don't understand poetry. It often happens that students, and sometimes strangers, show me their poems and I have nothing to say. This is a failing. It is embarrassing. I want to read more poetry.

During my boyhood in Patna, poetry meant finding poems to use during the elocution contest. The search for rhetorical thunder. Tennyson's 'The Charge of the Light Brigade' was a staple. '"Forward the Light Brigade! / Charge for the guns!" he said. / Into the valley of Death / Rode the six hundred.' You could be forgiven for thinking that poems always had cannons to the right of them, cannons to the left of them. Matching the artillery fire, when it came to Hindi elocution, there was the local deity, the fiercely nationalist poet Ramdhari Singh Dinkar. '*Khojo Tipu Sultan kahan soye hain? / Ashfaq aur Usman kahan soye hain? / Bombwaale vir jawaan kahan soye hain? / Veh Bhagat Singh balwaan kahan soye hain?*' Thousands of boys and girls across India declaiming in shrill tones. The Himalayas must be melting.

Later, bombast gave way to sentimentalism. To the damp poetry of Hindi film songs about *saawan* and *saajan*. Years would pass before somewhere in the middle of my teenage years, those lyrics began to appeal to me. I was stirred by their pathos. Partly because the words in the film songs were linked inextricably to the beauty of the women I was seeing in a new way on the screen. But Rafi singing Kamal Amrohi's lines about the delicate girl with the dusky skin—'*Kahin ek masoom nazuk si ladki, bahut khubsoorat magar saanwali si'*—suddenly seemed to take the form of language describing the people and real lives around me.

This sensibility—we can call it sensitivity—acquired a more playful edge in Gulzar. I was charmed by the way in Gulzar's lyrics the playback singers or actors interrupted their songs to engage in banter. How frantically I scoured the Palika Bazaar shops for a cassette from the film *Griha Pravesh*! In one song from it—'*Logon ke ghar mein rehta hoon, kab apna koi ghar hoga*'—Gulzar himself makes a cameo appearance, serious-faced and with oversized glasses. This was in the seventies. I was in my late teens. At that time, Gulzar's lyrics struck me as urban and utterly contemporary. The freshness of this poetry was its precise naming of our neighbourhoods, and the naming of our fears—with adequate attention given, of course, to Sharmila Tagore's luminous eyes and her smile.

A few years later, I began writing poems. I remember seeing a young woman removing a bindi from her forehead to stick it on the mirror before splashing her face with water—and telling myself that I needed to compose a poem about it. I wrote in English even though much of English poetry seemed alien to me.

An uncle of mine often asked me to recite Wordsworth's 'Daffodils', but neither he nor I had seen a single daffodil. Indian poets who wrote in English and were familiar to me, Nissim Ezekiel and A. K. Ramanujan, didn't appeal at first because I had read them in school. Like hospital food that always tastes of medicines, their poems smelled of the classroom. But that was then. Today, if I were a young writer I could pick up a collection like *60 Indian Poets*, edited by Jeet Thayil, and make exciting discoveries on my own.

One night in the early eighties, in the basement theatre of Shri Ram Centre in Delhi, I heard the Hindi poet Sarveshwar Dayal Saxena read his long poem 'Kuano Nadi'. This was my discovery. I had taken a DTC bus from Delhi University to Mandi House to listen to this poet without knowing anything about him. His reading changed me. His poem was about rural poverty and it took me away from myself; it presented a radical vision of art and the language he had used welcomed me as if it was the doorway of my home.

In the years since I have attended countless poetry readings but they are rarely like Saxena's. I have a dim sense of the ambition of the poet who, in a few lines, with a fine choice of words, invents a new language and new sounds. But it doesn't work for me. Poetry can be obscure. I'm a narrative man. I want a clear sense of time and place; I like a story with an arc. Yet, now and then, I go back to Hindi poetry from the heartland. This is a nostalgic act. Here, for instance, is my translation of a short poem 'Train' by Alokdhanwa, a poet from Patna: 'Every good man has a train / That goes towards his mother's house // Stretching its whistle / Blowing smoke.'

PARTITION LITERATURE

Each August, and not only on Independence Day, there are reminders of another August many years ago. August 1947. A documentary being broadcast on television, an article in a magazine or an ad about friends reunited after fifty years, a commentator judging once again the ambitions of men like Gandhi and Jinnah, a new film, a tear-jerker about love blooming like a flower among the gravestones.

It is the same each year. We remember, and in remembering one thing or another, we also forget everything else.

I wasn't alive then and my memories are made up mostly of what I have read in books. The unforgettable first line of Khushwant Singh's classic novel *Train to Pakistan* is one way I remember the past as a rupture: 'The summer of 1947 was not like other Indian summers.'

The novel quickly plunges into a description of the violence of the riots spreading across the subcontinent. The forced migration of millions, the brutal murders and rapes. But all this is summarily covered in a paragraph because what the writer is really interested in dwelling upon is ordinary culture, the way of life, that survives in his imagination. So, in the pages that follow, we are given a portrait of the village of Mano Majra, the rhythms of daily rituals guided by the passage of trains at the small railway station. The horror of the Partition will visit the village too but the readers and, one suspects, the writer, cherish the humanity that endures.

In the famous story 'Toba Tek Singh' by Urdu writer Saadat

Hasan Manto, we get a brilliant, biting commentary on the arbitrariness of borders. Manto's protagonist, Bishan Singh, lives in a lunatic asylum. He doesn't know whether his village, Toba Tek Singh, is located in India or the newly created nation of Pakistan. As much as the depiction of the madness of that time, what interests me in the story is the persistence of the ordinary. My throat catches as I hear what Bishan Singh's old friend Fazal Din says to him during a visit to the asylum: 'Soon you will be moving to India. What can I say, except that you should remember me to Bhai Balbir Singh, Bhai Vadhawa Singh and Behen Amrit Kaur. Tell Bhai Balbir Singh that Fazal Din is well by the grace of God. The two brown buffaloes he left behind are well too. Both of them gave birth to calves, but, unfortunately, one of them died after six days. Say I think of them often and to write to me if there is anything I can do.'

It is literature's task to record with an unblinking, democratic eye, both our triumphs and failures as individuals as well as a collective. Manto was a soldier in the war on error and hypocritical illusions about the human heart, but I have always nursed a slight suspicion about him. Like tabloid journalism, Manto seemed to enjoy the violence a little too much. I appreciate more the questioning stance adopted by Amrit Rai in his Hindi story 'Kichar' ('Filth') where what is mocked is the 'pleasurable attention' with which four men on Toofan Mail reminisce about the riots and the abduction of women: 'Lakhs of men had died, lakhs of children had been orphaned, lakhs of women had lost their homes and honour. Now all that remained were their stories, stories which were told and heard by people as they smacked their lips with an epicurean's delight.'*

Everyone will have his or her own favourite among the

*From *Stories of Partition, Volumes 1 to 3*, translated by Alok Bhalla, New Delhi: Manohar Publishers and Distributors, 2012.

documents about August 1947 and its ugly aftermath. Mine is M. S. Sathyu's film *Garam Hawa* ('Hot Winds'). The film starts with the shot of a train leaving for Pakistan, and we hear the puffing of its engines again and again. In the Mirza family, people are leaving India. The fate of a Muslim family in Agra, immediately after Independence, is criss-crossed by large historical forces beyond their control. But here's the small voice of the ordinary: during a meal, a little boy wants to know, 'Do they fly kites in Pakistan?'

Garam Hawa is based on an Urdu story by Ismat Chughtai, a writer sensitive to social currents but also alert to individual destinies, especially of women in homes. When I began writing this, I found *Garam Hawa* on YouTube and stopped at a scene that captures my point about civilizational continuities that defy the creation of nations. The old granny is told that they must move to another house. The haveli is no longer theirs. But her husband was buried there. The granny refuses to leave and hides in the woodshed. When her grandson forcibly carries her to the tonga waiting outside, she cries: 'Leave me here, leave me here. How can I face my husband on Judgement Day?'

LANGUAGE SE LAFDA NAHIN KARNE KA

The poet Arun Kolatkar, author of a stunning book, *Jejuri*, also wrote poems in the language of Mumbai's streets, the rough mix of Marathi and Hindi that would later find a flowering in Bollywood films. Kolatkar was sitting in an Irani restaurant when he heard one man narrate to another the following story: 'Main manager ko bola mujhe pagaar mangta hai / manager bola company ke rule se pagaar ek tarikh ko milega / uski ghadi table pay padi thi / maine ghadi uthake liya / aur manager ko police chowki ka rasta dikhaya / bola agar complaint karna hai to karlo / mere rule se pagaar ajhee hoga.'

Kolatkar turned Bombay patois into American English and his translation went like this: 'i want my pay i said / to the manager / you'll get paid said / the manager / but not before the first / don't you know the rules? / coolly I picked up his / wrist watch / that lay on his table / wanna bring in the cops / i said / 'cordin to my rules / listen baby / i get paid when i say so.'

I learned about Kolatkar's experiment from the poet Arvind Krishna Mehrotra. He too, in his fine translation of Kabir, infused the medieval bhakti poet's verses with American slang. '"Me shogun." / "Me bigwig." / "Me the chief's son. / I make the rules here." // It's a load of crap. / Laughing, skipping, / Tumbling, they're all / Headed for Deathville. // In the blink / of an eye, says Kabir, / The king will be / Separated from his kingdom.'

To save Kabir from smothering under solemn religiosity, and to ensure that his verses retain their earthiness, we must keep him colloquial. This is true of other old texts too.

I watched a performance of *Antigone* in Brooklyn with Juliette Binoche in the title role. I had only seen Binoche in films before that. Her wide-apart eyes, hair often cut short, I had seen her surrounded by succulent fruit, or desserts and chocolate, or beautiful landscapes. In *Antigone* she knelt in the bleak desert, mourning her dead brother lying unburied because he was a traitor.

The play's two millennia old but on stage everything was modern. Antigone wore an elegant black outfit and heels. The most recognizably contemporary aspect of the play was the language itself. In poet Anne Carson's translation of the play, the words appeared plucked from present-day parlance.

The colloquial language forced a turn to the recent past and I thought about the hangings of men like Afzal Guru and Yakub Memon. Whatever their deeds, proven or still in doubt, did their deaths not deserve to be mourned by a sister, wife, or child?

When I was in college in Delhi in the early eighties, I watched Girish Karnad's *Tughlaq* with Manohar Singh in the lead. The play was about the possibility of political idealism turning into tyranny. Karnad was using the fourteenth-century sultan as a device to comment on the disillusionment of his generation. Tughlaq's combination of vision and tyranny had a parallel in the problematic aspects of Jawaharlal Nehru's leadership, and the play later found new resonance when Indira Gandhi imposed the Emergency.

In 2018 I wrote to Karnad and asked him about the murder of Mohammad Akhlaq in Dadri over the suspicion of beef-eating. Was there an old story that would explain the present-day horror of lynchings?

In response, Karnad said that long ago he had written a play called *Bali: The Sacrifice* based on an ancient Jain myth. The myth mocked Brahmins who, yielding to the influence of Jainism and Buddhism, had started substituting animals made of dough for live sacrificial animals, arguing that they were thereby being non-violent. The myth declared that violence in intention—mental indulgence in violence—is as dehumanizing and corrupting as real violence.

In *Bali*, King Yashodhara is asked to perform an animal sacrifice. But he is a Jain and his faith forbids violence. As a compromise, instead of a live animal he decides to sacrifice a rooster made of dough. And then, just as he is about to plunge the knife into it, the rooster begins to crow.

The Hindi translation of *Bali* was launched in 2018 at the Jagaran Literature Festival in Lucknow. Karnad told me that instead of reading passages from the play he had merely quoted the BJP's union Minister of Culture, Mahesh Sharma, who had declared that from the nature of Akhlaq's wound it was clear there was no 'intention to kill' and that 'accident' was a more accurate description than 'murder'. Karnad also pointed to what the prime minister's long silence in the aftermath of the event implied in the context of the myth. Karnad said, 'The speeches and the silence could have been part of my play.'

THE LANGUAGE OF SMALL TOWNS

Politicians offer propaganda in a loud voice. Ditto for pundits. I love the small voice of literature. As Joan Didion said, we tell ourselves stories in order to live.

Writing about small towns or about provincial life is appealing because it too brings the gift of small particularities. R. K. Narayan built his entire career around it. However, a cultivation of quaintness in his fiction kept me at a distance. Then the kaleidoscope turned and, at least for me, the picture changed with Upamanyu Chatterjee's *English, August*, a wildly comic account of a metropolitan Indian, a young bureaucrat, in a mofussil town. And the language! The staidness of colonial English tickled, harassed, abused, and caressed by an irreverent writer for whom there were no sacred cows.

A few years passed and Vikram Seth's *A Suitable Boy* landed with a suitable thud, a grand achievement and not only for its portrait of life in the provinces. Set in a fictional town in Uttar Pradesh, it spoke in a voice that possessed all the nearness and transparency of a novel written in Hindustani. In its pages, English no longer sounded as a sociolect designed to set the elite apart from the unwashed masses.

I grew up in Patna, where Vikram Seth also attended school, and one recent work of fiction that celebrates Seth's connection to my hometown is Siddharth Chowdhury's *The Patna Manual of Style*. Chowdhury has woven all of his wonderful fiction around Patna and its scattered diaspora. The same characters wander in and out of the pages of his novels, they emerge from Kadam Kuan in Patna and stumble into classrooms in Delhi University, and sit down for a dose of litti-chokha and mutton at Yadavji Litti Centre in Paharganj.

Siddhartha is a friend of mine but the reason I possibly dislike him a bit, and this is writerly envy speaking, is because his writing is pure voice. I don't just mean the Patna lilt but also the confidence and a specific kind of cosmopolitanism. We see the hinterland populated with small-town managers of jugaad, those who wrestle fate and ultimately fail, and also others who have imagination (and maybe even ambition, if that's not too strong a word) borrowed from films and fiction. These latter could become writers like Chowdhury himself, except they wouldn't know how to write about sex with such bravado. Open Chowdhury's *Day Scholar* to its first page and read about Zorawar Singh Shokeen, landlord of Shokeen Niwas, in flagrant sexual congress with Mrs Midha, a section officer in Delhi University.

Goodbye, all genteel affectations! Farewell, Narayan!

The point is not sex, it is *seeing*. Seeing with the eyes of someone from the margins. NDTV's Ravish Kumar published a book of brief fictional pieces in Hindi, *Ishq Mein Shahar Hona*. Ravish explains that when he arrived from Patna, Delhi entered his consciousness as an image: on the balconies of the buildings visible from the street, women in nighties using washing machines to do laundry. India Gate or Ghalib came to Ravish later, or didn't properly come at all. Instead, it was the humble nightie that introduced him to his new urban reality.

What does that nameless, middle-class woman using the washing machine on her balcony have on her mind?

A question like that motivates Ratika Kapur's novel, *The Private Life of Mrs Sharma*. The titular Mrs Sharma is in her thirties; born in Meerut, she now lives in Delhi, where she takes the metro to work every day. One day at the Hauz Khas station she approaches a well-dressed young man. An affair begins. She doesn't tell the man at first that she is married or about her teenage son. Slowly she discovers a new self and a new city. The novel is narrated in her voice. This is the voice of the ordinary, the quotidian, even the banal—and it is to Kapur's credit that often she makes this voice sing.

The dominant imagination doesn't admit sex, except as scandal, in domestic spaces. This is particularly true of spaces inhabited by married women. In using a language that is idiomatically Indian, and recognizably middle class, Mrs Sharma provides a woman's plain testimony. Kapur has performed an act of literary ventriloquism, and only rarely does she slip into parody. We have seen such performances in Akhil Sharma's *An Obedient Father*, even in Aravind Adiga's *The White Tiger*; this novel also has a strand in common with an eye-opening story like Mohan Sikka's 'The Railway Aunty' which told us about Delhi housewives hiring gigolos.

But Kapur's protagonist is her own person. We accompany Mrs Sharma on the path of her discovery and her doom only because her voice is real. In Mrs Sharma, I heard the voice of the small town of her birth and also the tumult of the big city where she lives. Kapur is a writer not only with an eye for detail: she also uses her ear. And because Mrs Sharma sounds real, she is revolutionary.

THE NAME OF GABBAR SINGH'S HORSE

I wanted to meet him. The problem was that I had been told he doesn't see anyone. He is also quite sick, an invalid, confined to his bed. But I had a piece of paper with his address on it and I was standing at his doorstep in an ordinary housing estate near Jinjira Bazar on the fringes of Kolkata.

His name is Subimal Misra. He writes his stories in Bengali; over the last few years his work has appeared in English translation. When I read him for the first time, I saw that his stories rebelled against dominant literary conventions. His stories were anti-stories, a violent mix of fragmentary narratives and essays, even statistics, juxtaposed together to deliver a shocking statement. 'The bloodier the Naxalite movement in West Bengal grows, Vidyasagar's visage gets chopped off again and again, and the more the pavements of Kolkata become infested with sex-magazines.'

It was revealing that the first of his translated works carried the following dedication: 'To Jean-Luc Godard, who taught me language.' Like the French film-maker, Misra offered a montage of images. In one of his celebrated stories, the rotting corpse of a peasant's wife keeps appearing in unlikely places, including inside the crate that has brought Gandhi's golden statue from America.

Misra's work would have remained unknown to me had it not been for the dedication of his translator, V. Ramaswamy. A second volume of Misra's stories, *Wild Animals Prohibited*, has now been published. In these stories too we encounter the characteristic juxtapositions: images of poverty and protest jostle for space with piquant critiques of middle-class pretensions and sexual hypocrisy. News-items, scraps of dialogue, as well as commentary rub against each other, sometimes in stylized and varied font, calling attention to the fact that what we are reading has been *written*, it is an artifice, and ought to make us think.

It is possible to say that one cannot conceive of the existence of Misra's writing without the Naxalbari uprising. The rejection that we see in him of any pious celebration of postcolonial achievements or of the great Indian democracy returns us to the revolt of the late sixties.

But I'd be lying if I didn't admit that one of the main reasons I wanted to meet Misra was because of the persona he projects in his interviews. There, we learn that he has never sought mainstream publications, doesn't attend literary festivals, and instead of a price his books only have a suggested exchange amount. Once, when asked about his goal in writing, Misra said that he didn't have any goals in the commonly understood sense. And added: 'While watching *Sholay*, I only wanted to know the name of Gabbar Singh's horse.'

I read somewhere that Misra had once worked as a lecturer but he had torn up his degrees and started teaching at a school close to Sonagachi, Kolkata's red light district. In his classes were often the children of prostitutes. Before going to Mishra's home, I went to the school where he had once worked, Banga Vidyalaya. A pretty teacher there, one Miss Tudu, told me that her students, often poor and living on the streets, were 'fast learners'. In nearby Sonagachi, although it was still morning, women stood in clusters, waiting for customers, their hair still wet from their bath. Men with towels on their shoulders, greed in their eyes, urged me to follow them.

I went to Jinjira Bazar instead. A man outside Misra's building told me that Misra's sister lived in a flat on the floor above. The sister opened her door and then, after I had introduced myself, asked her husband to go down to find out if Misra would see me.

I said, 'I just want to pay my respects.'

Misra's flat was small. A female attendant was there too. I entered a small room, its shelves packed with yellowing books, and was then led into the bedroom. Misra was sitting up in bed, under a pink mosquito net, a quilt drawn around his shoulders. His hands shook when he raised them to return my greeting. His sister, speaking in Bengali, said that Misra had fallen off the bed one night and remained on the floor for hours.

The previous year I had taught a course called 'In-Between Novels'. The books in that course were part-essay, part-novel. Included were works by Elizabeth Hardwick (*Sleepless Nights*), Renata Adler (*Speedboat*), J. M. Coetzee (*Elizabeth Costello*), Teju Cole (*Open City*).

I might have said that I saw that Misra's work belonged in that course. I didn't tell him that I was also working on a book that mixed forms. I didn't thank him for his work nor did I feel I could ask any questions. Misra's brother-in-law took a picture of us together, my head inside the mosquito net beside Misra. Then I left. He hadn't said a single word.

THE ANTI-NATIONAL

If the police burst into your room while you were sleeping and, putting a gun to your head, asked you to name a literary work that was critical of the idea of the nation, which title would you reveal?

Those who read Saadat Hasan Manto in school will go back to that early memory. We all remember 'Toba Tek Singh'. The occupants of the lunatic asylum not being able to comprehend the Partition, and the old Sikh Bishan Singh lying in no man's land between the borders of the two countries, unable to decide where he belonged.

But the memory of this story is for me mixed with the white of my school uniform, the safety of home, and the taste of cornflakes in the morning. Which means the call of the nation begins to seem merely like nostalgia for lost childhood. Nationalism in this scenario becomes only an appeal to sentiment.

Let us go further afield, then, to a far country, to look for the literature of sedition.

I hope that even in my sleep I will be able say that my choice is J. M. Coetzee's *Waiting for the Barbarians*. Coetzee, born in Cape Town, South Africa, was awarded the Nobel Prize in 2003. *Waiting for the Barbarians* was published in 1980, a decade before Nelson Mandela's release from prison and the dismantling of apartheid. Its story is narrated by a magistrate, a loyal servant of the Empire in a frontier settlement. He is a man of ordinary virtues and ordinary vices. He reminded me of Hukum Chand, the magistrate in Khushwant Singh's *Train to Pakistan*. Like Coetzee's magistrate,

Hukum Chand possesses a sense of justice and a fondness for food and easily acquired female flesh. He is not noble but his flawed humanity is a bulwark against the rigid, annihilating certitudes of others around him.

In Coetzee's nameless country, the picture darkens with the arrival of Colonel Joll, the interrogation expert. The Colonel, with his trademark dark glasses, questions the tribesfolk living outside the settlement's walls. In precise prose, Coetzee describes Joll's art of torture. The magistrate protests—he has also become attached to a young tribal woman who has been tortured—and is thrown into prison. He is seen as an anti-national.

I haven't read much fiction by Indian writers that deal with authoritarianism or torture. Apart from what appeared in the wake of Naxalbari, our deepest and most despairing writing about the nation was in the context of the Partition. Of course, even before Independence, Tagore had written: 'Patriotism cannot be our spiritual shelter; my refuge is humanity.'

And the Partition stories worked because of their call to a shared humanity. Consider a story like Bhisham Sahni's 'The Train Has Reached Amritsar'. The narrator's focus is on a frail and nervous-looking Babu sitting in a train compartment who is mocked in a friendly way by three Pathan traders. The mood changes as the train passes towns where a riot is raging. The countryside is filled with fleeing refugees. As the train approaches Amritsar, the Babu has vengeance on his mind. He finds an iron rod. He is an angry nationalist now. He hits on the head a Muslim man who is pleading to get into the train. We feel the horror of the blows on a helpless man. The Babu's main regret is that he is unable to find the Pathans and take revenge.

Stories like 'The Train Has Reached Amritsar' succeed because they show that violence doesn't discriminate. The Hindus and the Muslims, Indians and Pakistanis, are all interchangeable in the most memorable Partition stories. You look at the murdered or raped figure—and you see that the victim could have been one of your own.

But that is a problem. Because our humanity isn't as universal as we often assume it is. Which explains why I like Coetzee's *Waiting for the Barbarians*. It presents a starker picture. The so-called barbarians don't look or behave like the townspeople. They appear aboriginal, live in the mountains, and speak a different language. The magistrate's attempts at finding a common humanity are fumbling and crude. They arouse suspicion. When he ministers to the young woman, what are his motives? He makes her his mistress before taking her back to her people. He is hoping for peace but there isn't any. There is only devastation.

I will be called anti-national for saying this but while reading *Waiting for the Barbarians* I thought of Govind Nihalani's *Aakrosh*. Remember the tribal Lahanya Bhiku, played by Om Puri, who is jailed by the forest contractor and the district officials on the charge of murdering his wife? But Bhiku hadn't killed her; the real story was that the contractor and his friends had raped Bhiku's wife. While reading Coetzee, the fiction of Mahasweta Devi also came to mind, the stories of state violence and Adivasi resistance in Singhbhum. Then, I thought of Soni Sori. Suddenly, Coetzee seemed to be telling the story of Adivasis who are tortured because they are suspected of being militants. I could close my eyes and see what is happening in Bastar today.

I TESTIFY THAT

A letter came from Los Angeles. It had been written by an upper-caste Marathi chemist. From this letter, an untouchable poet in Maharashtra found out that Indians in America were treated like dogs. This, I imagine, was in the 1950s or early 60s, before Ravi Shankar had played with the Beatles or Hollywood had used Gandhi to sell popcorn to millions.

The poet reading the letter was Daya Pawar. Beside a dusty rose bush in what was then called Bombay, with the news on the radio close by, our poet read the letter. His joy made him cry. He sat down to write a reply. 'I feel so damn good,' he wrote in Marathi. 'Now, you've had a taste of what we've suffered in this country for far too long.'

I received the story I have told above nearly thirty years ago. I was a new graduate student in the States. The friend who told me the story, a white woman from Minnesota, was translating Dalit writing into English. That is how Daya Pawar came into my life. I put his story into a long poem I was writing and didn't read Pawar again till I devoured with great hunger his autobiography, *Baluta*. It has been translated from Marathi to English by Jerry Pinto.

Pawar, who died in 1996, belonged to the Mahar community. Babasaheb Ambedkar was also a Mahar, a caste that Hindus considered polluting. The term 'baluta' refers to the share of the village harvest owed to a Mahar for the work done during the rest of the year—running in front of the horse of an important person who came into the village, announcing funerals, dragging away the carcasses of dead animals, chopping wood, playing music day and night at festivals, welcoming new bridegrooms at the village borders on their wedding days.

Baluta is a record of unspeakable humiliations in a caste-ridden society. Pawar spares no one, and least of all himself. This is the book's great strength.

Here's an example. When Pawar was still a schoolboy, his father died. Pawar's mother, unknown to the boy, was a couple of months pregnant at that time. A little later, an older man taunted young Pawar with a question: 'Your father's dead and gone but your mother's pregnant. How did that happen?' This threw the boy into turmoil. When his mother miscarried and lay in bed recuperating, Pawar asked her, 'How come you're pregnant when my father's dead?' The question was the wrong one, born out of an older man's malice, but this is what Pawar writes about his shame: 'If you had asked me about this terrible moment even a couple of years ago, I would not have been able to talk about it. But Aai made me promise to tell the whole truth to at least one person in my life. It was she who gave me the strength.'

Around the same time that I first heard about Pawar, I also read V. S. Naipaul's *India: A Million Mutinies Now*. In that book, Naipaul had described his meeting with Namdeo Dhasal, poet and founder of Dalit Panthers. What had made a greater impression on me was Naipaul's report of his conversations with Dhasal's wife, Mallika, the daughter of a Muslim father, who was a communist, and a Hindu mother. Mallika had written a book in Marathi, *I Want To Destroy Myself*. It was an autobiography that had caused a sensation. After all these years, I still remembered the bold title. And when I went back to Naipaul's book, I was reminded that Mallika's book was sexually frank and honest about the failure of her marriage.

'If I hadn't written the book, I would have gone mad,' Mallika had told Naipaul. She also said that Namdeo had supported his wife's right to say what she wished about her marriage. When I read those words, my mind went back to Pawar's *Baluta*. At his book's end, Pawar mentions seeing once or twice in a town-market the wife that he had abandoned years ago. She would be dressed in rags. I was struck by Pawar's candour, and his sense of shame. Pawar married again. Unlike his first wife, his second wife was educated. She also wrote an autobiography in Marathi, *Truth Be Told*...

Let's take the case of Delta Meghwal. Her story shows that a young Dalit woman in India might not get a chance to tell her life's story. On 28 March 2016, seventeen-year-old Delta called her father to tell him that she had been raped by her physical education teacher, Vijendra Singh. This happened after the warden of the hostel where Delta lived had sent the Dalit student to clean Singh's room. The next day Delta Meghwal's body was found floating in a water tank.

DEAD WRITER

The first book I read by the Tamil writer Perumal Murugan was *One Part Woman.** But the first words of his that I read were the ones he had posted on Facebook after he had been forced by religious zealots to sign a document withdrawing unsold copies of his book and deleting passages they found offensive: 'Perumal Murugan the writer is dead. As he is not god, he is not going to resurrect himself. He also has no faith in rebirth. An ordinary teacher, he will live as P. Murugan. Leave him alone.'

That note pierced me. A fireman leaving his job, or a politician quitting politics, even a young cricketer setting his or her bat aside, would most likely not be writing of quitting their profession as a death. And this was no ordinary death. In a simple but subtle way, Murugan was accusing his society of wanting to murder him.

I wanted to know more about Murugan. I feared for him but, to be honest, I also envied him a bit. A part of me felt that one wasn't a real writer unless one's writing had offended a section of readers. Murugan was a real writer.

From news reports I learned that Murugan taught Tamil literature at a college in a small town. His father was an illiterate farmer and, to find additional income, he ran a soda shop in a cinema hall. When Murugan married a woman from a lower caste, he was ostracized even by his own family. A lot of what he wrote reflected the divisions of caste and gender in rural society.

---

*Perumal Murugan, *One Part Woman*, translated by Aniruddhan Vasudevan, New Delhi: Penguin Books India, 2013.

When I read *One Part Woman*, I had further reason to envy Murugan. The novel was an affectionate portrait of a childless couple in colonial India; the narrative leads the reader to a carnival night during a festival when the rules of marriage are relaxed, and consensual sex between unmarried men and women is overlooked because all men are considered gods. I immediately recognized the novel as belonging to a genre we might call rooted literature. What Murugan was producing was locally grown literature, not a canned object sold on a supermarket bookshelf. It is rare to come across a writer who enjoys such intimacy with a land and those who live in close contact with it. One aspect that I admired so much about *One Part Woman* was that it was so rooted in the soil of tradition that its rebellion against it was all the more unexpected and moving.

It struck me, when I had finished reading the novel, that long before the protests and the controversies that exiled him into silence, Murugan was already a dead writer. What do I mean by this? I have in my notebooks a remark by Christopher Hitchens, his advice to writers: 'One should try to write as if posthumously.' What Hitchens was saying was that even the most independent-minded writer is never ever free of all of his or her inhibitions. And to be dead is to be relieved of all worry. You cannot be burdened with any concerns about how your writing is viewed. Hitchens wrote, 'You're free. Death is a very liberating thought.' Murugan's willingness or ability to look into the dark well of prejudice and see his own close society's face reflected there suggested that he was writing posthumously. This lack of fear, or radical honesty, gave his writing its power.

And so, if you follow my reasoning here, after *One Part Woman* had been published in its original Tamil, the violent protests and acts of coercion directed at Murugan brought him back from the dead. He began to live in fear. As he publicly remarked during the release of his book of poems, 'A censor is seated inside me now. He is testing every word that is born within me. His constant caution that a word may be misunderstood so, or it may be interpreted thus, is a real bother. But I'm unable to shake him off.'*

What is one to do if you are one-part alive and one-part dead? ('A walking corpse,' to borrow a phrase from Murugan.) You write. Or that is what Murugan did. Almost as if he were keeping a journal of his nightmare, he wrote down poems. They were published under the title *Songs of a Coward*.** These are his 'poems of exile'; they come accompanied by the dates on which they were written. A poem written on 23 May 2016 has the title 'About the Dead Man'. Another, written on 25 May 2016, is titled 'The Dead Man Speaks'.

A month later, Murugan wrote a poem called 'The Battlefield'. The poem begins with a declaration that he has 'no sword to wield / no spear / no arrow to aim.' This poet has 'no kingdom / no enemies.' The poem ends with the lines: 'Nevertheless / I set out from home / to the battlefield / every day / armed / armoured / with a battle plan / and an army.'

Murugan is saying he is prepared to fight. I believe he is also saying that he is not afraid of death.

---

*See Ellen Barry, 'A Censor Is Seated Inside Me Now: Hometown Wrath Tests a Novelist', *New York Times*, 22 August 2016.

**Perumal Murugan, *Songs of a Coward: Poems of Exile*, translated by Aniruddhan Vasudevan, New Delhi: Penguin Books India, 2017.

V

Form

LIGHT YEARS

I have mentioned earlier the lectures that James Salter delivered a year before his death at the University of Virginia. During one of those lectures, he told his audience about the difficulty of writing novels. The writer needs an idea and the characters. Also the story. And then, Salter added: 'You need, if I can put it this way, the form: What length book will it be? Written in long paragraphs? Short ones? In which person? A book that is going off in all directions? How dense? When you have the form, you can write the novel.'* There were other requirements that Salter listed, the related matter of style, for instance, the writer's prejudices and position, and of course the important matter of the book's beginning, but, for me, his description of form and what it entails gets to the heart of the matter. The authors of the books I like have this fact in common: they had a good idea for a book, yes, but what they had really succeeded at doing was figuring out the book's form.

---

*James Salter, *The Art of Fiction*, Charlottesville: University of Virginia Press, 2016. See p. 31.

PARANOID THEORY

There is a YouTube video from the New Yorker Festival in 2011 of Jonathan Franzen talking to David Remnick about the journey from his earlier books to the time he wrote *The Corrections*.* What was the break? A lot of it had to do with the death of Franzen's father but also his letting go of, among other things, hard-core academic theory. In the video, Franzen describes the latter as 'paranoid theory', reading the text for signs of what's wrong with society. ('All of them, the Marxists, Freudians, Derrida, Foucault, Lacan, although I never quite understood Lacan.')

By the time he came to write *The Corrections*, Franzen says he was also giving up on the wish to be encyclopaedic and the wish to construct a narrative that would include everything. What I find touching about this is Franzen's admission that this was humiliating. It was humiliating to give up the sense of power that came from oppositional thinking—and writing a book instead about a Midwestern mother getting to celebrate Christmas at her home with her grown-up children. ('How can that be my story and yet there was more and more evidence that that was the story. That was, in fact, *the plot*.') It makes sense to me, this admission, as does the desire Franzen describes earlier in the interview: 'To translate that which I loved so much about modernism, which is the touchstone for me literarily, into something that my parents could read.' He goes on: he was trying to find a form that takes on a modern sensibility, and a modern consciousness about method, but results

*https://www.youtube.com/watch?v=JA2Ajqwc_yQ

in books that appear welcoming to non-specialists.

Despite his claims on having given up on theory, I have always felt that his reading of the thinkers he named in his interview was responsible for the reason why not only Franzen's fiction but also his non-fiction, by which I mean his essays, possess a certain weightiness. How, for instance, is he able to lucidly connect disparate strands (in an essay entitled 'Farther Away', everything from a record of travel to a remote island to the history of the novel to the death of David Foster Wallace is discussed) and make something greater than the sum of individual parts?* When I asked him about it, Franzen said it probably had to do with his father who was a civil engineer and designed bridges. There were phrases that Franzen's father, Earl, used regularly: 'sturdy structure' and 'redundant members'. Franzen remembers that in his childhood when they passed a bridge his father would remark that people were crossing that bridge. Franzen said that it became intuitive for him to think in terms of structure. His father, he said, 'was very respectful of things because they could break'. A different kind of theory, entirely, onc interested in getting people and cars from one side to the other.

There is one other thing I want to say about structure, although this too has something to do with fathers and sons. It is a story about the non-fiction writer John McPhee and his father on his deathbed. But first, I have a story about McPhee and a teacher he had in his first three years at high school, Olive McKee. For each week of school during those three years, Mrs McKee allowed the students to write anything they wanted to, but each piece of writing had to be accompanied by a structural outline. The outline had to be done first. McPhee writes, 'It could be anything from Roman numerals,

*Jonathan Franzen, 'Farther Away', *New Yorker*, 18 April 2011.

I, II, III to a looping doodle with guiding arrows and stick figures.'* McPhee followed his teacher's example in his own classroom:

> Structure has preoccupied me in every project I have undertaken since, and, like Mrs. McKee, I have hammered it at Princeton writing students across decades of teaching: 'You can build a strong, sound, and artful structure. You can build a structure in such a way that it causes people to want to keep turning pages. A compelling structure in nonfiction can have an attracting effect analogous to a story line in fiction.' Et cetera. Et cetera. And so forth, and so on.

McPhee goes on to share his diagrams outlining the organization of various pieces he has written over decades but nothing about his sense of structure impressed me as much as the following account about him in a magazine.** The piece in question is a profile essay by Sam Anderson. It mentions the title piece of a future volume by McPhee, an essay about his father's death.*** The elder McPhee is in a hospital, after a stroke, and the son begins to talk to the unresponsive father about one thing they did together—fishing. He starts by talking about the pickerel he had recently been catching in New Hampshire. There is great specificity here in the description of the pickerel. ('Pickerel that have been found in the stomachs of pickerel have in turn contained pickerel in their stomachs.') Then, the trips when father and son had gone fishing ('did he

---

*John McPhee, *Draft No. 4: On the Writing Process*, New York: Farrar, Straus and Giroux, 2017. See pp. 18-20.

**Sam Anderson, 'The Mind of John McPhee', *New York Times*, 28 September 2017.

***That essay by McPhee first appeared in the *New Yorker*. See John McPhee, 'The Patch', *New Yorker*, 8 February 2010.

I went back to read 'The Patch' after reading Sam Anderson's profile-essay on McPhee. The point Anderson makes about McPhee's structural organization in 'The Patch' is a good and subtle one, and I'd only add that the moment that Anderson notices is only amplified, to devastating effect, by the way in which McPhee has structured the essay's ending.

remember the sand sharks off Sias Point? the rainbows of Ripton? the bullhead he gutted beside Stony Brook that flipped out of his hand and, completely gutless, swam away?'). Anderson informs the reader that after this 'there is a section break, some white space, then a paragraph of fish facts that in the context of his father's impending death, reads like a prose poem.' How could a paragraph of mundane details about fish possess such magic? I don't exactly know but I think a lot of it has to do with structure, this expert casting of the line so that it catches a sense of loss and the terrible yearning to overturn it:

> With those minutely oscillating fins, a pickerel treads water in much the way that a hummingbird treads air. If the pickerel bursts forth to go after prey, it returns to the place it started from, with or without the prey. If a pickerel swirls for your fly and misses, it goes back to the exact spot from which it struck. You can return half an hour later and it will be there. You can return at the end of the day and it will be there. You can go back next year and it will be there.

THE SOUND AND THE FURY

While I was in graduate school, I read an academic essay by Kumkum Sangari on narrative technique in the works of Gabriel Garcia Marquez and Salman Rushdie. I can't claim I understood much in what was being said in sentences like the following one: 'The double disjunction of a hybrid simultaneity and of the economic and ideological deformations of neocolonialism is the condition within which the real is perceived and also the condition within which both authors and texts are produced.'* The sentences I was reading were about writers I admired, but Sangari's own sentences aroused very little interest. Except that on one page I suddenly found materialist explanations for why writers produce the sentences that they do. In the case of Henry James, the elaborate, complex sentences served as 'the site for the formation of an aristocratic bourgeois consciousness'.** A different order of complexity in Joseph Conrad's fiction gestured 'toward an ineffable universe wherein mystery begins to underwrite and overdetermine imperial history'. Were these empty generalizations? I didn't think so. On the one hand, the analysis teetered close to reductiveness, but, on the other hand, because it paid attention to the shape of sentences, I found the readings suggestive. I was learning that it wasn't simply what the novel spoke about, nor even the novel's structure, but the form of the individual sentence that was perhaps

*Kumkum Sangari, 'The Politics of the Possible', *Cultural Critique*, (Fall 1987), pp. 157-186. The quote appears on p. 161.

**Ibid, p. 167. All following quotes are from the same page.

its most eloquent unit.

There was more to come in Sangari's piece. For instance, the insight that the long sentence in Faulkner becomes 'a sign of the incestuous involution of the American South and simulates the relentless claustrophobia of oppression that leaves no space to breathe or time to punctuate and is impossible to stem or stop'. A large element of determinism was present in this analysis, and yet I do not remember finding it disconcerting. Instead, I have never forgotten the words Sangari used to describe how Marquez's sentences were different from all the other writers she had so far analysed. In Marquez's fiction, Sangari wrote, 'the long sentence is an index of the *fecundity* of the repressed, of the barely begun and unfinished—*not uncertain*—stories simmering beneath the strident sounds and tight enclosures of dictatorship, and so gestured toward unopened possibilities'. There was an indication here that the conventions of grammar worked as constraints, and still, the voices that had been silenced in history would come tumbling out in bright, even boisterous, sentences.

How exciting! Except that my own sentences were laboured constructions, difficult to understand, and impossible to enjoy. I wasn't alone in writing like this; every postcolonial scholar was doing the same. In doing this, we were unlike the writers we were analysing. Salman Rushdie—who was also the subject of Sangari's essay, except that she had said nothing about him that I could easily parse—had launched a thousand dissertations. Yet, he was also the writer whose sentences, even in non-fiction, had very little in common with his commentators. This was the contradictory world I inhabited: unlike my new classes on postcolonial theory, where a writer's meaning was glimpsed, if at all, through the thick fog of nearly impenetrable verbiage, Rushdie's words were clear, even conversational. His intelligence was evident everywhere, and yet one didn't feel that his insights were weights dragging you to the bottom of the sea. I read everything he wrote and wanted to use his words in my work.

Don't get me wrong. I did my best to sound like my teachers, and wrote sentences whose texture was inevitably thicker than cement. Still, Rushdie could always be trusted to provide the perfect epigraph—by turns elegant, cutting, or comic—for the challenging edifices of prose that I was building. I would still construct my academic platforms of multiple subordinate clauses and reinforced concrete, but a line from Rushdie sat on the top, like a glorious, fluttering pennant.

I had to wait many years till I got to ask Rushdie any questions about his writing. During a public conversation with him on stage, I asked if he had any writing advice for postcolonial writers. 'I have a rule that I offer to young writers,' Rushdie said. 'There must be no tropical fruits in the title. No mangoes, no guavas. None of those. Tropical animals are also problematic. Peacock, etc. Avoid that shit.' He was equally blunt about the difficulty of his craft. 'Writing is an act of love. If you don't love it, go do something else for God's sake. Go get a job.' I then pressed him on the question of postcolonial theory. 'When I'm making a book, I'm not thinking of theory,' he replied, and later, when I asked him to elaborate by email, Rushdie wrote: 'The truth is that while I do have some awareness of literary theory it doesn't have much to do with the way I think when I'm making work. So while I am interested, I'm also wary of reading too much literary criticism about my own work, because I don't want to end up writing from theoretical positions. I'm grateful for the critical interest in my work, but I think it's probably best that I do the writing and let others theorize about it.'

COLLABORATIVE FORM

An old teacher in my hometown, Patna, told me that when he was young, and very poor, he didn't have enough money to eat. And yet, even during those hungry days, he was accepted as a poet in Patna. He was seventeen or eighteen at that time and was regularly invited to poetry meetings; he would be on stage with well-known Hindi poets like Harivansh Rai Bachchan and Gopaldas Neeraj. Every evening poets and writers gathered in a place called Janta Hotel on Govind Mitra Road, which is now a store selling medical supplies. Giants of contemporary literature who were passing through Patna would also visit the hotel. Anyone who had written a new piece would stand up and recite their work. When the old man was telling me all this, what grew in my mind was a picture of cultural ferment in Patna. To be alive, and to be an artist, was to be involved *in conversation* with others.* That, to me, is the essence of collaboration. It means that your work and those of others around you is shaped collectively, through the recognition of similarities and the airing of differences. Your art occupies the same contemporary moment, and a shared cultural

---

*Standing in a large room at the MoMA, looking at the paintings by Picasso and Braque hung side by side, I was conscious not so much of individual genius as much as creativity as a shared *social* force. How many meetings in studios, how many cups of coffee or glasses of wine shared, to examine and articulate the historical challenge at that moment in art? The similarities between Picasso's *Ma Jolie* and Braque's *Portugais* demonstrate an idea of collaboration, to borrow Braque's words, of two 'mountaineers roped together'. See Michael Brenson, 'Picasso and Braque: Brothers in Cubism', *New York Times*, 22 September 1989.

space, and you measure your response to this time and place by critically examining other responses around you. When you hear other voices raised in appreciation or debate, you also know that you are not alone.* Is that what academic conferences do for us?** Or are they too professionalized and busy, spaces of anxiety and hectic hustle? I ask these questions in order to remind myself and others to find spaces for collaboration.***

A few years ago, Teju Cole asked me to write brief essays to accompany his photographs for an exhibition. Cole is a friend of mine but a part of our friendship owes its strength to an idea of shared striving; over the past decade my work has been in dialogue with him through conversations both public and private. Last Christmas, when I asked him to explain his interest in collaboration, Cole cited an Igbo proverb: 'Where one thing stands, another will stand by it.' This was a proverb that Cole had often heard Chinua Achebe invoke. Cole then supplied another image: 'I'm walking through the landscape, holding a shoe, looking for the other one.' Real work will always draw you towards other people, Cole believes, towards the idea of the collective that is suggested by the South African notion of 'Ubuntu' ('I am because we are').

---

*I want to celebrate sharing and also caring. At a Worker Writers School workshop, a participant handed out little instructions for mutual care. I learned this from a friend who was attending. My friend's card said: 'Cook or bake something, then give it to a friend. (Be mindful of food allergies and restrictions.) When they ask why, say, "Because I treasure you as a friend."'

**One reason I'm against disciplinary conferences is that I welcome cross-disciplinary collaboration. Here is the requisite academic quote to support my position:
'To be inside and outside a position at the same time—to occupy a territory while loitering skeptically on the boundary—is often where the most intensely creative ideas stem from. It is a resourceful place to be, if not always a painless one.' Terry Eagleton, *After Theory*.

***'I feel, in a lot of ways, the fun thing about working collaboratively with someone is that you literally come to terms together.' Fred Moten in an interview with Stevphen Shukaitis. Stefano Harney and Fred Moten, *The Undercommons: Fugitive Planning and Black Study*, Wivenhoe: Minor Composition, 2013. See p. 105.

I would argue that collaboration is a basic tenet of Cole's formal aesthetic. You can read an essay of his and you will find that no idea is presented alone. I remember Cole telling me that he tries to find three different ideas, often images, to put together in one of his photography columns for the *New York Times Magazine*. For our project, the photographs Cole had sent me were in pairs, images of places twinned together, paired images that, Cole said, 'endorse and fortify each other'. We called our ekphrastic project, 'Who's Got the Address?'* I cite it as an example of an argument that writing does not—need not—happen alone.

*'Who's Got the Address?' was presented at the International Centre, Panjim, Goa, and at the Art Chamber, Calangute, Goa; both in December 2012. It was shown at the Handwerker Gallery, Ithaca College, Ithaca, between 9 April and 3 May 2013. To view and read the project in its entirety, please check the online magazine *Guernica* https://www.guernicamag.com/whos-got-the-address/. The piece was posted on 15 March 2013.

TRADE BOOK

When can an academic be considered to have written a trade book? According to this book's editor, the term 'trade' properly refers to a title published by a serious or big-time publisher for a general audience. Such a book cannot be confused with a 'crossover' book (a title that might have a cross-disciplinary appeal) or with 'academic trade' (a title given trade discounts or publicity by university presses). A good example of a trade book in recent years would be Matthew Desmond's *Evicted: Poverty and Profit in the American City*.* This book was brought out by Crown Publishers, a subsidiary of Penguin Random House. Desmond, a sociologist at Harvard, has won numerous awards for the book, including the 2017 Pulitzer Prize for general non-fiction. I read the book with interest because it addressed a pressing social problem, but I was also drawn by its style. Is there a particular kind of refusal of academic norms that makes it possible for a manuscript to be published as a trade book?

The first thing that can be said about *Evicted* is that it never allows learning to come in the way of life. Serious scholarship undergirds Desmond's exploration of evictions in Milwaukee from May 2008 to December 2009, but the book's real strength is the quality of its seeing. The quality of its reportage is such that instead of dead statistics we are witness to the complicated lives of the people portrayed. Till I had read Desmond, I had not understood why a woman who is suffering from domestic abuse would rather

*Matthew Desmond, *Evicted*, New York: Crown Publishing, 2016.

not call the police—it could get her evicted. In another scene we watch movers at an eviction. Desmond throws out a useful statistic or two about the race-based reduction in wealth but what is arresting, and heartbreaking, is the plain list of things being removed from the children's rooms and the reaction on the faces of those whose lives are being so rudely undone.

In the author's note, Desmond has written that often the very people he was studying taught him how to see. Nevertheless, he missed much, at least at first, 'not because I was an outsider but also because I was overanalyzing things'. When I read those words, my senses went on alert. I felt that here was a warning for academics. Desmond went on: 'A buzzing inner monologue would draw me inward, hindering my ability to remain alert to the heat of life at play right in front of me'.* There it was! For me, the definition of the trade book was present in that admission. I'm generalizing wildly, but academic books find safety in explanations that reduce the chaos of social life. To write what is not dead on the page, one has to be open to all kinds of disturbances and challenges and confusion. And skilled writers show us a way (Susan Sontag, Toni Morrison, Denis Johnson, Ralph Ellison, Jesmyn Ward—these are some of Desmond's models) to draw out a more difficult story out of all that pain and frustration.

When I asked Desmond if he had conceived *Evicted* as a 'trade' book, he said that he resists such categories. 'I wanted to write a book that did justice to people's stories, showing the human wreckage of the affordable housing crisis through ethnographic reporting and original statistical studies. I wanted that effort to make a difference, which means I wanted to write it for readers inside and outside the academy.'

And that was another clue to understanding 'trade'. If you want to make a difference, calling for affordable housing for all

---

*Ibid. See p. 324.

Americans, you will write fresh sentences. Not sentences that read like footnotes, stuffed with scholarly references.

IN DEFENCE OF THE FRAGMENT

Sarah Manguso's *300 Arguments* is a short book, only ninety pages long.* The pages are small, nearly pocket-sized. On the dust jacket on the back is printed one of the 300 arguments presented in the pages inside: 'Think of this as a short book composed entirely on what I hoped would be a long book's quotable passages.'** A great number of the passages are near-aphorisms. Several of these are a writer's statements, including a few on the form of the book we are holding in our hands: 'I used to write these while playing hooky on what I hoped would be my magnum opus. Assigning myself to write three hundred of them was like forcing myself to chain-smoke until I puked, but it didn't work. I didn't puke.' All right, then. But others among the 300 are about life, sexuality, desire, death. The fragmentary form makes it possible to easily move from one subject to another. A few of the entries here took me back to an essay on envy Manguso published in the *New York Times Book Review* before this book came out;*** unlike the thousand-word newspaper essay, all the entries in the book are at most only a few lines long. The fragmentary design gives Manguso freedom to cover

*Sarah Manguso, *300 Arguments,* Minneapolis: Graywolf Press, 2017.

**Another contemporary attempt at writing in fragments, particularly suited to the Facebook age, is Jeff Nunokawa's *Note Book*, New Jersey: Princeton University Press, 2015. Nunokawa's essays in the book were all originally written as 'Notes' on his Facebook page. In conversation with literary as well as philosophical sources, and expressed with touching candour and a desire for a connection with the reader in the Internet era, Nunokawa's fragments represent a brave stylistic experiment.

***Sarah Manguso, 'Green-Eyed Verbs', *New York Times Book Review*, 29 January 2016.

far more ground and to do so in a way that is nearly novelistic. Not all of Manguso's arguments are compelling or incisive but I was impressed by the way in which the form allowed her to soon follow a note on editing with another one on the memory of a kiss. And yet, these fragments are bound, one suspects, by a narrative arc. The novelistic feel comes from the kind of stories that Manguso tells—moving from caustic self-help for writers and fly-by-cultural-commentary to disclosures about relationships and marriage and parenting—but it also comes from a vague shift in the position from which the arguments are being made. This shift has to do with the acquiring of something like hindsight or from the application of memory. Manguso is a delicate writer so the change is suggested by small things, as if what was being said had been altered through a subtle dropping or adding of a comma or some other punctuation mark. I'm not always convinced that these pieces succeed, but I want to champion such books as possible models for new writing in academia.

KIDS

Kids determine the form in which you write, and sometimes how much you write.

The playwright Sarah Ruhl was speaking to students at my college. She was reading prose she had written; they were very short pieces, and sounded like aphorisms. Ruhl has small children and she talked of the 'vaporous lack of memory that comes from lack of sleep'. After her twins were born, there was little time and energy to write, and Ruhl said she engaged with 'short form as a way of maternal survival'.

Ruhl read out short pieces that were later compiled in a book—these brief essays were about the interruptions that kids brought to the writing. They were funny. Also likely to induce despair, but funny still. I don't remember now whether Ruhl read out the following lines but I read them with great pleasure in her book—I think they can be adopted as a mantra:

> I found that life intruding on writing was, in fact, life. And that, tempting as it may be for a writer who is also a parent, one must not think of life as an intrusion. At the end of the day, writing has very little to do with writing, and much to do with life. And life, by definition, is not an intrusion.*

---

*See Sarah Ruhl, *100 Essays I Don't Have Time to Write: On Umbrellas and Sword Fights, Parades and Dogs, Fire Alarms, Children, and Theater*, New York: Farrar, Straus and Giroux, 2014. See pp. 4-5. Ruhl also quoted from a letter that Virginia Woolf wrote to Vita Sackville-West: 'Style is a very simple matter; it is all rhythm. Once you get that, you can't use the wrong words.' See Ruhl, ibid, p. 92.

RECOMMENDATION LETTER

Form matters. Style is everywhere, and nowhere. It is seldom in evidence in what academics so often write—recommendation letters. And in that scenario, I want to make a recommendation.

To Whom It May Concern:

I am writing to recommend to you a novel by Julie Schumacher with the marvelous title *Dear Committee Members.**

This is an entertaining epistolary novel made up entirely of that least promising of forms: letters of recommendation. The sender of these letters is Jason Fitger, a cantankerous professor of creative writing. He belongs to a recognizable type: an early book he wrote met with success but his productivity has since dwindled, if not entirely vanished. Fitger is employed at a less-than-distinguished institution in the Midwest with a telling name, Payne University.

The letters go out to a vice provost, department chairs, a literary agent, managers of grocery stores and other captains of industry overlooking dead-end jobs, even former girlfriends in positions of power in administration. Because Fitger is an uninhibited over-sharer, the novel's narrative advances easily. He presents us at every turn a vivid picture of the academic workplace as a disaster zone, of literature as a beleaguered discipline, and last, but not least, the writer as truth-teller.

This might be the right place to swerve away from my subject, as letters of recommendation often do, and offer for your consideration personal, somewhat self-indulgent, anecdotes about myself. In the

*Julie Schumacher, *Dear Committee Members*, New York: Random House, 2014.

early nineties, while I was beginning my work on a dissertation, I sent out several applications for an assistant professor's job. I was lucky to get a few interviews and then one campus visit to a university in the American South. This was a trip out from the snows of Minnesota in deep winter to a place that was warm and sunny. I felt I was being rescued.

After the campus visit, I waited for the call. One afternoon I was reading when the phone rang. It was the department chair, a former nun, whom I remembered by her mannerism, a child's habit really, of using the back of her hand to regularly wipe her mouth and round face. She told me that the English department had voted to hire me, and that I could join in the fall. She was halfway through telling me that I would also be paid moving expenses when she suddenly stopped.

'I'm terribly sorry,' she said. 'I've made a mistake. You're not our top candidate.' I felt bad for her, especially because I understood how embarrassed she must be feeling, more so when she thought it necessary to next ask me to repeat my name. I imagined her sitting with a list in front of her, and when I gave her my name, I wondered whether she was now scratching it out.

A week or two later the phone rang again.

It was the same voice and I felt excitement flutter in my heart. The chair laughed and said that this time she knew what she was doing. She had a job offer for me. The person who had got the first nod from the department had chosen to go elsewhere. She said I had a week to decide but I wanted to erase the memory of her mistake: I told her I would take the job. This time she completed the sentence about paying a small amount for moving expenses.

I disliked the chair and I grew to dislike her successor; the bitterness of a small salary and small-stakes rivalries in each office along the corridor gave me for several years a skewed sense of academe. And yet, I'm sure that I didn't once write a recommendation letter of the kind that Jason Fitger routinely writes in *Dear Committee Members*. Here's an example:

> *You have asked for my candid assessment of Tamar Auden, applicant for the position of assistant professor, tenure track, with concentrations in British literature, rhetoric, and creative writing…Here's the pertinent question: Who in god's name, given the ad your department placed, would argue to turn Dr. Auden down? DiCameron is a small college with limited means: you've clearly been charged with hiring a jack-of-all-trades. And Dr. Auden is that mythical creature you seek: fully qualified to teach British and American literature, women's studies, composition, creative writing, intermediate parasailing, advanced sword swallowing, and subcategories and permutations of the above.*

Although I didn't write letters as Fitger does, the novelist Padgett Powell, who was my colleague at the university from the story I've told you above, tried valiantly to breathe life onto the page. I served on a committee where our main job was to read letters by English department faculty evaluating graduate student teaching. Padgett's letters were always different from the rest. I could see that he was fighting boredom but it took me some time to realize that the boredom he was fighting was one that comes from having to hide the truth. One year, a student named Tom Kenny whose teaching was being evaluated also happened to be my neighbour; when he showed me Padgett's letter evaluating his teaching, I promptly photocopied it and hung it in a frame in my bathroom for all visitors to see. Here's what Padgett had written in his characteristically whimsical, and witty, style:

> *I tender this evaluation without benefit of form not because I find the ranking numbers not merely invidious but invidious in a silly way, but because I do not have a form.*
>
> *I observed a class of Mr. Kenny's last Friday that was without a doubt the most unmalleable bunch in the history of education,*

and already I have misstated the matter. They were not unmalleable, they were hen's teeth; no, bumps on logs; no, blood of turnip. That's it—I need no form because Mr. Kenny squeezed the turnip and squeezed the turnip and that turnip do not bleed.

During this prodigious effort on Mr. Kenny's part, he gave a charming explication of 'Rappaccini's Daughter' that ran a good vernacular gamut; 'Who's Rappaccini and what's the deal with his daughter?' should have opened the floor to his neat delineation of Puritan oppositions and reversals in the story, an explication which made for me at least Hawthorne as interesting as he's supposed to be.

Mr. Kenny's syllabus and course in general suggest good, tough, old-fashioned rigor, and his method—despite somnolent troops—was alert, nuanced, and his Socratic questions had a genuine interrogative lilt to them that made me want to try a couple answers myself. I'd say Mr. Kenny does the University fine; the University, in locating this group of degree petitioners, has failed him.

As I said, I framed the above letter and kept it on display in my bathroom for the years I stayed at that dismal institution in the South. I took delight in Powell's flouting of the role he had been assigned, but it wasn't just the rebellion that delighted me; instead, I reveled in the creativity he had shown in responding to a writing task that is often performed as if by rote. Reading the letter I imagined the pleasure Powell had experienced in writing it. I was energized by the power that language possesses—how the words you use can transform a dull, seemingly awkward conversation into a cutting report that is refreshing to read.

In the case of Schumacher's Fitger in *Dear Committee Members*, it is a delight to read letters whose writer is not regurgitating familiar phrases and is attentive to language: 'A cursory glance at her transcript, with its tidy, monotonous fishing line of A's, should suffice to recommend her.' Yes, there is a faint stirring of veiled criticism there, a typical feature in the design of recommendation letters—often, the only feature through which any light creeps inside. But Fitger is routinely more outspoken. Even his parenthetical remarks bristle with energetic—well—recommendations: 'If you don't know Hanf's word: please head straight to the library or bookstore—I give you leave to put this letter aside and come back to it later—to find a copy of *Testimony in Red*, a finalist for the National Book Award, which, in the absence of cronyism among the judges that year, would have won.' Often, Fitger's awareness of the genre pushes him to alert the reader to the expected diction of recommendation letters and, on occasion, he is able to highlight the fact that truth-telling in recommendation letters is often an exceptional condition: 'Louise Frame is applying for the position of associate administrator in your department; happily, I am able to recommend her to you without reservation and with a clear conscience.'

The letter of recommendation, as a genre, demands hyperbole. It takes the writer hostage: you are a prisoner of its form. Which means that, in order to be freed, you have to pay. This is done through unearned praise and a clever concealment of truth. (The same holds true for what can be called the counter-recommendation. Just read the reviews on Amazon! Or, in the interest of honesty, consider the things I have said about that department where I once worked. Not a word so far about the friendships I formed, the students I still interact with, the support I received from colleagues as well as the university.) Returning to the letter of recommendation, however, the entire enterprise feels hollow because this exorbitant payment is nothing but a few rote phrases. Your conscience will not let you rest unless you exaggerate your praise; once this work is done, your conscience will stay troubled because you have heaped lies.

I can honestly say that I have written only one letter in my life that I'm not proud of. A student who had never taken my classes asked me to write a letter for her. This was a good fifteen-twenty years ago. I remember asking if her committee members wouldn't do a better job and she said no. It was a short letter and it must have reflected poorly on the student; at no point was I in any doubt, however, that the letter reflected most poorly on me. Why did I write it then? I believed I was sharing the truth about the student, that my letter was a statement about her professional abilities. But I wish I had been more direct and addressed this fact openly in my letter—that would have been a more generous and collegial act. Or I could have just kept saying no when I was asked if I could please write a letter. This last path is the one I have chosen ever since. It doesn't make me a hero, but it makes me less of a coward.

Which brings me back to Padgett Powell who, unlike the fictional Jason Fitger, is the real hero of my story. Years after I had left that place in the sun where we had been colleagues, I wrote to Padgett and asked him if he could give me rules for writing recommendation letters. This was for a book I was planning to write on style and academia. Padgett wrote back saying he didn't have any such rules. But, he said, he had an observation. I quote it here in full:

> This year we included in our application packets—the ones we look at to base admissions on—for the first time the letters of recommendation. We thought we should, after all. After reading about twenty of these sets of letters, I think we all realized that if we got, say, 240 applications for 6 spots, and we read the letters of recommendation, we would admit 240 candidates. I prudently discontinued including the letters in the packets.
>
> I saw, in the twenty or forty letters I read, one that was candid and telling; it included negativity. It was from Jamaica Kincaid, not an academic. It is the only letter I read

> that I trust. Had the writing of the candidate been stronger, we would have taken her over other candidates with equal writing who had but glowing this-is-a-genius letters.
>
> Years ago we had an applicant who had a story that was hauntingly strong, like something that had been found in an early drawer of Tennessee Williams or Truman Capote. The other sample was average and weak. We happened to read a letter of recommendation. It so began:
>
> 'The last time I saw Ms. _____ she was standing wet and naked on a chair, holding a smoke alarm, while living on an island for a week in my home. The story that I suspect she has applied to your program with she stole from me.'
>
> We decided the letter writer was crazy and threw the letter out and got a fourth to replace it and admitted the student and were wrong. She never wrote anything approaching the stolen story.

Dear committee members, I don't want to turn all lit-crit on you but that letter of recommendation Padgett quotes is startling, thrilling in its vividness, and certainly disturbing—the tone is proprietary, and not just about the work. It is so personal that it seems unprofessional and yet, in the context, perhaps not unprofessional at all. I like its excess.

In May 2015, the Princeton mathematician John F. Nash and his wife were killed in a car accident. Nash was a Nobel laureate, famous for his work in game theory and even more famous for having his life turned into an Oscar-winning film, *A Beautiful Mind*. In the days after Nash's death, a letter of recommendation was widely circulated on social media.* It had been written to help Nash get admitted to Princeton. The letter was simple and short, but like a math equation, it suggested something more profound. It

*Dylan Matthews, 'This is the best letter of recommendation ever'. Vox.com. http://www.vox.com/2015/6/6/8738229/john-nash-recommendation-letter

contained only three sentences; the first two provided perfunctory information, and the final sentence read: 'He is a mathematical genius.'

I marvelled at Nash when I read that line but I was also full of admiration for the writer of that letter. Such economy! Plain speaking like this would appear almost eccentric in today's academe.* Letters of recommendation say as much about the writer as they do about their subjects. In Schumacher's novel, Jason Fitger is often prolix. He has got much more on his mind and who could blame him. Academic institutions increasingly kowtow to corporate interests and hapless faculty often submit to unimaginative administrators. Teaching literature is a rebellion against the sterility of spirit. Or so Fitger believes, and I guess I do too. Kafka's famous line (written in a letter to a friend and not, alas, as a part of a letter of recommendation) goes something like this: 'A book must be the axe for the frozen sea within us.' For Fitger at least, that is what a letter of recommendation also must do. He is staging a protest, even if he is almost aware that it is all futile, and I recommend him most enthusiastically. Please give his letters the attention they deserve.

Sincerely, etc.

*'I read the applications for grad school (and junior hires) and am almost always struck by how similar and how un-vagrant their projects are. I search, usually in vain, for an unexpected adjective, a distinctive verb.' From my interview with Sukhdev Sandhu, author of two fine works of literary reportage criticism and cultural reportage: *London Calling* (London: Harper Perennial, 2003) and *Night Haunts* (London: Verso, 2006). I interviewed Sandhu because while he is an academic he writes for newspapers. He says of his readers: 'They prefer the thermodynamics of enthusiasm to the hermeneutics of suspicion.' I asked him if he had a manifesto for academic writing. He did. It began: 'The citational impulse is a baneful malady.' Sandhu also believes that our writing should have 'as much personality and as distinctive an authorial voice as a good novel.'

VI

Breath of Life

VOICE

In his excellent documentary, *Grizzly Man*, the filmmaker Werner Herzog also provides the voiceover. His voice is as inexorable and objective as the voice of death. Why do I find this voice exemplary? The main reason is that he is alert to what is ordinary but also what is extraordinary. In the opening minutes, Herzog is describing the more than hundred hours of footage collected by Timothy Treadwell in the wilds of Alaska. He says that although Treadwell might have only intended to show the grizzlies in their natural habitat, the footage goes 'beyond a wildlife film' and what lies dormant in the footage is 'a story of astonishing beauty and depth'. He hits the high note right away—using phrases like 'human ecstasies and darkest inner turmoil'. No use pussyfooting with qualifying phrases or more mundane observations. The details he offers are essential only to set the context and provide a storyline. We get a clear and immediate picture of Herzog as a serious filmmaker.

After an ecologist reads out on camera some of the hatemail directed toward Treadwell, Herzog sketches out his own defence of Treadwell 'not as an ecologist, but as a filmmaker'. Herzog says, 'He captured such glorious improvised moments, the likes of which studio directors with their union crews can never dream of'. While we hear this, we are watching Treadwell's footage: the camera is turned up at the blue roof of the tent, and we see the black outlines of a fox's paws as it moves about on the other side. We are looking at the world now through Herzog's eyes, and soon we are treated to what Herzog calls 'the inexplicable magic of cinema'. What he is referring to is the unanticipated arrival in the frame of the friendly fox and her cubs. In other words, a way of looking, what we usually call a well-defined position, and, going with it, an openness to surprise. And because Herzog is approaching Treadwell as a filmmaker, his commentary acquires additional texture and even rigour. Herzog says of Treadwell that as a filmmaker he was 'methodical' and he sometimes repeated 'takes fifteen times'. We in the audience now find more not only about Treadwell's but also Herzog's aesthetic as we listen to the voiceover: 'In his action-movie mode Treadwell probably did not realize that seemingly empty moments had a strange secret beauty. Sometimes images themselves develop their own life, their own mysterious stardom.' From here, Herzog makes a leap to the point that one suspects had been of interest to him from the start: Treadwell's use of the camera to explore 'his innermost being, his demons, his exhilarations'. Herzog celebrates Treadwell's film that has taken on 'the quality of a confessional'. We watch snippets of such footage but once again Herzog's rigour, although I could as easily call it his honesty, shines through when we are told what was left out of the confessional. For instance, how Treadwell's stylization of himself as the lone guardian of nature meant that his girlfriend Amie Huguenard's presence was excised from the frame. And speaking about his own film, Herzog says: 'Amie Huguenard remains a great unknown of this film.'

Grizzly Man works as a film because it eschews easy condemnation, of course, but also because it resists any sentimentality. Once again, I return to Herzog's voice, the essayistic voice of the documentarian, the voice that is also the voice of the imaginative critic. Did Treadwell ignore the 'harsh reality' of wild nature? Herzog makes his viewpoint clear when showing footage of Treadwell coming upon a bear cub's paw with the rest of the body missing. In that clear voice of doom, Herzog intones: 'Male bears sometimes killed cubs to stop the females from lactating and thus have them ready again for fornication.' Immediately afterwards, when an anguished and tearful Treadwell sits beside a slain fox cub, we hear Herzog deliver what is precisely the opposite of a sentimentalized view of the wildness and, indeed, of the world: 'Here I differ with Treadwell. He seemed to ignore the fact that in nature there are predators. I believe the common denominator of the universe is not harmony but chaos, hostility and murder.' It is only proper that after this judgement is delivered we are served Treadwell's footage showing more evidence of death and drought.

By the time the film comes to an end, we have come close to the moment of Treadwell's demise that had already been revealed at the beginning. The final minutes of the documentary preserve some of the mystery of Treadwell's life—and death—but also make his end both expected and nearly inevitable. Herzog keeps his viewpoint consistent. He focuses on the footage. Remarking about the bear that probably killed Treadwell, Herzog shows footage from Treadwell's last video-tape: Bear #141 diving to the bottom of the river in search of the last remaining salmon carcasses. Herzog comments: 'Treadwell keeps filming the bear with a strange persistence.' We see the bear close behind Amie. We see her face, almost for the first time. Then, the camera moves for a close-up of the bear, its massive head moving back and forth, gaze unfocused like a myopic's. As we look at the bear, Herzog's final judgement comes in language that is as forceful and damning as it is lyrical: 'What haunts me is that in all the faces of all the bears that Treadwell ever filmed I discover no kinship, no understanding, no mercy. I see only the overwhelming indifference of nature. To me, there is no such thing as a secret world of the bears. And this blank stare speaks only of a half-bored interest in food. But for Timothy Treadwell this bear was a friend and a saviour.'

Writing manuals ask you to 'find your voice'. But what does that mean? Better to start with something smaller and more concrete. 'Find your topic'. I like very much Umberto Eco's *How to Write a Thesis* for its generous offering of intelligent and focused advice to students.* At one point early in his book, Eco makes it clear that thesis writers must choose their topics carefully. If a student presumes to 'solve the question of God or define the concept of freedom' in a few, scant pages, the result can be 'tragic'. Eco writes: 'My experience is that a thesis like this usually turns out to be short and unorganized, and resembles more a lyric poem than an academic study.' I understand Eco's point and agree with it, but I'd go further and say that sometimes even for a lyric poem you need the kind of specificity that Eco finds attractive. Perhaps specificity is what brings us closer to the idea of voice, which I think is just another word for distinctiveness. It all depends on the question you are asking. Even in a lyric poem. Bhanu Kapil Rider's *The Vertical Interrogation of Strangers* is a book made up of responses given by women in different countries to one of twelve questions.** Questions like 'Where did you come from / how did you arrive?' and 'Tell me what you know about dismemberment.' When I first came across them, and ever since, I've found the questions startling. 'Dismemberment' is an abstract term too, of course, but for Rider it has specific connotations drawn from memory—hence this response in her book: 'I swore I'd never do anything as English as write a book about art. I said I'd write, instead, the book of blood. Chapter One: At the border, Hindu women are tied to Muslim eucalyptus trees. It is 1948, and so they are naked. Their wombs are hanging out of their stomachs. Chapter Two: there is no Chapter Two.'

---

*Eco, *How to Write a Thesis*, p. 14.

**Bhanu Kapil Rider, *The Vertical Interrogation of Strangers*, Berkeley: Kelsey St. Press, 2001.

I read an interview in which Rider described how her project took root:

> … the first question I asked, to a young Muslim woman at the Air Turkmenistan ticket counter—Indian parents, thick Glaswegian accent, 'Who was responsible for the suffering of your mother?' She burst into tears. That was how it truly began. I said, 'I'm working on a project where I ask Indian women these questions….' I invented questions as I went, centering upon these core twelve when I put the book together…. I have to say, too, that when I began, I was simply scrawling things down in my notebook. That first girl or woman—the flight was delayed for seven hours, I was taking my father's ashes back to India from London via a former Russian republic…a very dodgy aeroplane—was so open. She was so open to that question, and in the same breath, asked that I not use her name. Thus, the main reason I decided to intersect/collage the voices, rather than individuate them as sources, was that—at that time, it was challenging to speak or write openly about the body. For an Indian or Pakistani woman. In that era. In the places that I was. As it was for myself. As it still is.*

---

*Bhanu Kapil by Katherine Sanders, *BOMB Magazine*, 22 September 2011.

BUT LIFE

First, these words from the writer and editor William Maxwell: 'After forty years, what I came to care about most was not style, but the breath of life.'

SUGARED VIOLETS

Another seeming negation of style. John Cheever in his journals made a note about Nabokov and his 'sugared violets'. 'The house I was raised in had its charms, but my father hung his underwear from a nail he had driven into the back of the bathroom door, and while I know something about the Riviera I am not a Russian architect polished in Paris. My prose style will always be to a degree matter-of-fact.'* Style reduced to class, and at first it strikes me as true, and then, the next moment, not. There's so much elegance in Cheever's prose. Coming up with a phrase like 'sugared violets' isn't a plumbing job, whatever that means. And that image of the nail driven into the bathroom door—there's a lot more than just the underwear hanging from it.

*John Cheever, *The Journals of John Cheever*, edited by Robert Gottlieb, New York: Vintage, 2008. See p. 184.

FAILURE

While doing research for his book *Maximum City: Bombay Lost and Found*, a finalist for the Pulitzer for non-fiction, Suketu Mehta would interview several people each day. On one occasion, while talking to men from a right-wing Hindu group about the riots in Bombay, Mehta asked: 'What does a man look like when he's on fire?' And got the following answer: 'A man on fire gets up, falls, runs for his life, falls, gets up, runs. It is horror. Oil drips from his body, his eyes become huge, huge, the white shows, white, white, you touch his arm like this…the white shows, it shows especially on the nose… Oil drips from him, water drips from him, white, white all over.'*

Mehta's new book is on New York City, where he lives and works. It has long been clear to me that people reveal truths to Mehta, truths that you suspect they are discovering at the same time as the writer. It is a unique relationship he develops with his interviewees. It wouldn't be wrong to say that more than the cities that Mehta writes about, it is his subjects' inner selves that stand exposed in his writing—the place of darkness, the complicated paths to the past, the outskirts of feeling.

In the nineties, the *Village Voice* had carried Mehta's first major story, a report on the aftermath of the tragedy in Bhopal. But things had gone wrong. The editors had made too many cuts and the story's point had changed. Mehta said, 'They ran it as if they

---

*Suketu Mehta, *Maximum City: Bombay Lost and Found*, New Delhi: Penguin Books India, 2004.

were ashamed of it.'

There had also been a long wait. Once, even after he'd been shown the proofs, his piece was missing when the issue hit the stands. Another time, the *Voice* editors said that it was appearing as the cover story. Mehta arranged for a party, the champagne cooling in the fridge. But then, at the last moment, the story was replaced by a news-report—Tupac Shakur had just been shot.

There was need for money. Mehta had paid for the trip to Bhopal himself. He was not employed, and his wife was pregnant. Before it was accepted by the *Voice*, his essay had been rejected by all the major publications in New York. Mehta said, 'I felt like a failure.'* Once, on the road back from Connecticut, he thought he'd welcome death. The tale he was telling me began to sound like a Bollywood story.

Then, Mehta took a friend's advice and contacted Ian Jack who was the editor at *Granta*. Jack had liked his Bhopal piece and wanted Mehta to write something for him. Maybe Suketu could write about Gandhi in Africa, Jack suggested.

'And then he said the words that changed my life: "Have you heard of a man called Bal Thackeray?" I said, "He is the man who has ruined the city in which I grew up."'

The essay that Mehta wrote for *Granta* earned him a book contract and a substantial advance for *Maximum City*—he moved to India for several years—but the point that he keeps insisting on is that it all came out of the 'colossal failure' of the work he had done in Bhopal. The failure that lies behind the success of the book must also be true of those thousands of interviews that Mehta did

---

*A footnote on failure. While I was waiting for news recently about a book's fate, help arrived in the form of a video interview with Daniel Handler aka Lemony Snicket in the PBS News Hour 'Brief But Spectacular' series. Here's Handler on rejection: 'A writer's relationship with rejection is like that of a fish to water. It's all that's there. I think you should feel it and feel utter despair and then move on.' Available online at https://www.pbs.org/newshour/brief/191740/lemony-snicket. Accessed on 4 April 2017.

for his book. After all, when it comes to people, there's no happy teleology describing a path from failure to success. Thousands of conversations, thousands of streets or alleys, false signs, roads ending in places he thought he had been before, dead ends.

MISERY

When I see the above sign at airports or office buildings, I feel that if I were to break the glass what I would find inside, or perhaps what I would *want* to find inside, is this quote from Joan Didion:

Misery is feeling estranged from people I love. Misery is also not working. The two seem to go together.*

---

*I found the Joan Didion quote in this report on *Vanity Fair's* Proust Questionnaire: https://www.brainpickings.org/2014/10/02/joan-didion-proust-questionnaire/ Accessed on 7 June 2018.

Another quote: 'Every book about writing addresses, in one way or another, the difficulty of writing. Not just the technical problems (eliminating clutter, composing transitions) but the great existential agony and heebie-jeebies and humiliation involved—the inability to start, to finish, or to progress in the middle. This is one of the genre's great comforts: learning that you are not alone in your suffering.' Sam Anderson, 'The Mind of John McPhee.'

EXAMINED LIFE

Another clipping from the time when I first began taking notes for this book. This one is about a documentary that had just come out—philosophers out on a walk, talking about philosophy—and the clipping has a date scribbled underneath it: 25 February 2009.

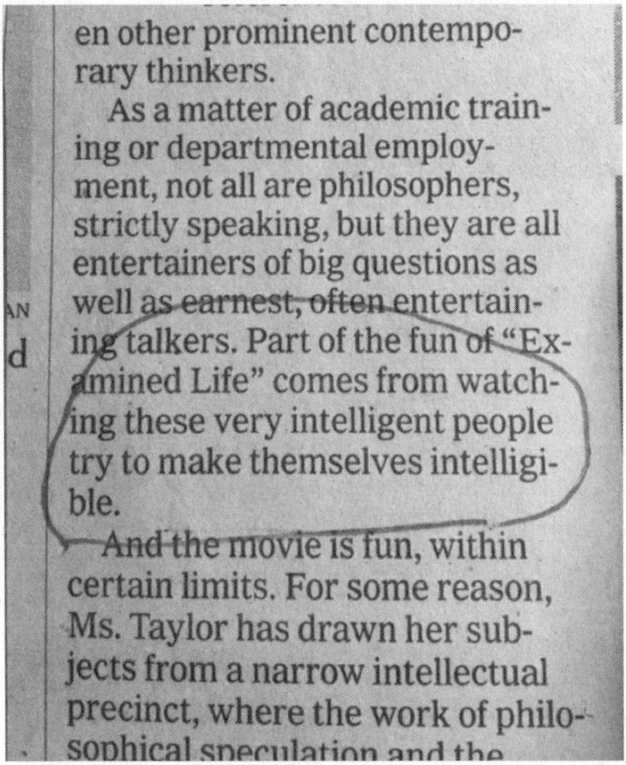

en other prominent contemporary thinkers.

As a matter of academic training or departmental employment, not all are philosophers, strictly speaking, but they are all entertainers of big questions as well as earnest, often entertaining talkers. Part of the fun of "Examined Life" comes from watching these very intelligent people try to make themselves intelligible.

And the movie is fun, within certain limits. For some reason, Ms. Taylor has drawn her subjects from a narrow intellectual precinct, where the work of philosophical speculation and the

DEPEND ON YOUR DUMBNESS

On the right side of my writing desk in my study is a black wooden bookshelf with thick, box-like sections where I keep books I need for my current projects. But on the wall in front, the wall that I face while I write, is a bookshelf on which are kept the books I know I will return to regularly. These are the books that have made me who I am: they hold the key to the kind of writer I want to become. These titles are my personal classics. On the top of the shelf there is a boxed set of *Paris Review* interviews and the framed photographs of my two children, and below them, in the first row, a line of hardbound books in their white cardboard cases. These are the Library of America editions of Philip Roth's writings.

I must have already read three or four novels of Roth's before he became central to my thinking. Why did this happen? Perhaps the change occurred one night in Delhi. I was in my late thirties. By then I had published books of criticism, reportage, and a literary memoir. During a visit to India, the country of my birth, a young writer I admired took down Roth's *American Pastoral* from his crowded bookshelf. We were sitting on the floor in his living room, drinking rum and coke. This writer is a man of unusual sensitivity and, although he downplays this part in conversation, he is a powerful editor of a national newspaper. He also stammers. From the page he had opened in *American Pastoral*, my friend began to read a passage which ended with the following words: 'The fact remains that getting people right is not what living is all about anyway. It's getting them wrong that is living, getting them wrong and wrong and wrong and then, on careful reconsideration, getting them wrong again. That's how we know we're alive: we're wrong.'

I remember asking my friend to read the entire page again and, for my sake, he did so with many pauses. When I came back to the US, I bought a paperback copy of the novel. The lines that had been read to me in Delhi appear early in *American Pastoral* and what they catch quite effectively is a kind of shocked bewilderment in the face of angry social change. I'm talking now of the late 1960s in America. Roth's novel is about the unsettling of middle-class notions of success and stability. But the above passage also presents a literary credo. Its essence was captured by Grace Paley when she argued that the writer, in contrast to the critic, writes not out of expertise but out of bafflement and urgent, unfailing interest. In an essay called 'The Value of Not Understanding Everything', Paley distinguished criticism from literature with disarming lucidity: 'What I'm saying is that in areas in which you are very smart you might try writing history or criticism, and then you can know and tell how all the mystery of America flows out from under Huck Finn's raft; where you are kind of dumb, write a story or novel, depending on the depth and breadth of your dumbness.'

I like Roth for his monumental dumbness. His lack of understanding of the mystery that is his life—this also explains why he sometimes seems to be writing the same book again and again—is interesting because it is paired with a particularly male, even arrogant, set of certainties. The struggle for understanding is examined with great frankness. Roth generates enormous energy in *American Pastoral* by putting beside the voluble, expressive sharing of rage, and sorrow, and befuddled despair, an impressive array of precise observations. Think, for instance, of the detailed description of glove-making in Newark.

It's not just that Roth's characters can be so completely sure, and then so incredibly filled with doubt. Very few writers are capable of showing how *they* get things wrong, how they get *themselves* wrong.

But let me make this argument by using Roth's own words. Here is an anarchic poet named Ralph Baumgarten talking to Roth's narrator, David Kepesh, in the novel *The Professor of Desire*: 'For me the books count—my own included—where the writer incriminates *himself*. Otherwise, why bother? To incriminate the other guy? Best leave that to our betters, don't you think…'

English departments in this country are full of our betters. Roth teaches me to be a bit more honest.

NOT WRITING

You are probably going to think I'm out of my mind but I recommend that if you aren't writing, you should nevertheless perform the ritual of sitting down to write about what you are not writing. (You can write other things down. Write down what you see outside your window. Or what you remember of your dream. Or what your plans are for the day or the week.) The best thing I've read about this is a poem actually entitled 'Not Writing' by the wildly talented Anne Boyer.* The poem is a sharp, funny, rueful, even painful, list of what Boyer isn't writing. For instance: 'I am not writing Facebook status updates. I am not writing thank-you notes or apologies. I am not writing conference papers. I am not writing book reviews. I am not writing blurbs.'

---

*Anne Boyer, *Garments Against Women*, Boise, Idaho: Ahsahta Press, 2015. See 'Not Writing' and 'What Is 'Not Writing'?' on pp. 41-46.

VII

Academic Interest

DIANA STUDIES

A 1998 article in *The Independent* reported on the birth of Diana Studies.* 'She may have left school without an O-level to her name, but Diana, Princess of Wales, is rapidly becoming the Professors' Princess.' There was mention of a slew of conferences on Princess Di, attended by sociologists, psychoanalysts, and literary figures. Specialists from a wide variety of disciplines, including art history, feminism, psychology, media studies, and religious studies, were described as eager to have a say. The report's mention of a course on Diana in a university in Berlin took on an even more farcical air. The German organizers were 'snowed under with enquiries'. What were these enquiries? Like the gleeful report in American newspapers of titles of MLA papers, *The Independent* provided a list: Was Diana a 'living simulacrum' or a symbol of 'faux modernity'? Could the reaction to her death be described as 'grief-lite'? What does the public mourning for her tell us about 'uncertainty and social psychological responses'? This list of questions was followed by the sad speculation: 'It is perhaps only a matter of time before such questions are appearing on examination papers'. Well, if they are, then one could only hope that these questions would arrive with some narrative context—because, in the report, they serve as ridiculous buzzwords and not really as tools of analysis. The article's headline could also be submitted to a quick literary examination.

*Clare Garner, 'Diana phenomenon becomes a matter of academic interest', *The Independent*, 9 February 1998. See also the section that follows in this book, 'Occupy Writing'.

'Diana becomes a matter of academic interest' was literally true, but its effectiveness, of course, lay in the malicious pun, so that we were to see the matter as the dictionary defines it—'of no consequence, or without relevance'.

How to brush this phrase 'academic interest' against the grain and read it in a radically different way?

~

Here's one attempt. I understand it as 'a stubborn holding on to complexity'. A friend posted on Facebook the text of the speech that Stuart Hall had delivered on Raymond Williams's death. I found that I was reading the text to find both the complexity one expects from academics and also the lucidity one associates with people like Williams and Hall. There was one line about Williams that drew me back again and again. : 'In his writing and speaking—those slow, exploratory sentences that turned back on themselves, tracing the actual lived movement of his mind—he insisted on the effort to reach out beyond any specialized intelligentsia to a wider audience and to link intellectual work with a broader social and political purpose.'

How to understand what Hall says about Williams' sentences? Hall had earlier quoted a few stellar lines from *Politics and Letters*. And then he had added his own brilliant touch. Here are both paragraphs, first from Williams, and then from Hall unpacking them for his listeners:

> I am very powerfully moved by the early churches, by the great cathedrals, and yet if I don't see the enormous weight of them on man, I don't altogether know how to be a socialist in the area where I work…if we acknowledge them as a contribution, we must also acknowledge them as an obstacle… The cathedrals are not just monuments to faith, the country houses are not just buildings of elegance. They are constantly

> presented to us as 'our heritage', inducing a particular way of seeing and relating to the world, which must be critically registered along with our acknowledgement of their value. I always see them as profoundly ambivalent. (Williams)
>
> Everything about the man—his mind, his way of writing and speaking, his political intelligence—is in those few sentences. His range, connecting and spanning things which our compartmentalized ways of thinking routinely separate: the stubborn holding on to complexity—the 'elegance' together with the 'weight', the two ends of the chain; the perception that everything is part of this 'giving and taking of descriptions' and affects our 'way of seeing and relating to the world'; the long parentheses, which try to hold, so to speak, at the margin of the field of vision of any one sentence, the other connections waiting to be made; the relating of this critical exercise to the question of how to be a socialist, now… (Hall)

I want to come to the issue of 'academic interest' in another way; I see it as a refusal of easy consolations. This is a quality I find in the memoirs, written by academics, that I read while writing this book. Unlike the memoirs lapped up in mainstream culture, books that inscribe an arc of redemption, scholars retain a quality of intelligent skepticism. A good example is Christina Crosby's *A Body, Undone: Living On After Great Pain.** Crosby, a professor of literature at Wesleyan, was in a terrible bicycle accident that left her paralyzed. Most accounts of trauma and recovery follow what Crosby calls 'the dictates of the realist consensus', describing the ways in which

*Christina Crosby, *A Body, Undone: Living On After Great Pain*, New York: New York University Press, 2016.

the writer overcame setbacks and found once again a semblance of wholeness. The idea in such accounts is to offer an uplifting message. Crosby's account, more honest, less sentimental, focuses instead on the brutal details of the pain she suffered. A similar note is struck in Susan Gubar's *Memoir of a Debulked Woman: Enduring Ovarian Cancer*.* In Gubar's book too we find the same vigilance, and a similar erudition, and, last but not least, the same awareness of narrative conventions that determine how we discuss disease. Or, in a different vein, the memoir-essays of Terry Castle which are sharp and witty, not to mention scathingly honest and revealing.** And, in a different vein still, Daniel Mendelsohn's *The Lost*, an account of a search for the particulars of the experiences of his family members during the Holocaust.*** There is an arc here but again what is so valuable is the attempt to convey difficulty: 'There are no miracles, no magical coincidences. There is only looking, and finally seeing, what was always there.'**** (And then, too long to quote here, the beautiful, sad and haunting, paragraph that follows.)

'Academic interest' is a contradiction—the phrase signifies, on the one hand, a pursuit without consequences, and, on the other, a search, and, moreover, a search without heed or subservience to the dictates of the market. Stefano Harney and Fred Moten come to the contradictions of that term in a different way. They write that, at least in the United States, 'it cannot be denied that the university is a place of refuge, and it cannot be accepted that the university

*Susan Gubar, *Memoir of a Debulked Woman: Enduring Ovarian Cancer,* New York: W.W. Norton, 2012.

**Terry Castle, *The Professor and Other Writings*, New York: HarperCollins, 2010.

***Daniel Mendelsohn, *The Lost: A Search for Six of Six Million*, New York: HarperCollins, 2006.

****Ibid, p. 486.

is a place of enlightenment.'* For Harney and Moten, the true work is done by 'the subversive intellectual in the university' who 'disappears into the underground, the downlow low-down maroon community of the university, into the *undercommons of enlightenment*'.** I like this insistence on radical hope because it is utopian (the undercommons is 'where the work gets done, where the works gets subverted, where the revolution is still black, still strong') and also because it is so well-written, the beautiful poetry of the future. This project that is sketched by Harney and Moten is for me a real interpretation of the idea of 'academic interest', and intersects with how to think about writing, because of its hopeful elaboration of what it means to have an intellectual orientation and exist socially. It offers an orientation for writing. Here is Moten in an interview that he and Harney gave to Stevphen Shukaitis:

> …is there a way to be in the undercommons that isn't intellectual? Is there a way of being intellectual that isn't social? When I think about the way we use the term 'study,' I think we are committed to the idea that study is what you do with other people. It's talking and walking around with other people, working, dancing, suffering, some irreducible convergence of all three, held under the name of speculative practice. The notion of a rehearsal—being in a kind of workshop, playing in a band, in a jam session, or old men sitting on a porch, or people working together in a factory—these are various modes of activity. The point of calling it 'study' is to mark that the incessant and irreversible intellectuality of these activities is already present.***

To see it in this way is to understand 'academic interest' as an

---

*Stefano Harney and Fred Moten, *The Undercommons: Fugitive Planning and Black Study*, Wivenhoe: Minor Composition, 2013. See p. 26.

**Ibid, p. 26. Emphasis in the original.

***Ibid, p. 110.

intellectual stance, and to produce writing, then, that is a part of what Moten in the interview calls 'a whole, varied, alternative history of thought'.*

*Ibid, p. 110.

OCCUPY WRITING

In a video available online, Judith Butler, philosopher and winner of a bad writing award,* is speaking to a crowd at the Occupy Wall Street protests.** It is a short speech, pointed and incantatory, and Butler is brilliant.

A wonderful innovation of the Occupy Wall Street movement was the use of the human microphone—the name given to the body of the audience repeating, amplifying, each statement made by the speaker. This practice was probably introduced because there was a ban on the use of megaphones. During Butler's speech, the repetition by the human microphone helps. It produces for us the image of her words being taken up by the public (so that we see philosophy as a public act) and we, her listeners, also get a chance to think through her words in the process. Critics of the Occupy movement, Butler says, either claim that the protesters have no demands or that their impossible demands are just not practical. And she then adds, 'If hope is an impossible demand, then we

---

*The philosopher Dennis Dutton (1944-2010) was a founder of the website 'Arts & Letters Daily' but a part of his fame, or notoriety, was attached to his stewardship of the Bad Writing Contest. Dutton declared that his interest was in finding the 'most egregious examples of awkward, jargon-clogged academic prose'. The contest awarded its 'prize' to such writers as Fredric Jameson, Homi Bhabha, and Judith Butler. There is much to complain about academic writing but there is also a great deal of anti-intellectual angst directed at such prose, especially if such prose is deemed 'theoretical'. My task in this book is neither to praise Dutton, nor to bury him, but to consider academic writing that is difficult to categorize, or is challenging in a new way, or is noteworthy for its inventiveness.

**https://www.youtube.com/watch?v=JVpoOdz1AKQ Accessed on 15 July 2015.

demand the impossible.'

Butler's performance as a public intellectual is impressive because she is both lucid and difficult. (Is *difficult* really the word I want?) Put differently, I'm struck by her quick arrival at a knotty question and then the magnificent unfurling of, as if it were a flag being waved at the barricades, the repeated phrase about demanding the impossible.

Less than two years after that speech she read from her phone at Occupy Wall Street, I found myself seated next to Butler at a dinner at Vassar College. I asked her about the speech, and Butler said that she had written it 'on the subway between West 4th and Wall St.'

I could not reveal at dinner that the reason I had asked Butler about her speech was my interest in having her talk to me more about the truth and pitfalls of the charge that academics are bad writers. In her performance on Wall Street, I had seen a retort to those accusations. Later, I sent an email asking Butler if she could help unpack the meaning of the phrase 'of academic interest'. I chose that phrase because it seems to gather together rather succinctly the general dismissal of the work we do, or the questions we ask, and even the language we use.

Soon, I received a response. This time Butler wasn't addressing a crowd of protesters, and the register was understandably different. She wrote that 'the phrase presumes that there is a firm line that divides the academy from the real world, and it is a way of marking a certain uselessness to what academics do or what happens inside the academy'. The phrase implied that what academics do makes sense only within their own, closed-off world, but, of course, part of what happens in the academy is the development of a set of questions about the world. Butler pointed out that the academy is sometimes the place where we call into question what we know and our sense of the world that has become naturalized over time. This leads to a certain disorientation that might be resisted by those who wish to remain in what Husserl called 'the natural attitude'. Those who dismiss academics, Butler wrote, 'fail to see that a reorientation toward the world' is also taking place within academe, one marked by greater knowingness and a heightened ethical or aesthetic responsiveness.

What form might this reorientation take?

In the documentary film *Examined Life*, we see Butler walking with the artist Sunaura Taylor in a wheelchair.* Butler says to Taylor, 'I thought we should take this walk together' and talk about '*what it means* for us to take this walk together.'

Taylor, who was born with arthrogryposis, says that she goes out for walks nearly every day, and that, like other disabled people, she always uses that word: 'I'm going for a *walk*.' Butler asks her about the environments that make it possible for Taylor to take a walk, and in describing urban features like curb cuts and public transportation, Taylor explains how physical access leads to social acceptance. Butler's questions help develop a discussion not only about what she calls the technique of walking but also a proposition that calls into question the alleged self-sufficiency of the able-bodied person.

For me, this is philosophy in action. In a discussion that is less than fifteen minutes long, we have moved from what was a deceptively simple question about going out for a walk to a place where the ideology of individualism has been effectively challenged. Academic work here is embodied and urgent—and its language is as simple, and as complicated, as taking a walk.**

**Examined Life*, directed by Astra Taylor, Zeitgeist Films, USA, 2008, 88 minutes.

**I interviewed the film's director, Astra Taylor, about her interest in taking philosophy out of the classroom. My questions were about process. Taylor says that while searching for a form for the film, she found inspiration in Rebecca Solnit's book, *Wanderlust: A History of Walking*. Here is an excerpt from my interview with Taylor where she explains how the sequence I've written about here came about—I include it here also because it gives succinct proof of how academic interests shape—and save—lives:

The Judith Butler and Sunaura Taylor sequence certainly has the most interesting backstory. I was long interested in Butler's work and ultimately interviewed her for an essay I wrote that was published in *Salon* after her book *Precarious Life* came out. So we had had some limited contact before I invited her to be in the movie.

Sunaura, of course, is my younger sister. In the film she recounts her discovery of disability studies and the profound impact that had on her self-understanding and conception of the social world; disability was no longer simply personal, it was social and political. She read everything from Foucault's *Madness and Civilization* to Eli Clare to Marta Russell to Joseph Shapiro's *No Pity* and the transformation these books helped cause was pretty amazing. Within months she went from living with me, having never gone anywhere by herself or paid for anything in her life, to living independently and falling in love. Ideas can be extremely powerful.... That was right when I was dropping (or rather, drifting) out of graduate school, tired of the whole game, and her experience partly accounts for my drive to connect this type of subject matter with people outside of the usual academic context. I'm not sure if I would be as committed to the cause of theory, or if *Zizek!* or *Examined Life* would have been made, if all this had not transpired.

Flash forward to 2007 and I am meeting with Butler for the second time to discuss *Examined Life*. I decide to invite my sister, who was studying for her MFA at Berkeley. They hit it off and by the end of the meeting Butler invited her to come to the shoot; the next day she invited Sunaura to join her on the walk. Butler intuited, rightly, that they would have a fabulous conversation. I believe Judith didn't want to play herself; she wanted to learn something and to share the spotlight, which is very generous. I was excited by the prospect but a bit nervous, as was my sister (who tried to back out many times). In fact, I didn't even tell my executive producer that my sister was part of the shoot for fear of being reprimanded somehow. I was over the moon after the first few screenings when that sequence turned out to be one of the scenes that garnered the strongest, most visceral response and when I realized that viewers also believed it served to connect all the various themes of the movie (vulnerability, interdependence, embodiment, walking).

ACADEMIC SENTENCE

On the website of the University of Chicago's Writing Program, there is a link that you can use to generate a random academic sentence.* When I last clicked on it, this is what I got: 'The idea of the proper-name effect allegorizes the de-eroticization of normative value(s).' The site also says that if you are 'the do-it-yourself type', you may write your own sentence. You are to choose one word from each of the four drop-lists, and then all you need to do is click on 'Write It!' If the result doesn't please, click on 'Edit it!' (If you start enjoying what you're doing there's also a third button, 'Reset'.)

I will now list some of the words and formulaic phrases in each drop list. One: 'the public sphere', 'the gendered body', 'power/knowledge', 'agency'; Two: 'discourse', 'politics', 'legitimation', 'construction'; Three: 'post-capitalist hegemony', 'the gaze', 'pop culture', 'civil society'; and Four: 'epistemology', 'emergence', 'logic', and 'culture'. Simply by choosing a word or phrase from each category, it is easy to write sentences like the following: 'The emergence of civil society may be parsed as the legitimation of the public sphere.' This was among the more intelligible results I got. When I clicked on the cheerful and encouraging 'Edit It!' link, I got the following, rather perfect, result: The legitimation of civil society may be parsed as the emergence of the public sphere.

All this is funny, at least for a short while. When an academic friend of mine posted the above-mentioned link on her Facebook page, another friend asked in the comments section whether she

*http://writing-program.uchicago.edu/toys/randomsentence/index.htm

could use the sentence generator to complete her dissertation. That joke was a wonderfully precise one. More than anyone else, it is the academic initiate, the graduate student or, in some cases, the young scholar seeking tenure, who must reveal his or her proficiency in the use of the sacred tongue. Style is assumed to be a feature only of senior living, a part of what you do later in your career, when you have acquired the necessary academic credentials. And till you have amassed the capital of years of professional membership, the luxury of innovation or originality is frowned upon as irresponsible and excessive. Recitation by rote is encouraged. It is to assure all, or at least some of us, that we belong to a community, or at least a tribe with shared rituals and a common language. In a rather obvious way, then, the academy is the original random sentence generator.

I know, I know, I'm saying all this, and I agree with it, but I also get a bit defensive about the academy. So, let's start all over again.

Consider this sentence: 'If such a sublime cyborg would insinuate the future as post-Fordist subject, his palpably masochistic locations as ecstatic agent of the sublime superstate need to be decoded as the "now all-but-unreadable DNA" of the fast industrializing Detroit, just as his Robocop-like strategy of carceral negotiation and street control remains the tirelessly American one of inflicting regeneration through violence upon the racially heteroglassic wilds and others of the inner city.'

This quoted extract appeared in a *Sacramento Bee* article entitled 'No Contest: English Professors Are Worst Writers on Campus'*; the writer David Foster Wallace cited the above extract in a review-essay in which he also quoted Orwell who had famously opined that when

*David Foster Wallace, 'Tense Present: Democracy, English, and the Wars Over Usage', *Harper's Magazine*, April 2001.

reading art criticism and literary criticism 'it is normal to come across long passages which are completely lacking in meaning'.* Wallace went on to say that the 'pleonasm and pretentious diction' as well as the 'opaque abstraction' found in a lot of academic writing had as its real purpose 'concealment' and its main motivation was 'fear'. That is what he said he was tempted to believe, and I am too, but not without asking further questions about what exactly is being concealed and what particular set of easily recognizable fears beset academic souls. One can linger with the popular speculation that the rise of more arcane forms of theorizing in literary or cultural studies in the Western academy was directly proportional to the diminution of real political power as well as popularity that the left intelligentsia enjoyed under Reagan and Thatcher. But the more intriguing question here is why Wallace, a writer whose work best represented a near-scholarly rigour in search for complexity, didn't cut us academics any slack? With his interest in language (its philosophy and play, but also, more broadly the difficulty of representation), his broad range of references, his intellectual interest in popular culture, and yes, his footnotes (Wallace's 1996 novel, *Infinite Jest*, runs to 1,079 pages and includes a hundred pages of footnotes), *wasn't he really one of us*?**

*George Orwell, 'Politics and the English Language', *Horizon*, April 1946.
As far as old, but perhaps by now over-familiar, jokes go, one can cite Orwell's translation of the line from Ecclesiastes 'I saw under the sun that the race is not to the swift' into what he called 'modern writing' (and David Foster Wallace called 'Academic English'): 'Objective considerations of contemporary phenomena compel the conclusion that success or failure in competitive activities exhibits no tendency to be commensurate with innate capacity, but that a considerable element of the unpredictable must invariably be taken into account.' Wallace wanted Orwell's parody 'tattooed on the left wrist of every grad student in the anglophone world'.

**In his introduction to *The Best American Essays 2007*, for which he was the guest editor, David Foster Wallace wrote that his attitude to academic writing was a complicated one 'that a clinician would probably find easy to diagnose in terms of projection or displacement.' He added: 'As someone who has felt a lot of trouble being clear, concise, and/or cogent, I tend to be allergic to academic writing, most of which seems to me

DISSERTATION BLAH

The protagonist of Ali Smith's novel *Autumn* is Elisabeth Demand, a young lecturer in the history of art.* But many years earlier, when she was eighteen, Elisabeth had discovered an old catalogue from an exhibition of paintings by a British Pop Art painter, Pauline Boty. (She got into an argument with her tutor who was opposed to the idea of Elisabeth writing a thesis on Boty—why write on a subject about which there wasn't much critical material, etc.) Later, while working on her dissertation, Elisabeth is watching the film *Alfie* starring Michael Caine and with Pauline Boty in a small role. This film had been made a year before Boty died, and she also happened to be pregnant in those shots. We see Boty in the movie with Elisabeth's eyes: 'She was wearing a bright blue top. Her hair was the colour of corn.'** This is immediately followed by another more self-conscious, or self-reflexive, observation on the nature of academic writing:

> But you can't write that in a dissertation. You can't write, *she made it look like a blast*. You can't write, *she looked like she'd be really good fun, like she was full of energy*, or *energy comes off her in waves*. You can't write, even though it's a lot more like the language expected, *though she's in that film for less*

---

willfully opaque and pretentious. There are, again, some notable exceptions, and by "academic writing" I mean a particular cloistered dialect and mode; I do not just mean any piece written by somebody who teaches college.'

*Ali Smith, *Autumn*, New York: Pantheon Books, 2016.

**Ibid, p. 224.

> *than twenty seconds she adds something crucial and crucially female about pleasure to its critique of the contemporary new and liberated ethos, which was indeed what she was also doing with her aesthetic.*
>
> Blah.

Really? The scene described above is set in the spring of 2004. I don't think a feminist analysis, about female pleasure, would be frowned upon today. Certainly not in the US, but perhaps things are different across the Atlantic. And yet, if I ponder the question, thinking for a moment about a college in small-town India, any college, even a women's college, I have little doubt that such freedom would indeed be denied.

A page later Elisabeth is pondering Boty's famous missing painting, *Scandal 63*. She writes in pencil on a page of her pad a bit of slightly incomprehensible academic prose. Immediately below, the phrase: 'Dissertation blah'. The novelist's description that follows shares nothing of the language of Elisabeth's handwritten note. Now the writing is sharp and straightforward, factual without being dull. ('No one knew who'd commissioned this painting. No one knew where it was now, if it was still anywhere, if it still existed.') The contrast in the language is so vivid that it is clear that Ali Smith is doing what creative writers often do. (It is something I'm guilty of doing too.) She is mocking the language, if not also the culture, of academe. Not a new preoccupation apparently. As I was writing this, I saw a tweet that quoted Virginia Woolf's *To The Lighthouse*:

> She supposed it was all right leaving him to his own devices, Mrs. Ramsay said, wondering whether it was any use sending down bulbs; did they plant them? "Oh, he has his dissertation to write," said Mr. Ramsay. She knew all about *that,* said Mrs. Ramsay. He talked of nothing else. It was about the influence of somebody upon something. "Well, it's all he has to count on,"

'It was about the influence of somebody upon something.'* That is what you want to say when you don't say 'Dissertation blah'.

*Virginia Woolf, *To the Lighthouse*, first published 1927, New York: Harcourt Mifflin, 1989. See p. 66.

YOUR JOB IS TO KNOW A LOT

Masha Gessen, acclaimed author of books on Russian politics and a columnist for the *New Yorker*, had a piece of advice for fellow journalists: 'Now, academics are not always the easiest people to talk to, and the scholarly papers aren't always the easiest papers to read, but frankly, psychology papers, especially papers and books on terrorism, are very easy to read, and journalists should be reading them… It takes longer than talking to somebody on the phone, but that's what you should be doing.' After sharing a panel with Gessen at a literary festival, I asked her to explain her praise for academic modes of knowledge. She said, 'Journalists are dilettantes by nature: even the lucky experts among us are ultimately tasked with knowing a bit about a lot. We should not forget to talk to the people whose job it is to know a lot about a little. It is such a luxury for a journalist to talk to an academic who has spent years thinking about something or someone—especially when the academic can communicate *how* this someone or someone can be thought about.'

TERMINOLOGY

Disciplines of study need their own terminology, an entire universe of self-contained discourse that makes communication possible. When we want to be dismissive, we use the word *jargon* to describe the employment of this specialized terminology.* I understand the value of a discursive universe and a shared vocabulary, especially in technical or scientific fields, but, as a writer, it is fascinating to witness the tear in language—and in reality—when a set of specialized words are peeled away to reveal a more ordinary reality. So, for instance, from an article about the ethics of primate research at the Eunice Kennedy Shriver National Institute of Child Health and Human Development: 'Suomi's research involved keeping

*Would I use the word 'jargon' to describe this abstract? No, not necessarily, but the abstract raises the same questions that most jargon-laden prose does: what poverty of thought is this language trying to cover up? (I initially thought the abstract below was a parody but an online search revealed that it was genuine. Many others on the Web, including quite a few who were genuinely right-wing in their other beliefs, also revealed a similar confusion.) 'This article examines the symbolic whiteness associated with pumpkins in the contemporary United States. Starbucks' pumpkin spice latte, a widely circulated essay in *McSweeney's* on 'Decorative Gourd Season,' pumpkins in aspirational lifestyle magazines, and the reality television show *Punkin Chunkin* provide entry points into whiteness–pumpkin connections. Such analysis illuminates how class, gender, place, and especially race are employed in popular media and marketing of food and flavor; it suggests complicated interplay among food, leisure, labor, nostalgia, and race. Pumpkins in popular culture also reveal contemporary racial and class coding of rural versus urban places. Accumulation of critical, relational, and contextual analyses, including things seemingly as innocuous as pumpkins, points the way to a food studies of humanities and geography. When considered vis-à-vis violence and activism that incorporated pumpkins, these analyses point toward the perils of equating pumpkins and whiteness.'

infant monkeys in near-isolation and investigating their responses to stress and alcohol consumption. In research argot, his team members produced primate models of neuropsychiatric disorder. In more conversational terms, they drove monkeys mad.'*

---

*Brandon Keim, 'Reconsidering Research on Primates', *Chronicle of Higher Education*, 9 December 2016.

ANTI-ANTI JARGON

'Of the hundreds of academics I have talked to about their work as scholarly writers, only a few have mentioned books about writing as a significant source of their learning either during or beyond the PhD.' I read this in Helen Sword's informative book, *Stylish Academic Writing.** Sword conducted interviews with academics and then researched more than a hundred books and articles recommended to her in different disciplines to come up with an idea of what precisely made for eloquence or elegance in academic writing. The resulting list includes such features as interesting titles, first-person asides, use of concrete nouns, numerous examples, broad set of references, humour, etc. These are important points to keep in mind, and Sword helpfully provides examples from published work in different fields. Her recommendations ought to be taken seriously because Sword came to the conclusion that 'wordy, wooden, weak-verbed academic prose finds few if any explicit advocates *but vast armies of practitioners*' (emphasis added).**

Sword wishes to rid writing of the disease she calls 'jargonitis'. An example: In her one thousand-article data sample, she found eighteen articles that mentioned Michel Foucault at least once in the first few pages. Especially when the French philosopher's name was used in its adjectival form, Sword found that the knowledge of

---

*Helen Sword, *Stylish Academic Writing.* See p. 25.

**Ibid, p. 10. One of the recommendations Sword makes is that you post a sample of your writing on her Writer's Diet Web site (http://www.writersdiet.com) and find out whether your sentences are 'flabby or fit'. See pp. 60-62.

Foucault's work was often only second-hand. In such cases, there was no real engagement with Foucault's writings and the invocation of his name could be seen as an empty exercise.

In an article in the *Chronicle of Higher Education*, published the same year as her book, Sword made the following criticism of academic writing:

> In my survey of 100 recent writing guides, I found that 21 recommend against disciplinary jargon of any kind; 46 caution that technical language should be used carefully, accurately, and sparingly; and 33 make no comment on the subject. I have yet to discover a single academic-style guide that advocates a freewheeling embrace of jargon. Nevertheless academic journals are awash in the stuff...*

That sounds accurate to me but there is at least one academic-style guide, and a very good one at that, which adopts a stance that its author, Eric Hayot, calls 'anti-anti-jargon'.** In *The Elements of Academic Style*, Hayot allows that jargon and clichés 'often conceal emptiness in thought' but he also remains unconvinced by anti-jargon arguments. Doesn't each scholarly field have its own language, he asks. And do people complain that they can't understand articles written by physicists or economists? Hayot also clarifies that he is not pro-jargon because that would be 'like being pro-gonorrhea'. Except, what Hayot still insists on is that graduate students in the humanities, if they are to succeed as academic writers, must learn 'how to use "problematic" in a sentence or "stage" as a verb'. I don't agree.*** Everything I have said in these

*Helen Sword, 'Inoculating Against Jargonitis,' *Chronicle of Higher Education*, 3 June, 2012.

**Eric Hayot, *The Elements of Academic Style: Writing for the Humanities*. New York: Columbia University Press, 2014. See, in particular, pp. 178-79.

***Here's the narrator in Sam Lipsyte's novel *The Ask*: 'We used words like "systemic," "interpolate," "apparatus," "intervention." It wasn't bullshit, I remember thinking at the time. It just wasn't not bullshit.' (Exactly, but it is important for me to know: did he mean

pages runs counter to the notion that it is essential to learn to use words like 'problematic' in a sentence. The idea of a stock vocabulary is a certain way to produce language that is stillborn.

~

William Germano, author of *Getting It Published*, told me that scholarly prose isn't as bad as people say, but it could be a lot better.* He said, 'It's not entirely fair to tell scholars they have to write like trade writers. Most can't. Do we really want every scholarly book to sound like a PBS tie-in? I don't think so.' He first said that we have moved away from some of the most boring models of scholarly writing, and then allowed that they were still out there, and more could be done. Germano offered 'a two-stream model of scholarly production'. His advice to academics is that they write 'the book you need to write for other professionals in your field'. ('Try not to make the writing too gassy, too long, too self-regarding. It's a book, not a catalogue of your footnotes. Don't write your homework, just the results of your homework.') The second step is to try and write a book 'for a non-professional audience interested in your subject'. ('Youth culture in contemporary Iran. The idea of money in early modern Europe. Histories of family illnesses and how they affected the work of great writers. Turn your prose inside out. Tell stories about your scholarly knowledge. Risk clarity, even if that feels slightly unprofessional.') The ambition that each one of us could have is that we get known scholars willing to speak to two very different audiences—'maybe a local seniors group and an academic conference—on the same subject in the same academic year'. Germano's term for this was a 'new scholarly bilingualism'.

'interpellate' instead of 'interpolate'?) Sam Lipsyte, *The Ask*, New York: Farrar, Straus and Giroux, 2010. See p. 51.

*William Germano, *Getting It Published*, Chicago: University of Chicago Press, 2016.

Here, again, I stand at a distance from such advice, pragmatic and well-intentioned as it might be. We can do better. There's so much evidence of young academics producing fresh work that we must model ourselves as better advocates of stylish writing. Examples: Christina Sharpe's *In the Wake* for its personal, passionate framing of the never-ending erasure of black bodies.* Plus, Sharpe curates in her book an impressive array of black art. Or Hua Hsu's *A Floating Chinaman*, which avoids the sin of dragging the reader in its first thirty-forty pages through tedious debates about everyone who has heretofore been wrong in their consideration of Asian American subjectivity or representation. More importantly, the book tells the story of an unknown, eccentric immigrant to America from China, a writer named H. T. Tsiang who remains resistant not only to glory but also to any kind of academic omniscience.** Or, to cite a more recent title, Alexis Pauline Gumbs's *M Archive*, an example of a writer-activist fashioning, in a language that is poetic and in a style that is experimental, a critical response to the work of influential theorist, M. Jacqui Alexander.

*Christina Sharpe, *In the Wake: On Blackness and Being*, Durham: Duke University Press, 2016.

**Hua Hsu, *A Floating Chinaman: Fantasy and Failure Across the Pacific*, Cambridge, MA: Harvard University Press, 2016.

A CLEAN ENGLISH SENTENCE

Among academics, perhaps the most interesting, if also prickly, proponent of the argument for legibility is Stanley Fish. In publications like the *New York Times*, Fish has expressed alarm at the inability of his graduate students 'to write a clean English sentence'.* In Fish's eyes, these graduate students also make bad teachers of composition because rather than focus on the 'craft of writing' they spend time discussing 'a variety of hot button issues—racism, sexism, immigration, globalization'. Although Fish concedes that these are serious topics that are worthy of attention, he feels that what should be taught in a composition course is 'grammar and rhetoric and nothing else'. Which is to say, politics cannot be allowed to trump pedagogy.

A part of me understands the argument that Fish is making. Often, the belief that we are making a progressive political argument blinds us to the fact that the language we are using is rigid; our ideas might be intended to strike the reader as trenchant, but given the deadening familiarity of the terms we use to mobilize critique, our writing is quite dull and unoriginal. Let's go along with Fish. How to write better sentences? I'm not much of a sentence man myself, although I wish I were, but I have a notion that those who *are* usually express their fetish by quoting *first* sentences from novels. ('Call me Ishmael.' 'It is a truth universally acknowledged, that a single man in possession of a good fortune, must be in want of a wife.' 'A screaming comes across the sky.' 'Many years

*Stanley Fish, 'What Should Colleges Teach?', *New York Times*, 24 August 2009.

later, as he faced the firing squad, Colonel Aureliano Buendía was to remember that distant afternoon when his father took him to discover ice.' 'Lolita, light of my life, fire of my loins.' Etc.) In his book, *How to Write A Sentence*, Stanley Fish devotes a chapter to first sentences and another to last sentences, but his taste isn't reducible to a vulgar fetishism.*

Part-formalist, part-forensic reader, Fish is interested in drawing our attention to a wide range of sentences and then explaining to us why they work. Here's an early example from Fish: John Updike's sentence telling us of the home run hit by Ted Williams in his last at-bat in Fenway Park in September, 1960: 'It was in the books while it was still in the sky.' This is part of what Fish has to say about what makes the depiction of that instant so effective in this sentence:

> … he confers that mythical status on the moment before it is completed, before the ball actually goes out of the park. Indeed, in his sentence the ball never gets out of the park. It is 'still in the sky,' a phrase that has multiple meanings; the ball is still in the sky in the sense that it has not yet landed; it is still in the sky in the sense that its motion is arrested; and it is still in the sky in the sense that it is, and will remain forever, in the sky of the books, in the record of the game's highest, most soaring achievements. On the surface, 'in the book' and 'in the sky' are in distinct registers, one referring to the monumentality the home run will acquire in history, the other describing the ball's actual physical arc; but the registers are finally, and indeed immediately (this sentence goes fast), the same: the physical act and its transformation into myth occur simultaneously; or rather, that is what Updike makes us feel as we glide through this deceptively simple sentence composed entirely of monosyllables.

*Stanley Fish, *How to Write A Sentence*, New York: HarperCollins, 2011.

You, dear teacher, could use the above passage to teach your undergrad to slow down and appreciate what he or she had just read. But Fish's aim is more specific and goes further: he wants your student to try to write a perfect sentence. To write a sentence like Updike's, your student will have to take note of the form and imitate it by 'arranging clauses in somewhat the same way'. Fish is upbeat about the results, including his own, and quite encouraging: 'And once you get the hang of it—of zeroing in on a form that can then be filled with any number of contents—you can do it forever.'

You cannot get the sense of form from, say, Strunk and White. Fish is emphatic about this. On National Public Radio, he calls the old instruction manual useless. Advice from that book, like 'Do not join independent clauses with a comma', presumes too much knowledge on the part of the writer; instead of rote learning of that kind, Fish wants writers to grasp that '(1) a sentence is an organization of items in the world; and (2) a sentence is a structure of logical relationships.' Several chapters of *How to Write A Sentence* introduce the formal devices through which we might understand a variety of syntactic structures, e.g., the additive style or the satiric style. *But does this allow me to write a better academic sentence?* Does the sort of advice that Fish is offering work only among what we now call the younger demographic? I could ask the question in another way: all the examples that Fish has presented in the book are from literary fiction or non-fiction, and is he saying that he hasn't encountered any memorable sentences in critical writing? Let me quote in its entirety the opening paragraph from the *New York Times* piece by Fish that I had cited earlier:

> A few years ago, when I was grading papers for a graduate literature course, I became alarmed at the inability of my students to write a clean English sentence. They could manage for about six words and then, almost invariably, the syntax

> (and everything else) fell apart. I became even more alarmed when I remembered that these same students were instructors in the college's composition program. What, I wondered, could possibly be going on in their courses?

Fish's article focused on a writing curriculum for undergraduates but the opening words cut into me. I recognized myself in that description, especially that part of me that wrote papers for my grad seminars twenty years ago, papers that had words like 'hegemony' or 'historicization' in their titles. So, there was that anxiety that persisted in my reading of the Fish book on sentences. When I finished reading it, I admitted that I had taken delight in some of the lines Fish had quoted, and also his facile (in a good way) readings of those sentences, but I still wanted to know what language of criticism would he approve?

When I sent him a note asking for an example of a good sentence written by a literary critic, Fish wrote back saying this: 'Here's one I like, Terry Eagleton's example of a theoretical question: "Why do we have all these practices, utterances and institutions rather than some others?"' I confess I found the sentence ordinary, quite unremarkable, and I wrote back to Fish, requesting him to share with me his reasons for singling out this sentence.* Within minutes, he had sent back this response: 'Because it invites us to ask a series of questions—what are the practices we have and the institutions we inhabit, where did they come from and how do new ones emerge?—which, if followed through, will lead to an entire course in literary and cultural theory. It a question posed in a very simple vocabulary that just keeps opening up.'

That was helpful, but I guess I wanted more. As I said before,

---

*This would be the right place to mention that perhaps the most memorable sentence of Fish's to my mind is the following one: 'Academics like to eat shit, and in a pinch, they don't care whose shit they eat.' From Stanley Fish, 'The Unbearable Ugliness of Volvos' in Susan Gubar and Jonathan Kamholtz (eds.), *English Inside and Out: The Places of Literary Criticism*, New York: Routledge, 1993. pp. 102-08.

I'm not so much a sentence man. I like detail, it allows any piece of writing to gather individuality; but what gives any prose greater force is a conflict at its heart. (This might be a story of a contradiction that grows so large it threatens to shatter the assumptions with which we had begun. The conflict or crisis is an essential element but it can inhabit countless forms; the writing can go in many directions, what is crucial is that silence it induces, the silence in which we pay the writer our maximum attention.)

A day or two after my exchange with Fish I sent him another note:

> Hello again.
>
> This is probably bad form, at some level, but I couldn't resist asking you, especially because you're intellectually feisty and self-confident, if you'd in any way also relish pointing out how or why these sentences work, especially the second or the last ones (or if you'd at least say something as simple as 'look at p.__ of my book *Sentences* to understand what is good about these lines by Eagleton): *Stanley Fish, lawyer and literary critic, is in truth about as left-wing as Donald Trump. Indeed, he is the Donald Trump of American academia, a brash, noisy entrepreneur of the intellect who pushes his ideas in the conceptual marketplace with all the fervour with which others peddle second-hand Hoovers. Unlike today's corporate executive, however, who has scrupulously acquired the rhetoric of consensus and multiculturalism, Fish is an old-style, free-booting captain of industry who has no intention of clasping both of your hands earnestly in his and asking whether you feel comfortable with being fired. He fancies himself as an intellectual boot-boy, the scourge of wimpish pluralists and Nancy-boy liberals, and that ominous bulge in his jacket is not to be mistaken for a volume of Milton.*

Once again, Fish responded quickly. Once again, I was reading a clean, clear sentence. Fish had written, 'Sorry, this time I'll have to decline.'

VIII

Self-Help

THE 90-DAY BOOK

Ottessa Moshfegh is a young American writer whose novel *Eileen* was a finalist for the Man Booker Prize. Moshfegh told *The Guardian* newspaper that she didn't want to 'want to wait 30 years to be discovered…so I thought I'm going to do something bold'.* She bought a book called *The 90-Day Novel* by Alan Watt. Moshfegh understood the limits but, nevertheless, she persisted. ('It's ridiculous, claiming that anybody can write a great book, and quickly too. And I thought if *I* were to do this, what would happen, would my head explode?') She carried on with the exercise for 60 days, and *Eileen* was born. In the interview, Moshfegh had said that 'the Booker people' would be 'disgusted' with this story of her novel's origins, but I embrace it wholeheartedly. Because the point of course is to get the start you need and then put the imprint of your talent, your personality, your obsessions, on the work you are doing.

~

Many years ago, a near-stranger in Mumbai gave me a book called *Advice to Writers.*** Walking on the Dadabhai Naoroji Road, this used-book in hand, I came across a quote from E. L. Doctorow: 'Writing a book is like driving a car at night. You only see as far as your headlights go, but you can make the whole trip that way.'

---

*Paul Laity, 'Ottessa Moshfegh interview: *Eileen* started out as a joke—also, I'm broke, also I want to be famous', *The Guardian*, 16 February 2016.

**Jon Winokur (ed,) *Advice to Writers*, New York: Vintage Books, 1999. See p. 46.

This was almost two decades ago, and I have always remembered those words when struggling with a new book. If I had to name one single quote that I have gone back to sustain me, it would have to be the one by Doctorow. On a bookshelf in my study, I also have a quote from Sylvia Plath. I have now forgotten where I found it but this is what it says on the index card: 'The worst enemy to creativity is self-doubt.' Both the Doctorow statement and the one by Plath can be helpful when you are starting or are in the middle of a project. What will happen when your work is finished and your book is published and gets reviewed? For any number of reasons, the following quote won't help you—it is not meant to—but it will help to keep it in mind: it comes from an obituary for the writer Denis Johnson after his death in May 2017. This is what Johnson had once told the journalist Lawrence Wright: 'A bad review is like one of those worms in the Amazon that swims up your penis. If you read it, you can't get it out, somehow.'*

*Lawrence Wright, 'Remembering Denis Johnson', *New Yorker*, 26 May 2017. Wright's piece also shares Johnson's three rules of writing, including this one, my favourite, not least because it is so difficult to follow: 'Write in blood. As if ink is so precious you can't waste it.'

READ NO SECONDARY LITERATURE

I wanted to meet Anuk Arudpragasam after I read on the jacket of his beautiful novel, *The Story of a Brief Marriage*, that he was completing a dissertation in philosophy at Columbia University.* We met at the Hungarian Pastry Shop near the Cathedral of Saint John the Divine. I felt envy that he had used his time in graduate school so well. Where had his resolve come from? Arudpragasam told me he had started writing the novel during his first semester. In fact, he had joined a PhD program to earn himself a period of seven years ('a funded holiday') to do this work. But why philosophy, why not do an MFA in creative writing instead? His answer was clarifying. To his mind, an MFA was for Americans. It would have meant that his work 'would be read and judged and filtered through a middle-class white American literary sensibility'. He wasn't interested in people who weren't interested in what he represented.

And why philosophy in particular? Arudpragasam wanted me to know that he hadn't read more than five to ten philosophy books in the past six years he had spent in the graduate programme. He revealed that his choice of a dissertation topic had been a strategic one: a subject on which there was no secondary literature. He wasn't required to read too much, although his way of presenting this point was a bit different: 'You are not beholden to the banality or pedantry of scholarship.' (Arudpragasam's dissertation focuses on early twentieth-century American philosophy—he had completed

*Anuk Arudpragasam, *The Story of a Brief Marriage*, New Delhi: Fourth Estate, 2016.

two chapters. When I met him at the café, he was reading a book on Sri Lanka published by University Teachers for Human Rights in Jaffna.) However, philosophy was important to him. 'The impetus to study philosophy,' Arudpragasam said, 'is the same impetus that leads me to write. As a writer, I'm really not interested in stories for the sake of stories. I'm not really interested in the world. I'm not interested in describing a society, describing a culture, describing a milieu. I'm not really interested in socio-political issues—it happens that my work is infused by the Sri Lankan Tamil problem but that is because that's who I am, not because I have some idea that I need to describe or understand that condition. Instead, I'm interested in understanding, in the broadest sense, the inner life, the life of moods, the different stances and attitudes, the various self-deceptions, the various psychological structures.'

The writings of introspective philosophers like William James, Jean-Paul Sartre, Martin Heidegger, and Maurice Merleau-Ponty come close to the kind of writing that is of interest to Arudpragasam. He told me that he wasn't a fan of academic philosophy but what he liked in philosophy in general was 'a sense of mystery, a sense that things are unknowable, a sense that we are proceeding in the dark and that any misstep can trip us over and that we have to move very slowly not knowing whether the ground under is stable or not.' This was wholly missing in the kind of writing produced in academe. 'To succeed in academia,' he added, 'what is necessary above all is the performance of authority.' In philosophy, specialization and taxonomies mean that the range of answers to questions is limited. This means that 'everything is domesticated' and there is 'no surprise'. This feeling of what one might go so far as to call antipathy toward academic writing was present also in Arudpragasm's response to my question about the research he did for his novel. He said he disliked the word. It represents a distant anthropological relationship to the subject. 'To use the word research is to suggest a forced and artificial division between one's life and one's writing,' he said. His listening to interviews with survivors or his conversations with the only Tamil psychiatrist in the war-affected region in Sri Lanka weren't driven by the narrow end of writing a book about them; instead, the visits as well as the writing that followed were conceived by him as expression of the same deep interest in the subject. Arudpragasm described for me the experience of looking at the images that he found on the Internet of the war in Sri Lanka, how he would dwell on them for a long time, and in some cases print them out and pinn them to the walls of his room. He said, 'I was doing this not for the book but for me.'

READ JUNK

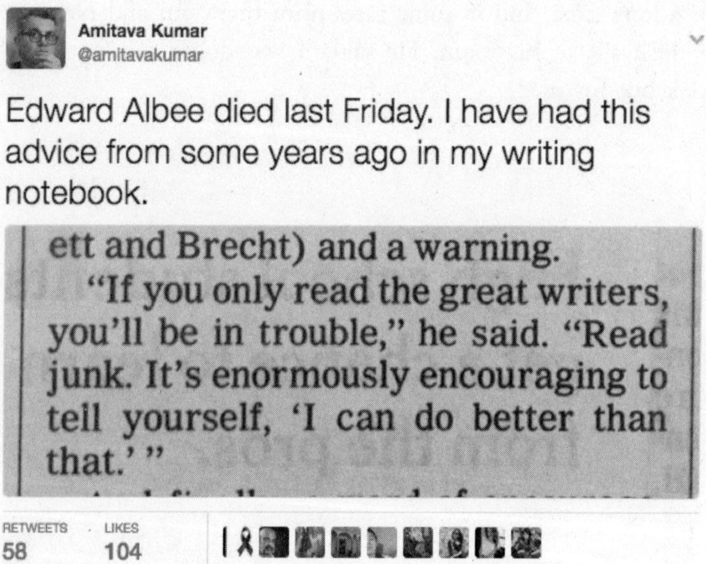

Amitava Kumar
@amitavakumar

Edward Albee died last Friday. I have had this advice from some years ago in my writing notebook.

ett and Brecht) and a warning.
"If you only read the great writers, you'll be in trouble," he said. "Read junk. It's enormously encouraging to tell yourself, 'I can do better than that.' "

RETWEETS 58 LIKES 104

11:08 AM - 21 Sep 2016

BUT WHY ONLY JUNK?

W. G. Sebald used to offer the following advice to his students: 'If you look carefully you can find problems in all writers. And that should give you great hope.'

GOOD SENTENCES

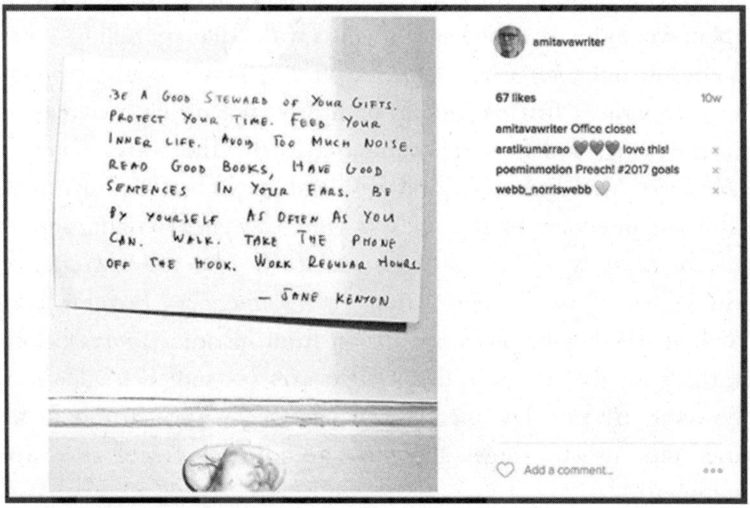

RUNNING

There is a book of interviews with non-fiction writers—most of them would be described as journalists with a literary calling—that I consult often for what it has to offer in terms of advice about how to write a first paragraph, or tips on organizing materials or interviewing, and how to conduct research. The book's name is *The New New Journalism* and is edited by Robert S. Boynton.* The last interview in the book is with Lawrence Wright, author of *The Looming Tower: Al-Qaeda and the Road to 9/11*, winner of the Pulitzer Prize for non-fiction. In the interview, Boynton asks Wright whether he seeks permission from his interviewees before turning on the tape recorder. Wright says yes and then adds that however reluctant his interviewees might be at the start about its use, 'they usually forget about the recorder's presence after five minutes'.**

I can't tell you how many times I've remembered this quote, and felt encouraged by it, when I'm in the act of taking the tape recorder out of my bag during an interview. But the part of the Wright interview that I have had reason to recall even more times is the following one:

> Boynton: What do you do if you get knotted up during the day?
>
> Wright: I sometimes go for a run because I find it mentally

---

*Robert S. Boynton, *The New New Journalism*, New York: Vintage Books, 2005.

**Ibid, p. 446.

> liberating. Oftentimes I'll solve the problem that is frustrating me after only five hundred yards. I get so many ideas when I run that I bring along notepaper and a pencil.*

I keep a set of golf pencils just for my walks or the occasional jog at the nearby Vassar farm. A small pencil and an index card folded in half. Those tools simply sit in my pocket. I forget about their presence after five minutes. And then remember them because an idea has come into my head—an answer to a question I had about the structure or the voice or anything else in the piece I was working on at my desk only fifteen minutes earlier.

Several years after I had read the interview with Wright, we met in India. We were both headed to a literary festival in Jaipur, but even before we reached our destination, both of us stopped in Delhi where Wright released a new book of mine.** I mentioned to Wright how much, over the years, I had appreciated his interview with Boynton.*** Over the next several days, I found Wright open

---

*Ibid, 450-51.

**My book, *Evidence of Suspicion* (New Delhi: Picador, 2010) was published outside the subcontinent under a different title, *A Foreigner Carrying in the Crook of His Arm a Tiny Bomb* (Durham: Duke University Press, 2010).

***I had occasion to conduct an interview with Boynton in front of my journalism students. Later, we had an email exchange. Here is a brief excerpt:

AK: Your book, *The New New Journalism*, is a wonderful introduction to method. I read it to learn what writers I admire do, how they gather their ideas, how they follow-up on them, what they have learned through their long practice. What pieces of advice have you yourself picked up from those writers?

RB: Pick a system and stick to it. The worst thing to do is to flounder around, driven by your mood or whims.

AK: At the end, can you give us a short list of your stylistic advice to your students working on their own literary reportage?

RB: Structure is the most difficult, and most important thing to do. Sometimes you need to forget everything about your subject and create a structure in order to know what to do with your material. I use scenes to structure my pieces. Find your best scenes, think

and generous. During his public interview in Jaipur that year, he opened his black backpack and began taking out one by one everything that was inside. He wanted to explain his method as a non-fiction writer by listing all the contents of his bag. I found it extremely revealing and helpful, and suspect that the list would be of use to scholars working 'in the field':

Sunglasses
Sleepmask (To be able to sleep in public places)
Computer cables
Small phone to be used in foreign countries with a local chip
Business cards
Fountain pens (Ball-point pens can be painful to use if you're writing for 8-10 hours, which Wright sometimes does when he is interviewing)
Ink
Tape recorder
Imodium pills
Sleeping pills
Aspirin
Notecards (In noting down things, Wright says he is already outlining in his mind his material and what he is going to say to his reader)
Batteries
Extra pens ('Redundancy is key in the business')
A book (At which point, he held up a copy of my book and offered praise)
A newspaper
Travel itinerary
Legal pad (Legal pads because they have about 50 pages and 20 lines, thus offering more space to the reporter; they also

---

about what kinds of ideas/themes they embody, and start by figuring out what order they should go in. The rest is easy! (Yeah, right).

provide a hard surface to write on)
Another legal pad with a list of contacts and names of potential interviewees
A sweater
Water and food

(I sent the above list to Wright and he wrote back immediately, wanting to 'round off the list'. Below are his additions.)
Earplugs
A spare tape recorder
Flash drive
$100 cash in a hidden pocket (a little money can get you out of a lot of trouble)

SLEEP

I am in favour of naps.

On days I can nap, I am able to think much better and even write late at night. A few years ago I received a note from a reporter at the *Chronicle of Higher Education* who was writing a piece on 'napping in academe'. She wanted to know if I napped. Only for a moment did I entertain the thought of mentioning that one of my children was still little and I rarely got a full night's sleep. The truth is that I have always napped. The reporter asked if she could call me: she had questions about any rituals that accompanied my napping. I wrote back that I had just woken up from a nap, and couldn't talk because I was still to have my tea. That was my ritual. But we talked in the morning the next day. Here is what the report said about our conversation:

> Amitava Kumar, an English professor at Vassar College, is similarly frank. Every day he takes a short walk home from the campus, closes the blinds in his study, turns off the phone, switches on his white-noise machine ('I go for rain,' he says), and lies down on a futon for 'a magical hour.'
>
> 'People joke a little bit about it,' he says. 'Maybe it is the triumph of multiculturalism that people are usually forgiving. They think, "He's Indian, it's okay for him to nap."'
>
> The academic schedule is generally perfect for nappers, says Mr. Kumar, with one exception: job-candidate visits. 'They fill every minute of these visits with some kind of meeting,' he says. 'If you could put it as a public service in

your article: Perhaps people who plan these itineraries, if they would allow some time to nap.'*

*Jennifer Ruark, 'Spring Forward, Fall Back (and Take a Nap)', *Chronicle of Higher Education*, Volume 54, Issue 26, p. A1.

KITCHEN TIMER

A colleague of mine said that I should try the Pomodoro technique.* The technique presents itself as 'a simple yet very effective way' to improve what bad self-help books call 'time management'. What is even better, the basic requirement of the Pomodoro technique is simply that you set 'a kitchen timer to 25 minutes'. The same colleague who swears by the Pomodoro technique was also responsible for inviting me to a meeting where she paired senior faculty with new junior faculty members that we could mentor. At that meeting I heard a colleague describe how she uses a timer that rings every 15 minutes. For her, those 15 minutes are the basic unit of work-time. When I came out of the meeting that day, I bought a battery-operated, red Polder timer that I've now been using to do quick bits of work—not the kind that gets done when you have an hour or two to switch on the Freedom app but instead the guerilla writing that you use to ambush time and save the task that was taken hostage the day—or the month—before. In fact, I am making this entry under 'Kitchen Timer' while the seconds fade in rapid succession on the Polder lying to the right of my computer.

One other thing. In my notebooks, I have recorded from I no longer remember where the following story: Sinclair Lewis was invited to talk to some students about the writer's craft. He stood at the head of the class and asked, 'How many of you here are really serious about being writers?' A sea of hands shot up. Lewis

*Check out pomodorotechnique.com

then asked, 'Well, why aren't you all home writing?' And with that he walked out of the room.

That is all I have in my notebook about the story. What did I think of it when I wrote it down? I'd like to believe that I recorded Sinclair's story and then, immediately, pressed the round black button on the Polder and began to write.

SELF-HELP

What advice can one give? *Get out more, love what you do, and try to write daily.* But that sounds suspiciously like Garrison Keillor on the *Writer's Almanac*, signing off with a 'Be well, do good work, and keep in touch.' To which the only proper, if sardonic, response can be the one made by August Kleinzahler: 'You bet, Garrison, I'm right on it.'* Perhaps one can only presume to give advice to the young. But even to them, I can only repeat what Barbara Kingsolver has said, 'It is harrowing for me to try to teach 20-year-old students, who earnestly want to improve their writing. The best I can think to tell them is: Quit smoking, and observe posted speed limits. This will improve your odds of getting old enough to be wise.'**

And if I were to dispense advice, would it be as if I were writing a self-help book? Would this not be looked down upon by the authorities in the academic cultural industry? I thought of Alain de Botton's wonderfully-titled book *How Proust Can Change Your Life*.*** The front dust-jacket quotes the following from a review: 'A

*August Kleinzahler, 'No Antonin Artaud with the Flapjacks, Please', *Poetry*, April 2004. Also at http://www.poetryfoundation.org/journal/article.html?id=146880

**2008 Commencement Address at Duke University delivered by Barbara Kingsolver on May 11. The speech can be accessed at http://www.dukenews.duke.edu/2008/05/kingsolver.html

***Alain de Botton, *How Proust Can Change Your Life*, New York: Vintage, 1997.

self-help manual for the intelligent person.' I had used *How Proust Can Change Your Life* in my classes and I wrote a brief message to de Botton sharing my worry.

As you are probably aware, de Botton writes clever, charming books that carry their learning lightly. He is not interested in writing for the four or five discriminating members of a dissertation committee: he wants his writing, whether about art or travel or philosophy, to reach a wider audience and bring delight. One way this can happen is if a direct connection is made between ideas and experience. A part of the pleasure of reading de Botton is to be reminded that knowledge can have practical use in our daily lives. In his books, de Botton is likely to ask questions like the following: How does philosophy help you grieve? How does literature help you love? How did our sense of well-being come to be a supreme object of managerial concern? These questions are such that they at once make much of what we know in academia enormously important but much of what we write as academics often irrelevant. (Early in his book, *The Pleasures and Sorrows of Work*, we get a sense of what de Botton thinks of academic writing. He observes that the practice of converting passion into facts has 'an established pedigree, most noticeable in academia, where an art historian, on being stirred to tears by the tenderness and serenity he detects in a work by a fourteenth-century Florentine painter, may end up writing a monograph, as irreproachable as it is bloodless, on the history of paint manufacture in the age of Giotto. It seems easier to respond to our enthusiasms by trading in facts than by investigating the more naive question of how and why we have been moved'.)* When I asked de Botton to tell me if he thought it was a good idea to write a book that offered self-help for academics, he responded: 'For two thousand years in the history of the west, the self-help book stood as a pinnacle of literary achievement.'

*Alain de Botton, *The Pleasures and Sorrows of Work*, New York: Pantheon, 2009, p. 27.

He listed the ancients who were masters of that form, including Epicurus, Seneca, and Marcus Aurelius. Christianity, de Botton said, had continued in the same vein. The Benedictines and Jesuits poured out handbooks to help one navigate the perils of earthly life. 'The assumption behind this long tradition was that the words of others can benefit us not only by giving us a practical advice, but also—and more subtly—by recasting our private confusions and griefs into eloquent communal sentences. We feel at once less alone and less afraid.'

How did this practice decline and self-help books lose their prestige? De Botton blamed the modern university system that 'in the mid-nineteenth century became the main employer for philosophers and intellectuals and started to reward them not for being useful or consoling, but for getting facts right'. Another feature of modernity was the 'growing secularization of society which emphasized that the modern human being could do the business of living and dying by relying on sheer common sense, a good accountant, a sympathetic doctor and hearty doses of faith in science.'

This abandonment of writing that emphasizes utility has meant that the genre of self-help is flooded by practitioners who traffic in offering salvation. Those who smother any intelligence-seeking under the blanket of cheerful optimism. De Botton reminded me that the noble predecessors of today's writers insisted on hard truths instead of pablum. Seneca, for example, asked: 'What need is there to weep over parts of life? The whole of it calls for tears.'

De Botton wanted me to contemplate the prospect of Virginia Woolf having a shot at writing a self-help book. But I was thinking of someone more along the lines of Thomas Piketty ('A Guide to the Long Run'). Or Martha Nussbaum ('Ten Questions to Answer Before You Vote'). And Wendy Doniger ('How to Be a Hindu').

IX

Exercises

BAD WRITING

An invitation came by email to contribute to a teaching volume. A brief piece, only a few hundred words long, was needed. Describe a favourite teaching exercise from your literature classes. The word 'fun' was also used. I responded immediately. The previous semester I had asked my creative-writing students to do a simple exercise in class. They were required to produce bad writing.

Hemingway's short story 'Hills Like White Elephants' is a classic of its kind. It illustrates Hemingway's 'iceberg theory', which requires that a story find its effectiveness by hiding more than it reveals. In 'Hills Like White Elephants', the conversation between a man and a woman waiting for a train at a station in Spain turns on the discussion of an imminent operation. Neither party uses the word 'abortion'. What is omitted in the discussion adds to the tension felt by the reader of the story.

Here is the exercise I suggested: The students can come to class having read 'Hills Like White Elephants'. Ask them to rewrite the dialogue where the iceberg is tipped, so to speak, allowing students to see for themselves what is lost when we state the obvious. Here's a sample of the work that students produce during in-class writing:

> *'It's really a simple operation, honey,' he said. 'It's not really an operation at all, abortions aren't a big deal these days.'*
>
> *The girl had an ambiguous look on her face that possibly hid some crucial emotion behind it. She said nothing. Sometimes, silence speaks volumes.*

> *'I know you'll be fine in there when they do it, it's no big deal, just to get rid of the baby.'**

Bad writing as a conscious goal is liberating for students: They are freed to be creative in a new and different way. I try to use this exercise in other classes, including non-fiction. In my journalism class for undergraduates, I take the poem 'Waiting for Icarus' by Muriel Rukeyser and ask students to rewrite it as a bad news report.** The point of the exercise isn't simply to teach students to avoid stating the obvious but, in the broader context, to prompt them to become better critics of what is conventional or clichéd.

Teju Cole, the author of the novel *Open City*, was visiting my writing class. He said that editors of non-fiction want whatever is important to be revealed in the first two paragraphs. They'll ask, 'Why are you burying this? Put it in the lede.' But it is different in fiction. In a work of fiction, Cole said, 'you pretend to be giving a lot of interesting information but actually you're burying the lede. You're going to release the information you want to *when* you want to. And in fact you probably don't need to release as much information as you think you need to.' As an example, Cole said that nowhere in *Open City* does he tell the reader the narrator's last name. ('Even though I know it… It is none of your business.')

I asked Cole to read the novel's opening lines and then participate in the exercise of bad writing. Here are the actual lines:

> And so when I began to go on evening walks last fall, I found Morningside Heights an easy place from which to set out into the city. The path that drops down from the Cathedral of St.

---

*Ernest Hemingway, 'Hills Like White Elephants', in Wendy Martin (ed.), *The Art of the Short Story*, New York: Houghton Mifflin, 2006, pp. 590-93.

**Muriel Rukeyser, 'Waiting for Icarus'. Available online at https://www.poemhunter.com/poem/waiting-for-icarus/.

> John the Divine and crosses Morningside Park is only fifteen minutes from Central Park ...*

Cole said, 'To me, the wrong way to begin it, knowing what the book is about, would be: "As a Nigerian-German psychiatrist, living in New York City in my mid-thirties, I found myself quite melancholic to be in the shadow of the Twin Towers five years after they went down. In order to sort through my feelings both about the historic past of the city of New York and my own unsorted neuroses regarding my mother and my grandmother and my dead father I decided to wander around the city."'

I sent off my brief submission to the teaching volume and then began to wonder what passage I would choose to give to graduate students in a criticism course if I wanted them to do bad writing. Which example from a critic or theorist would you choose, as I had done with Hemingway, to encourage students to write badly? Or, more provocatively, which passages would you choose to illustrate such writing?

---

*Teju Cole, *Open City*, New York: Random House, 2011. See p. 3.

PROMPT

The use of the word prompt to mean incitement or cue has probably been around for 500 years or so, but its use in a narrower sense, as an instruction or directions for a writing assignment in class, is new to me. I swear I hadn't even heard it until maybe a couple of years ago. 'Professor, what is the prompt for next week?'

'Did you check the syllabus? Take this poem by Muriel Rukeyser, "Waiting for Icarus", and rewrite it as if you were a reporter filing a story. Interview the speaker, etc.'

Everyone understands the idea of prompts. The use of #hashtags on Twitter, in my opinion, offers the most succinct example of incitement to writing. Teju Cole has used Twitter #hashtags to provoke public writing and image-making among his 265,000 followers. This exercise can become an extraordinarily creative, collaborative act.* Cole is on a temporary (or maybe permanent) break from Twitter, but he has been producing a new set of essays on Instagram—for instance, reposting photographs of the Mona Lisa taken by visitors to the Louvre, and accompanying them with his analysis of social photography, the ritual function of icons, and the optical qualities of digital compression.

Last year, on the first day of freshman composition, I introduced students to the essay form through Cole's tweets about drones.**

---

*Robinson Meyer, 'When the World Watches the World Cup, What Does That Look Like?' *The Atlantic*, 15 July 2014.

**Available online at https://storify.com/joshbegley/teju-cole-seven-short-stories-about-drones

(E.g. 'Mrs. Dalloway said she would buy the flowers herself. Pity. A signature strike leveled the florist's.') Here was an elegant, eminently literary, entry into the contemporary world: a quick rewriting of the opening lines of the classics. I wanted students to throw away the five-paragraph costume-armour of the high-school essay. They were already masters of that particular form; they could now break rules and become inventive writers. We would explore other conventional as well as unconventional essays later in the course, but that first day I asked my freshmen to write essays about their first day at the college in 140 characters, #hashtag included. Cole also came in handy for my beginning journalism students, whether they wanted to offer critical commentary or report on news in more creative ways.*

In a scene early in *Open City*, Cole's protagonist, Julius, wanders into the American Folk Art Museum, and sees an exhibition of paintings by John Brewster Jr.** Julius finds Brewster's portraits of children unsettling. Later, he discovers that Brewster's subjects, like Brewster himself, were deaf. Julius's reading of the paintings, precise and slow, served in my class as a prompt for a visit to Vassar College's art museum and writing about any one of the art works on display.***

---

*See, for instance, Teju Cole's 'Small Fates' project on Twitter. A report on it is available online at http://www.newyorker.com/books/page-turner/teju-coles-small-fates. Accessed on 24 March 2017.

**Cole, *Open City*. See pp. 36-40.

***Prompts are everywhere. A newspaper lying on my dining table informs me that the singer Feist, about to embark on a promotional tour, has a 'Pleasure Questionnaire' for the strangers she will meet: 'What are 10 words to describe the way you experience your sadness?' 'What makes you feel tenderness?' 'Describe a lonely day in one sentence.' 'Feist's Potent, Positive Solitude,' *New York Times*, 9 April 2017.
Or, consider the journal my middle-school-going daughter picked up at the local bookstore. The journal contains prompts like the following: 'Rewrite the Gettysburg Address for today's audience'; 'You're the White House head chef, preparing a state dinner for the president of India. What do you serve, and how does it turn out?'; 'Five things you wish your mother had never told you.' *642 Things to Write About, by the San*

Careful seeing and critical commentary are part of the apparatus of *Open City*. The novel was praised by James Wood in the *New Yorker* for providing a rare example in contemporary fiction where literary theory was neither satirized nor flaunted to establish the author's credentials.* In return, the book has been popular in university courses. Cole told me that his readers in academe are enthusiastic about *Open City* because it 'takes for granted some of the language that they use to think about the world'.

When I asked him if we could think of a writing prompt to which the response is the novel *Open City*, Cole said that a novel was an answer to a question or a set of questions, and you are only able to figure out what the questions are after writing the novel. And what did he realize after finishing his own book? That he had been responding to questions about mourning in the post-9/11 moment, that he had been working through how historical innocence and guilt affect personal innocence and guilt. And there was something else he discovered quite late: The novel was also 'trying to be responsible to academic insight as part of the texture of life'.

Academic insight? Yes.

One of the questions *Open City* did not know it was setting out to answer, Cole said, was the following: 'What does a novelistic space look like if the work of Barthes, Fanon, Butler, Foucault, Said, etc., are taken seriously as part of the world? Because, after all, they are indeed part of the world, and have actually helped improve it.'

Francisco Writers' Grotto, San Francisco: Chronicle Books, 2011.

Or, for that matter, one of the more popular memes on Facebook: '20 Things You Don't Know About Me.'

*James Wood, 'The Arrival of Enigmas', *New Yorker*, 28 February 2011.

POST-ITS

A friend posted a news item on his Facebook page about a postal carrier in New York City who, over a decade, stashed about 17,000 pieces of undelivered mail.* The reason the carrier gave for doing what he had done was that he felt 'overwhelmed'. Beneath my friend's post on Facebook, someone had written: 'That is how I sometimes feel about grading.'

Exactly. I have sometimes felt overwhelmed when writing this book—I needed to edit the many interviews I initially did as I began to develop this project, so many engaging books to read with a new publication of interest every month, what to do with the many gaps in my knowledge, and the endless problem of finding time. I try to remember the story from decades ago that Anne Lamott recounts about her brother who was ten at that time.** As Lamott tells it, as the summer ended, her brother was desperately trying one night to write a report on birds. He had had three months to do the assignment and attempting to do it at the last moment left him feeling—I guess the right word is 'overwhelmed'. Seeing the boy close to tears, Lamott writes, their father put his arm around his son and said, 'Bird by bird, buddy. Just take it bird by bird.' Such good advice! I have had reason to offer it not only to my own children but also to my students and myself.***

---

*Luis Ferré-Sadurní, '"Overwhelmed" Postal Carrier Hoarded 17,000 Pieces of Mail, Officials Say', *New York Times*, 21 April 2018.

**Anne Lamott, *Bird by Bird*, New York: Anchor Books, 1994. See pp. 16-20.

***Lamott also offers another consolation—although the word I like is *caution*. She repeats a line whose principal sentiment is attributed to Hemingway: 'The first draft of anything

Lamott writes that she keeps a one-inch picture frame on her desk to remind her to perform her task in short assignments. In my composition classes, I pass around a stack of post-it notes and ask students to first write just enough to fill the small yellow square of paper in front of them. The post-it note, like the small-sized notebook I carry always in my pocket, gives comfort when I recall the Latin dictum *Nulla dies sine linea* (No day without a line).

is shit.'

REVISING

In creative writing classes, there is always a great emphasis on rewriting. (I once asked Colum McCann what his MFA classes were like. His reply: 'Blood runs out the door.') A similar emphasis on revising doesn't exist in graduate classes in other areas of the humanities. Unlike classes in literary theory, for instance, creative writing classes don't typically engage with questions of history or ideology, and that is their drawback. On the other hand, in creative writing workshops, attention paid to language at the level of the sentence makes for small miracles. This work doesn't happen—*doesn't need to happen*—only in workshops. It can happen on the table in your study, and on your page. Consider this example of a revision—the poet A. K. Ramanujan deletes 'mirrors' and replaces it with 'shopwindows'. Instead of the more routine word, we have the slightly unexpected one, and it makes perfect music:

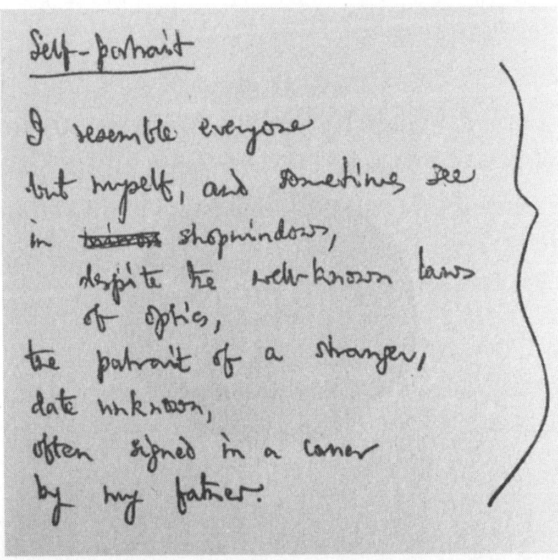

Self-portrait

I resemble everyone
but myself, and sometimes see
in ~~mirrors~~ shopwindows,
despite the well-known laws
of optics,
the portrait of a stranger,
date unknown,
often signed in a corner
by my father.

If you're a writer, you revise. Virginia Woolf even revised her suicide note. A letter to her husband, Leonard, began: 'Dearest, I feel certain that I am going mad again: I feel we cant go through another of these terrible times. And I shant recover this time. I begin to hear voices, and cant concentrate. So I am doing what seems the best thing to do. You have given me the greatest possible happiness....' The last sentiment is elaborated upon in the letter before Woolf returns to her illness. 'You see I cant even write this properly. I cant read. What I want to say is that I owe all the happiness of my life to you.' And then again, more lines acknowledging Leonard's love. In the revised version, which Woolf's biographer speculates was perhaps written ten days later, the writing is more compact. The fifth line is now the first. And the description that follows, of her illness, is swift and final. 'Dearest, I want to tell you that you have given me complete happiness. No one could have done more than you have done. Please believe that. But I know that I shall never get over this: & I am wasting your life. It is this madness.' Then the lines about the difficulty of writing the note. A fresh protestation of love, and then the request that Leonard destroy all her papers.*

The thing I try to remember when revising is this line from an interview with Jon Krakauer: 'Writers often fail to appreciate that removing 5 percent of a book can make that book *twice* as good.'**

---

*Hermione Lee, *Virginia Woolf*, New York: Knopf, 1997. See pp. 744-47.

**Robert Boynton (ed.), *The New New Journalism*, New York: Vintage Books, 2005. See p. 179.

EDITING

The writer Garth Greenwell was explaining in a newspaper article the process of revising, over the course of a summer in Madrid, his novel *What Belongs to You.** His editor sent him scans of the manuscript pages with her markings on it—'Find a better way' or

*Garth Greenwell, *What Belongs to You: A Novel*, New York, Picador: 2016. Also see Garth Greenwell, 'Topography of a Novel: Garth Greenwell on how he wrote *What Belongs to You*', *The Guardian*, 7 March 2016.

'Not good enough'—and Greenwell would work on the changes each day, 'often for ten hours a day'. I'm interested in process. I think we all are. And what was encouraging about Greenwell's description was how he felt lost or uncertain but slowly the editing and rewriting came to feel 'more and more like composition'. The part that stayed with me in Greenwell's story was about his visits to the museum in Madrid hosting an exhibition of El Greco:

> I'm drawn to art in which things are a little askew. Straight realism isn't very interesting to me; I like to see the interference of consciousness, the way perception is muddied by a unique interpreting mind. El Greco's paintings are eccentric, strange, willful; I loved them. Standing in front of his *Portrait of Fray Hortensio*, I couldn't help wondering what an editor would make of it: the obviously strange angle of the back of the chair, for instance, or the weird positioning of the hands. Wouldn't an editor want to make those less strange, to straighten those things out? And yet wasn't their strangeness the key to the greatness of the painting?

Do we have an answer to Greenwell's questions? It is all about process, the process of working with the criticisms and making changes and judging the new work, but process also includes the important matter of the working relationship with the editor.* Even with the latter part, you can begin with doubt and uncertainty, you can struggle with confusion, but the partnership has to arrive at an arrangement where it feels more and more like collaboration. As to the question about preserving strangeness or what is whimsical

*To get a realistic idea of how a more mainstream editor might be thinking, especially an editor who has to convince a publisher or even a bookseller to invest financially in a book, please read Susan Rabiner and Alfred Fortunato, *Thinking Like Your Editor*, New York: W.W. Norton, 2002. This book asks the academic writer to seriously consider issues of audience, proposal package and argument, understood as broader than merely research, with particular emphasis on the use of narrative devices, especially narrative tension, in writing.

in your work, a huge part of me believes that it starts with an understanding that language is your closest ally, and that if you align it with your desire for freedom, you will be able to live forever.

PERFORMING IT

I would like to make a case for writing that comes out of an idea of performance. (And also writing as performance.) An editor friend asked me a few years ago to go to several bookstores in New York City and ask: 'Where is your "White literature" section?'* I found the exercise thrilling and exhausting—in the middle of it, I got a sense of what it would be like to be the Sacha Baron Cohen of literary criticism—but it was also revealing of booksellers' attitudes about whose books counted as literature. That said, a writing exercise need not be a sting operation. It can generate stories by other means; for instance, by inviting public responses in an unusual and compelling way. I was very much taken by a book entitled *Jeff, One Lonely Guy.*** As David Shields writes in his introduction to that book, his student Jeff Ragsdale posted flyers in his neighbourhood in New York saying: 'If anyone wants to talk about anything, call me (347) 469-3173. Jeff, one lonely guy.' The flyer went viral after it was posted on Reddit. Ragsdale received more than 60,000 phone calls and texts from all over the world. The book is an edited record of those messages. (I myself was inspired by the book and posted questions about my hometown Patna when writing a biography of the city.*** Questions

---

*Amitava Kumar, 'Bookstores of New York' in Kumar, *Lunch with a Bigot.* See pp. 162-66.

**Jeff Ragsdale, David Shields, Michael Logan, *Jeff, One Lonely Guy,* Las Vegas: Amazon Publishing, 2012.

***Amitava Kumar, 'What Happens in Patna, Stays in Patna?', India Ink Blog, *New York Times,* 20 August 2012.

like 'Did you see Brando in Patna in 1967?' I got responses that I was then able to use in my book.)* A more recent, and also different type of book is *Bleaker House* by Nell Stevens.** A non-fiction account, *Bleaker House* tells the story of its author being awarded a fellowship to travel and write—and her choosing to go to a remote, snowy island in the Falklands where, for a long stretch of time, she is the sole human inhabitant. Of course, one could argue, quite logically, that many kinds of books, from travel to cooking to anthropology, are performance-texts; what makes *Bleaker House* unlike those other books, and more in line with what I'm advocating here, is that it is deliberate and unusual in its staging. It is definitely dramatic—and results in an engaging story. I was never quite convinced that Stevens had gone to Bleaker Island to write a novel, not least a novel that shared something with Dickens's *Bleak House*; but what was a winning part of the narrative was the author's choice of the locale for the residency. It was like Ragsdale's flyer: an instigating event that set into motion an interesting story. On Bleaker Island, Stevens is cold and hungry and lonely. She is afraid of getting depressed. On Skype, when she confides her fears to her mother, the response she gets is a question: 'Why do you do it to yourself?' But when she says the same thing to a novelist friend, the response is: 'That's the thing about being a writer. Every bad experience you have is good material.'*** Exactly. In choosing to undertake her trip, and to spend forty-one days on Bleaker Island in the unforgiving winter, Stevens has made a terrific choice. It is a performance; it gives her material. Of course, it is not *merely* performance either. This is even more true of a book like Barbara Ehrenreich's *Nickel and Dimed*.**** A serious exploration of

---

*Amitava Kumar, *A Matter of Rats: A Short Biography of Patna*, New Delhi: Aleph Book Company, 2014.

**Nell Stevens, *Bleaker House*, New York: Doubleday, 2017.

***Ibid, p. 120.

****Barbara Ehrenreich, *Nickel and Dimed: On (Not) Getting By in America*, New York:

the consequences of poverty on ordinary Americans, and a report on the struggle to survive on the low wages given for unskilled labour, *Nickel and Dimed* is nevertheless the product of what I'm loosely calling a performance: Ehrenreich pretends to be a divorced homemaker needing to do waitressing or cleaning to get by. She takes jobs with pitiful pay in places like Florida and Maine: if 30 per cent of the workforce toiled at that time for $8 or less an hour, Ehrenreich was going to find out how they were able to survive. What she finds at the end is that you can work harder and harder and still sink deeper and deeper into poverty and debt.* I love the book and have taught it in my classes several times. But what has always struck me is that no one told me during my days as a graduate student working on a thesis in cultural studies that one could do a project like Ehrenreich's. But that's what I'm advocating, that we find imaginative ways of entering zones of experience. That we produce reports on our new reality. When I came across the documentary *Super Size Me*, I was amazed at its simplicity and boldness.** From 1 February to 2 March 2003, Morgan Spurlock ate only McDonald's food. The physiological changes that were experienced by Spurlock told a revealing story about obesity in America.

'Sophie Calle is a first-person artist.'*** True enough but it isn't just that Calle's art draws upon her life stories; instead, what is fascinating is the part she plays in *engineering* these stories. Consider the opening entry in her opening entry from the text-and-photo project called 'The Shadow, 1981':

Metropolitan Books, 2001.

*Ibid, See especially p. 3 and p. 220.

***Super Size Me*, dir. Morgan Spurlock, 2004.

***Sophie Calle, *Sophie Calle M'as-tu-vue.* First published 2003. New York: Prestel, 2010. See p. 15.

> Thursday, April 1, 1981
>
> 10 A.M. I am getting ready to go out. Outside, in the street, a man is waiting for me. He is a private detective. He is paid to follow me. I hired him to follow me, but he does not know that.*

Calle's diary is followed by the detective's report and his photographs of his strange subject, Calle herself. An unusual collaboration, and just one of the many during a long career. (Twenty years later, another detective was hired to fulfil the same task of shadowing the artist.) Calle's work as an artist started with her following strangers and producing texts; other projects included working as a chambermaid at a hotel and going through the belongings of guests and photographing them; a room atop the Eiffel Tower where strangers come to tell stories to Calle as she lies in bed; in collaboration with Damien Hirst, giving her profile to psychiatrists for a psychological evaluation; in one, and I'm choosing here from scores listed in a catalogue, Calle meets the blind, those who have never had sight, and asks them what image of beauty they carry in their minds.** (The faces with their unseeing eyes are paired with the quotes and photographs of what is being described. 'The most beautiful thing I ever saw is the sea, the sea going out so far you lose sight of it.') Often, Calle's own writing style is simple and straightforward, in the present tense, structured like a report. The style doesn't defeat you with distractions. Her real daring lies in the situations she conjures. When in my own chosen discipline, English, I encounter endless studies of one writer or another, offering commentary on a book or more, I think of Calle. What would Sophie Calle do? What kind of brilliant or outrageous rendezvous would she

---

*See 'The Shadow', 1981, ibid, pp. 101-112.

**See 'The Blind,' ibid, pp. 377-384.

devise with the writer in question? I dream of fresh, provocative, unpredictable texts.

RITUALS

I am writing this at a writers' residency in the town of Ghent in Hudson Valley. I'll be here for a month and my aim is to finish this book that I imagine you, dear reader, holding in your hands in the not too distant future. There are words to be put on the page but the only way that is going to happen is if I stick to my rituals.

The writer Patricia Highsmith once said that she was rarely short of inspiration; she had ideas, she said, 'like rats have orgasms'. I cannot make the same claim. I don't think writers need ideas so much; what they really need is time.

Or, more accurately, the need is for those conditions of work, the meeting of place and habits, that allow the right words to emerge. I have on my desk here a book called *Daily Rituals.** It offers short accounts of how writers and artists work. The above quote from Highsmith is something I came across in the book. And the detail that Highsmith, probably in an effort to keep distractions to a minimum, ate the same food every day: American bacon, fried eggs and cereal.

According to literary legend (probably untrue), Edith Sitwell used to lie in an open coffin for a while before she began her day's work. This was supposed to serve as inspiration for her macabre writing. Maya Angelou could work only in hotel or motel rooms. Truman Capote couldn't begin or end anything on a Friday. Igor Stravinsky performed headstands when he needed a break and Saul Bellow did thirty push-ups. For the work to go on, John Cheever

*Mason Currey (ed.), *Daily Rituals: How Artists Work*, New York: Knopf, 2013.

required erotic release.

These examples appear to us as oddities but what needs to be stressed is the importance of ritual in the creation of work. I tell my students that they must 'write every day and walk every day'. (See Appendix A.) It is not essential that they write a lot; only a hundred and fifty words each day is enough. All that matters is the routine.

In *Daily Rituals*, the dancer Twyla Tharp presents the following account of what she does after waking up at 5.30 a.m..: 'I walk outside my Manhattan home, hail a taxi, and tell the driver to take me to the Pumping Iron gym at 91st Street and First Avenue, where I work out for two hours. The ritual is not the stretching and weight training I put my body through each morning at the gym; the ritual is the cab. The moment I tell the driver where to go I have completed the ritual.'

I understand what Tharp is saying. When I lace my boots, before stepping out for my walk, I'm entering a ritual. I'm mindful of the notepaper and the small yellow pencil in my pocket. The work of writing has begun. I was pleased to find out in *Daily Rituals* that it is extremely common for writers and artists to go on walks. As important as the act of shutting the door of the study has been the act of opening it and stepping out for a stroll. Gustave Flaubert, Charles Dickens, Leo Tolstoy were all walkers.

My rituals become more formalized, even concentrated, in a situation like a writers' residency. The work of reading and writing goes on through the day, interrupted by walks along the country road outside or on the grass that stretches out to the surrounding hills. The writers don't see much of each other during the day but we gather together for dinner at 7.30 in the evening. Then, soon after the dinner plates have been cleared, I look forward to ping-pong. Although I brought with me a new yoga mat, thinking that I'd like to stretch every day, it has stayed rolled up in a corner of my room. I'm satisfied with my routine, happy that I'm able to play ping-pong and sometimes even mix drinking shots of bourbon into the game. (This is the place, of course, to insert a quote from Thomas Mann's *Death in Venice*: 'Who can unravel the essence, the stamp of the artistic temperament! Who can grasp the deep, instinctual fusion of discipline and dissipation on which it rests!')

My first act on waking up is to pour the coffee from the thermos (I make the coffee in the communal kitchen each night before going to bed) and sit down at the desk to write. It appears that at least one-third of the writers and artists featured in *Daily Rituals* mention their dependence on coffee. I'm not surprised. What surprises me more is that writers like Graham Greene and Jean-Paul Sartre relied on amphetamines for their writing. Then there was W. H. Auden who took 'a dose of Benzedrine each morning the way many people take a daily multivitamin'.

I don't know about amphetamines but I can attest to the power of books. I have brought with me to this residency titles that appear elsewhere in these pages: these are books that I turn to when I'm stuck or need inspiration. (Today's text has been *Insectopedia* by Hugh Raffles. A work of astonishing breadth and beauty. Very quickly you learn about the nearly unimaginable fecundity of insects, the limits of the categories we have assigned to them, and what you also realize is that Raffles has produced his own organizational principle for his *Insectopedia*.* This innovative arrangement, not to mention the gorgeous language and teeming imagery, are closely allied with the book's aim: to present knowledge about the 'astonishing perfection' of 'the billions of beings' that surround us. A sense of strangeness of the world, and accompanying it, a feeling of awe, gives to many of its pages the same narrative quality that one associates with the fiction of W. G. Sebald or Michael Ondaatje.) I've also been reading just before falling asleep the diary of Virginia Woolf. The last passage I marked was from an

*Hugh Raffles, *Insectopedia*, New York: Pantheon Books, 2010.

entry she made on Wednesday, 13 July 1932: 'I've been sleeping over a promising novel. That's the way to write. I'm ruminating, as usual, how to improve my lot; and shall begin by walking, alone, in Regent's Park this afternoon.'*

---

*Virginia Woolf, *A Writer's Diary*, edited by Leonard Woolf, New York: Houghton Mifflin Harcourt, 1954. See p. 177.

I should add here that Woolf would probably have been ambivalent about my reading these writers I admire, including her, while trying to finish my own book. When correcting the proofs of *Orlando*, she recorded her experience reading Proust: 'Take up Proust after dinner and put him down. This is the worst time of all. It makes me suicidal. Nothing seems left to do. All seems insipid and worthless.' Woolf, ibid, p. 127.

FOR GRADUATE STUDENTS

When I came to the US for graduate study, I was lucky to have several inspiring teachers; to the best of my recollection, however, not one of them offered any advice to me about how to write. To make up for that deficit at this late date, I decided to ask some of the academic scholars whose books I was reading about the advice they gave to the students in their graduate seminars.

Andrew Ross, author of *Bird on Fire: Lessons from the World's Least Sustainable City**

When people ask me about my discipline, I say that I am an agnostic, and for academics, it is very difficult to achieve that. Finding my own voice (or one that I feel comfortable with) is the way I would describe the means to that end. At a certain point, I became more influenced by writers' styles than by the authority of their ideas. Writers as disparate as C. Wright Mills or Jonathan Raban, for example.

As far as a method goes—and this is what I tell my graduate students—it's more important to have a good sense of your object and the questions you want to answer, then you are in a position to choose your methods—i.e. how to get from A to B. In most disciplines, the method comes first, and is then applied to an object. For me, it's the other way around. The questions and the goals determine the methods. How will I answer those questions? Do I need to do interviews, or conduct surveys? Do I need to

*Andrew Ross, *Bird on Fire: Lessons from the World's Least Sustainable City*, New York: Oxford University Press, 2011.

visit sites, or consult archives? What kind of reading do I need to do, and what is the likely audience? In our American Studies programme, our students are encouraged to be flexible in their application of methods. They are much more likely to think of themselves as investigators, undertaking case-studies, rather than being motivated by general theoretical problems. Approaching research in this manner, it's more likely that they will find their own voice, or at least a voice that is uniquely theirs, rather than aping the consensus voice of their discipline, or whatever influential master thinker they have been weaned on.

~

Anna Lowenhaupt Tsing, author of *The Mushroom At the End of the World**

My favourite thing about anthropology is its ability to go back and forth between what you rightly identify as 'ordinary, lived detail' and 'abstract frames of intelligibility'. To me, it's the best gift of the discipline, the feature I am most passionate about sharing with my students. The best anthropology does not merely add scraps of information to the stockpile of scholarly knowledge; it asks big questions. At the same time, abstract thought alone is not enough. It is in the encounter between the details of life and the big questions that anthropologists find their insights.

I'm teaching a course right now in which I'm trying to get undergraduate students to do this, at least as readers. I ask them to work with some accessible ethnographies and to figure out how these ethnographies do theoretical work—often without trumpeting their interventions very loudly. At the same time, I want them to consider what details of life might contribute to those kinds of theoretical interventions. Why does the ethnography matter to the argument?

*Anna Lowenhaupt Tsing. *The Mushroom at the End of the World: On the Possibility of Life in Capitalist Ruins*, Princeton, NJ: Princeton University Press, 2015.

That back and forth between big theory and intimate ethnography is the key to what the discipline can do. And, more importantly, it might make curiosity about the world seem worthwhile.

I'm aware that this distinctive methodological approach does not always translate well to readers trained in other ways. Readers from other disciplinary backgrounds often interpret ethnographic work as detail that merely gets in the way of theoretical questions. As a result they too often miss the ability of the ethnography to change theory—and to change what we know about the whole world, not just a single place.

Some stubborn facet of my character takes this as a challenge. In my new book, I'm pushing as far as I can go in telling 'big stories', just to see what it might take to get heard. And then I taunt readers by arguing that the bigness can only be understood by attention to some intimate detail. '*This is the structure of global capitalism*,' I herald, only then to tell readers that I know this because I have studied how people pursue a particular mushroom. I can't say this strategy is always successful, but I'll also admit I'm having fun performing its outrageousness.

∽

Kathleen Stewart, author of *Ordinary Affects**

I've been having them read *New Yorker* articles that describe little worlds (there's a great one on the world of homing pigeon breeders). And other examples of creative non-fiction. I get them to bring in examples and to bring in their own writing. I try to keep the reading down so we can read what they write, using the classroom as a workshop.

∽

*Kathleen Stewart, *Ordinary Affects*, Durham: Duke University Press, 2007.

Rob Nixon, Princeton University, author of *Dreambirds**

I think it's often easier to theorize in the official codes of theory rather than to theorize lightly through scene, object, story, and incident in ways that keeps alive the sensual serendipities of language. This is not a question of being for or against theory, but rather of being suspicious of orthodoxies that concede, in advance, that what passes for theory must be signaled by a narrowing of diction, sentence rhythms, and sensual awareness. I'm in favour of surprise.

Before a graduate student embarks on a dissertation, I ask them to find two works of criticism that turn them on stylistically. At least one of these works they should disagree with intellectually, preferably vehemently so. Then I ask the student to photocopy a couple of pages and ventriloquize the voices of their chosen critics. It's not a matter of simply emulating someone's style but of absorbing, through concentrated exposure, certain ideas about how you'd like to sound.

In my early work on Naipaul I was—and remain—profoundly skeptical of the role he played as a public intellectual during the latter decades of the Cold War and the height of structural adjustment. Yet reading and rereading his work—the sheer variety of his sentence structures—was, though I didn't recognize it at the time, a profound blessing. Just to have that voice wash over me even as, intellectually, his ideas often enraged me.

I also encourage students to read literary criticism that is deeply personal yet formally inventive and intellectually expansive. I use your own *Bombay-London-New York*, Richard Mabey's *Nature Cure*,** Laura Miller's *The Magician's Book*,*** John Elder's *Reading*

---

*Rob Nixon, *Dreambirds: The Strange History of the Ostrich in Fashion, Food, and Fortune*, New York: Picador, 2000.

**Richard Mabey, *Nature Cure*, Charlottesville, VA: University of Virginia, 2007.

***Laura Miller, *The Magician's Book: A Skeptic's Adventures in Narnia*, New York: Little, Brown and Company 2008.

the Mountains of Home,* books that, whether through the work of Hanif Kureishi, John Clare, C. S. Lewis, or Robert Frost, offer unorthodox ways of doing double duty as literary criticism and as love letters to the power of literature per se. Passion can have a profoundly critical edge; it doesn't have to be sentimental. Look at the example of James Wood, an impassioned skeptic who sets the bar very high in terms of what he considers literary greatness. Yet I am moved by his immersion, his indisputable love for the wondrous shards that he finds and explicates even in novels that disappoint him. Sometimes I agree with his judgements, sometimes not, but I feel consistently enlivened by his profound attentiveness, which never seems cynically routine.

Recently, when I taught Anna Tsing's *Friction*, a graduate student asked: 'Could I get away with writing my dissertation like that?'** Yes, if you're committed, inventive, and, like Tsing, refuse to cut corners intellectually. Maybe you won't write something like that for your dissertation, but your career is long, so stay alive to the possibilities, not least the possibility of passion.

There is a whole slew of vocal options out there for you. And these options keep changing as the media environment around us morphs. Don't just find your voice, find your voices. If you're writing on the same subject for, say, an op-ed piece in the *New York Times*, *Critical Inquiry*, or *Slate*, flex your voice to fit the genre and the audience. Keep reading people who surprise and challenge you at the level of style. Yes, sometimes you will have to reread a sentence to grasp an author's meaning, but don't be overly seduced by the notion that difficult-looking writing is the most difficult to write. Theorizing lightly (which doesn't mean theorizing less seriously) is often harder than theorizing that announces itself as serious, as

*John Elder, *Reading the Mountains of Home*, Cambridge, MA: Harvard University Press, 1998.

**Anna Lowenhaupt Tsing, *Friction: An Ethnography of Global Connection*, Princeton, NJ: Princeton University Press, 2004.

professional, because its language is recognizably stillborn.

Josh Kun, author of *Audiotopia**

I am drawn to the figure of the DJ as a model of scholarship and research. I particularly like the idea of 'cross-fading' as a metaphor, or model, for what we ought to be doing as academics, public intellectuals, etc. One input channel with one flow of sound, a second with another flow of sound and the crossfader keeps them in dialogue with each other. The DJ blends, skips between them, juggles beats, merges melodic lines, finds the points of convergence, all while keeping each sound unique and singular. More and more I am drawn to points of convergence and connection, not only between cultures and communities, styles and genres, traditions and beliefs, but between the campus and the city, between the academy and the world the academy is meant to be in dialogue with. My heroes are poets, musicians, artists, scientists, and anyone else who follows the truths of their creative and intellectual missions to wherever they lead, refusing to judge the direction, refusing to police the site of arrival. The cellist Fred Katz was an anthropology professor, an arranger, a jazz innovator, a kabbalist, a Zen buddhist, and a magician. I'm drawn to polymaths I guess, line blurrers. As one whose work starts, always, with music and sound, I would be disloyal and dishonest if suddenly I became a disciplinarian—music and sound, by nature, drift and bleed, connect and cross. The challenge is to not take that for granted and to develop a critical language and a historical sensitivity to the process of connection and crossing. Not all connections are equal, not all easy.

I was trained to be deeply and immediately suspicious of humanism and yet more and more I find myself asking all of the

*Josh Kun, *Audiotopia*, Berkeley: University of California Press, 2005.

big, classic humanistic questions about self, truth, reason, justice, hope, etc. You can feel like in some of the utopian strains in *Audiotopia* and I confess that lately it really colours my teaching, which has become so driven by notions of the commons, notions of grand interconnectivity (deeply influenced by the Upanishads, for example), the kinds of inter-species politics popular among food justice activists and environmentalists, and the recurring sense that there really might be (must be?) such a thing as a global politics of love. I blame a newfound love affair with the poetry of Charles Wright, the art of Elias Sime, the music and writing of Daniel Barenboim, and the work of Eknath Easwaran.

Here are the texts I teach in my graduate seminar, Experiments in Critical Writing, very much inspired by a similar course I took as an undergraduate with the amazing Eve Sedgwick (the last text they read is one of your own—they have to write their own passport narratives):

Peter Turchi, from *Maps of the Imagination: The Writer as Cartographer*; Dave Hickey, 'Unbreak My Heart, An Overture'; George Orwell, 'The Politics of the English Language'; Jorge Luis Borges, 'Borges and I'; Nicholas Delbanco, 'In Praise of Imitation'; Annie Dillard, from *The Writing Life*; Trinh T. Minh-Ha, 'Commitment from the Mirror Writing Box'; Raymond Williams, from *Keywords*; Ambrose Bierce, from *The Devil's Dictionary;* Michael Jarrett, from *Sound Tracks;* Gustave Flaubert, from *Dictionary of Accepted Ideas;* David Bleich, 'Finding the Right Word: Self-Inclusion and Self-Inscription'; Eve Sedgwick, 'White Glasses'; Patricia J. Williams, from *The Alchemy of Race and Rights*; Joan Didion, *The White Album*; Roland Barthes, *Lover's Discourse*; Ryzard Kapuscinski, *The Emperor;* Mark Doty, *Still Life With Oysters and Lemon*; James Baldwin, *The Devil Finds Work*; Jamaica Kincaid, *A Small Place*; Neil Bartlett, *Who Was That Man?: A Present For Mr. Oscar Wilde*; Cherrie Moraga, *Loving in the War Years*; Samuel Delaney, *Times Square Red, Times Square Blue;* Carol Mavor, from

Becoming; John Berger, from *Another Way of Telling*; Geoff Dyer, from *But Beautiful*; Amitava Kumar, *Passport Photos*.*

---

*Peter Turchi, *Maps of the Imagination: The Writer as Cartographer*, San Antonio: Trinity University Press, 2004.

Dave Hickey, 'Unbreak My Heart, An Overture,' *Air Guitar: Essays on Art and Democracy*, Los Angeles: Art Issues Press, 1997.

George Orwell, *Politics and the English Language*, London: Penguin Classics, 2013.

Jorge Luis Borges, 'Borges and I', *Labyrinths: Selected Stories and Other Writings*, New York: New Directions, 1994.

Nicholas Delbanco, 'In Praise of Imitation,' *Harper's Magazine*, New York: July 2002, 57-63.

Annie Dillard, *The Writing Life*, New York: Harper Perennial, 2013.

Trinh T. Minh-Ha, 'Commitment from the Mirror Writing Box,' *Woman, Native, Other*, Bloomington: Indiana University Press, 2009.

Raymond Williams, *Keywords: A Vocabulary of Culture and Society*, New York: Oxford University Press, 2014.

Ambrose Bierce, *The Devil's Dictionary, Tales, & Memoirs*, New York: Library of America, 2011.

Michael Jarrett, *Sound Tracks - A Musical ABC*, Philadelphia: Temple University Press, 1998.

Gustave Flaubert, *Dictionary of Accepted Ideas*, New York: New Directions, 1968.

David Bleich, 'Find the Right Words: Self-Inclusion and Self-Inscription,' *Autobiographical Writing Across the Disciplines: A Reader*. Durham: Duke University Press, 2004.

Eve Kosofsky Sedgwick, 'White Glasses,' *Tendencies*, Durham: Duke University Press, 1993.

Patricia J. Williams, *The Alchemy of Race and Rights: Diary of a Law Professor*, Cambridge: Harvard University Press, 1992.

Joan Didion, *The White Album*, New York: Simon & Schuster, 1979.

Roland Barthes, *A Lover's Discourse: Fragments*, London: Vintage, 2002.

Ryzard Kapuscinski, *The Emperor: Downfall of an Autocrat*, London: Vintage, 1989.

Mark Doty, *Still Life with Oysters and Lemon: On Objects and Intimacy*, Boston: Beacon Press, 2002.

James Baldwin, *The Devil Finds Work*, London: Vintage International, 2011.

Jamaica Kincaid, *A Small Place*, New York: Farrar, Straus and Giroux, 2000.

Neil Bartlett, *Who Was That Man?: A Present For Mr. Oscar Wilde*, London: Serpent's Tail, 1988.

Cherrie Moraga, *Loving In The War Years*, Brooklyn: South End Press, 2000.

Samuel Delany, *Times Square Red, Times Square Blue*, New York: New York University Press, 2001.

Carol Mavor, *Becoming: The Photographs of Clementina, Viscountess Hawarden*, Durham: Duke University Press, 1999.

John Berger, *Another Way of Telling*, London: Vintage, 1995.

Seminar rule #1: Failure is the point.

Seminar rule #2: Always tell a story.

Seminar rule #3: For the next 15 weeks, think form first, content second.

~

Sudhir Venkatesh, author of *Gang Leader for a Day: A Rogue Sociologist Takes to the Streets.**

1. Write every day—so I was told by my advisers. Grocery lists, emails, dissertation chapters… it doesn't matter. Wake up and write something. Gin sometimes helps.
2. Being 'right' and being 'relevant' are not the same. Try and understand the difference. It will not only save your domestic partnership/marriage. Your work will have reach, it will breathe.
3. There is very little space between the emotional and intellectual registers. Even Descartes knew this. Stated another way: Think like a structuralist, make your appeal as a humanist.
4. Be an apprentice. Anyone can do it alone. It is a lot harder to give yourself up, wholly and honestly, to another's teachings.
5. See #1.
6. Try and finish this sentence once a day, 'I liked this [book, article, essay] because…' Any fool can snark.
7. Every two weeks, write at least five letters to people in the public: letters to the editor, to authors, to people in government… Don't email. Write.

~

Geoff Dyer, *But Beautiful: A Book About Jazz*, New York: Picador, 2009.

Amitava Kumar, *Passport Photos*, Berkeley: University of California Press, 2000.

*Sudhir Venkatesh, *Gang Leader for a Day: A Rogue Sociologist Takes to the Streets*, New York: Penguin Books, 2008.

Jack Halberstam, author of *Trans**[*]

Being a graduate student means never having to stick to one school of thought. You are here to experiment, to make mistakes, to fail well and fail often. Your writing will be evidence of this. When I was a grad student, I went through a Derridean stage, a psychoanalytic phase, a French feminism phase, but luckily for me, right as I was writing my dissertation, Judith Butler published *Gender Trouble* and I realized I could write about all things queer. My advice to graduate students has always been to follow their passionate investments rather than writing towards some imaginary market that may or may not hire them. Two of my former graduate students of whom I am very proud, Yetta Howard and Alexis Lothian, are just publishing their first books. Yetta Howard wrote *Ugly Differences* in which they ask what it would mean to turn towards rather than away from an ugliness that is always already queer. And in *Old Futures*, Alexis Lothian has written an astonishing account of futures past. They both wrote through queerness rather than about it and turned their projects into counter-intuitive studies of modes of thinking, assembling eclectic archives in the process. Students today seem to realize that on account of all kinds of new scholarship by intellectuals who are also truly writers—Amitava Kumar, Fred Moten, Saidiya Hartman, Maggie Nelson to name a few—the bar for academic writing has risen and in all the right ways. The best indication of this writerly turn has emerged in excellent dissertations that refuse to sacrifice form to content. The worse effect has been poor imitations of creative scholarly work in which self-confession predominates and full disclosure is the norm. As far as the topic of trans* goes, the trans* writer must always write the self because trans* bodies have been so poorly written about by non-trans people. But getting the balance right between personal accounts and abstract

---

*Jack Halberstam, *Trans*: A Quick and Quirky Account of Gender Variability*, Berkeley: University of California Press, 2018.

theory remains a challenge.

∽

Fred Moten, author of *Black and Blur**

My mantra for writing is that it has to be something very much like an everyday practice. I believe that the logic of the assignment has made writing anathema. The illusion of the finished assignment, the pressure to accomplish this illusion, drives professors crazy, I think, and they are generally left with no alternative but to pass that on, though students, who can far more easily divest from reading/thinking/writing tend to do just that. But, for me, reading/thinking/writing are 1) sacred and 2) inseparable. Along with the sociality of talking with people about whatever you've been reading/thinking/writing, that's what study is. Now this becomes more complex the more properly complex our notions of reading/writing/thinking, the more we understand their situational diversity, the more rich our understanding of the vast range of literacies. But for folks like us, situated in and around schools, our kind of writing has to be everyday and ongoing, a practice of revision and extension and opening rather than finishing, completion, closure. Anyway, an awkward sort of mantra, I know. The other thing I try to tell my students is that they should always pay attention to how they are writing sounds. Make it sound like something. Remember the little kid inside who loved Dr. Seuss. Consider that language is a toy for communicability rather than a tool for communication. Find a rhythm your readers, who are, more technically, your listeners, can feel. William Carlos Williams once said, 'If it ain't a pleasure, it ain't a poem.' He was right about that and I think this formulation should extend to the essay, too. And this means it should be a pleasure to write, too. And one way to get at that pleasure is to be attuned to the sound, to refuse the imperative to suppress play. We

*Fred Moten, *Black and Blur*, Durham: Duke University Press, 2017.

tend to drive that out of children very early on in the process of schooling and I think it makes our job, when it comes to writing, more like PTSD counselors than anything.

~

Hua Hsu, author of *A Floating Chinaman* and staff writer for the *New Yorker**

My academic writing is different from my journalism mostly in subject. Journalism is a wonderful outlet for those interested in pursuing an idea or theme very deeply but for a very limited window of time. I wrote a piece for the *Boston Globe* Ideas Section a few years back about literary hoaxes. While I enjoyed spending a couple of weeks immersing myself in that world and figuring out ways of translating ideas for a newspaper audience, applying academic scrutiny to the ins and outs of hoaxing was beyond my skill-set. My academic work tends to be about subjects I want to 'live' with for longer spells—a month, a year, etc.

I definitely go through wild swings—sometimes journalism seems like the perfect outlet, so direct, democratic and attentive; other times, it is the rigor, care and patience of academic work that feels like the only possible way to treat something one cares about. But ultimately, journalism and academic work aren't in competition. In both, I seek to refine my voice as a writer. Now I don't think I've found my 'voice' quite yet, but I realized recently that this is what I value the most when I pick up a magazine or journal. It is the writer's voice—the glimpse into someone else's imagination, sense of wit or style, code of ethics, etc.—that ultimately entrances me or inspires me to read further or write something of my own.

When I was on the academic job market, more than a decade ago, there was still a clear divide between academic and journalistic writing. There were people who worked in both worlds but, as a

*Hua Hsu, *A Floating Chinaman*, Cambridge, MA: Harvard University Press, 2016.

young scholar, I was encouraged to hide any aspirations to follow in their footsteps. For my first few years of graduate school, for example, I never mentioned my pop criticism to any of my professors, because I was under the impression that it made me seem less serious. Thankfully, things changed over time, and the line has blurred.

I have always gravitated towards figures who were comfortable in different settings—Michael Rogin was my thesis adviser at Berkeley and he had a gift for drawing from this impossibly expansive universe of knowledge to situate people like Tocqueville or Henry Adams in riveting new contexts. While in graduate school, I was heavily influenced by Werner Sollors and Luke Menand—the way they commanded a classroom, the way they wrote, their senses of humour. They showed me the intimate relationship between teaching and writing.

X

The Groves Of

ACADEME

Part of being a writer is taking notes when academic culture is being discussed. In the opening pages of Lorrie Moore's novel, *A Gate at the Stairs*: 'My brain was on fire with Chaucer, Sylvia Plath, Simone de Beauvoir. Twice a week a young professor named Thad, dressed in jeans *and* a tie, stood before a lecture hall of stunned farm kids like me and spoke thrillingly of Henry James's masturbation of the comma. I was riveted. I had never before seen a man wear jeans with a tie.'* Or, on a parody site on Tumblr called MLA Jobs: 'Ohio University announces that it will not be hiring in English this year, as part of the university's mission is to shrink the department to the size where you can drown it in a bathtub.'** Or, a parenthetical note in Curtis Sittenfeld's short story 'Gender Studies' in the *New Yorker*: '(Semi-relatedly, Nell was once the first author on a paper titled "Booty Call: Norms of Restricted and Unrestricted Sociosexuality in Hook-Up Culture," a paper that, when she last checked Google Scholar, which was yesterday, had been cited thirty-one times.).'*** Or, an article titled 'Why Professors

---

*Lorrie Moore, *A Gate at the Stairs*, New York: Vintage Books, 2009. See p. 4. (I have a shelf full of novels and short-story collections that take us into the classroom. Why are these authors—Mary McCarthy, Jeffrey Eugenides, Lore Segal, Alice Munro, Mary Gaitskill, David Lodge, Richard Russo, Jane Smiley, Randall Jarrell, Zadie Smith, Sam Lipsyte, Francine Prose, Jennifer Egan, Vladimir Nabokov, Elif Batuman, James Hynes, J. M. Coetzee, I could go on and on—so interesting? I think this is because fiction deals with time, with changes over time, and what better place to witness this than in the young lives unfolding on college campuses?)

**Accessed online at http://mlajobs-blog.tumblr.com/. See entry for 28 September, 2012.

***Curtis Sittenfeld, 'Gender Studies', *New Yorker*, 29 August 2016.

Are Writing Crap that Nobody Reads' with statements like the following: '82 percent of articles published in the humanities are not even cited once' and 'Half of academic papers are never read by anyone other than their authors, peer reviewers, and journal editors.'* Or, a response to the above article by political scientist Corey Robin on Twitter: 'It's time to declare a moratorium on the 'academic work that no one reads' genre.'** Robin had attached a screengrab providing an explanation: 'It's kind of hilarious—and outrageous—that in this day and age, in this era of neoliberal academy, we get articles like these. Let's be clear. The vast majority of professors, who are adjunct instructors, aren't writing anything at all, except comments on student papers. And those of us who are writing something on top of that, are often writing letters of recommendation, tenure and promotion reports, assessment reports, self-studies, responses to external evaluators, teaching observations, evaluations, email, bloody email, and making all manner of word salad just to keep accreditors or whoever the fuck it is, happy and well fed on blather and bullshit. To complain, in these circumstances, about academic papers that no one reads, seems inapposite.'

*Daniel Lattier, 'Why Professors Are Writing Crap that Nobody Reads', Intellectual Takeout Blog, 26 October 2016. http://www.intellectualtakeout.org/blog/why-professors-are-writing-crap-nobody-reads Accessed on 24 March 2017.

**Corey Robin on Twitter: https://twitter.com/CoreyRobin/status/794235173999091712

STONER

When the writer Jim Harrison died in 2016, I came across the following quote in one of the pieces that were being sent around on the Web:

> 'I wasn't very long at Stony Brook,' he writes in *Off to the Side*, 'when it occurred to me that the English department had all the charm of a streetfight where no one actually landed a punch.'*

I promptly put this quote up on Facebook. Those words appealed to me. They revealed the tensions that make academic interactions so very fraught, and they also told me that all the warring that goes on is quite pathetic and achieves little. There was a macho swagger to Harrison's statement, sure, but I was prepared to overlook it in favour of its honesty. Or what I was calling its honesty, because of my belief, as a naturalized citizen of an English department, that we fight, often for small stakes, and without any real result.

But is there a recognizable style to our fighting?

Trained as we are in the language of criticism, we are seldom afraid to practice it while conducting departmental business. But perhaps also because of this training, our severest rebukes are masked, the hostility veiled in formality of sorts, in a language that at least takes on the appearance of judicious discrimination. I rather appreciate this. It makes departmental meetings tolerable. Over twenty-five years, in the different institutions where I have

---

*Tom Bissell, 'The Last Lion', *Outside*, 31 August 2011.

worked, I have witnessed shouting and open insults and tears only twice. At other times, I have had occasion to sit back and enjoy the deployment of irony.

This reflection on style was instigated by my reading of *Stoner* by John Williams, a 1965 novel that has witnessed a revival in the last few years.* The protagonist, William Stoner, is a professor of English at the University of Missouri. There is a plainness to the novel, and yet I found it profoundly affecting. *Stoner* also contains the portrayal of an implacable enmity between Stoner and his colleague, Hollis Lomax. The sections about Stoner's clashes with Lomax ought to be made compulsory reading for graduate students contemplating a career in the academy. I say this because these sections serve as an introduction to a culture: the cause of the grudge has been forgotten, but it can last as long as a career.

In one of the most dramatic renditions of a matter as unpromising as a thesis examination, Stoner and Lomax square off. We are seeing things from Stoner's point of view. The qualities that I have mentioned above as characteristics of tense academic exchanges, at least in English departments, are all there. But there is something else too that I have neglected to mention: intense self-consciousness and, despite the righteous rage, some regret. Here are two paragraphs, divided from each other by the space of a few pages, that I want to share with you:

> During this time Stoner did not speak. He listened to the talk that swirled around him; he gazed at Finch's face, which had become a heavy mask; he looked at Rutherford, who sat with his eyes closed, his head nodding; and he looked at Holland's bewilderment, at Walker's courteous disdain, and at Lomax's feverish animation. He was waiting to do what he knew he had to do, and he was waiting with a dread and an anger and a sorrow that grew more intense with every minute that

*John Williams, *Stoner* (Copyright 1965). New York: New York Review Books, 2003.

> passed. He was glad that none of their eyes met his own as he gazed at them.
>
> Relentlessly Stoner continued his questioning. What had been an anger and outrage that included both Walker and Lomax became a kind of pity and sick regret that included them too. After a while it seemed to Stoner that he had gone outside himself, and it was as if he heard a voice going on and on, impersonal and deadly.

So much emotion! So much truth! And, not least, a clear confirmation of what I had long suspected, that a few of our departmental exchanges can easily turn into an out-of-body experience. And the only way to represent them is to cast oneself as a distant, detached observer, speaking in a voice that we don't even recognize as our own.

TITLES

I received an email from a stranger: 'Dear Professor Kumar, I would greatly appreciate receiving a PDF copy of your article "Imbalanced oxidant and antioxidant ratio in myotonic dystrophy type 1" which appeared in Free Radic Res 2014, Apr; 48 (4): 503-10.' I was relieved to inform the sender of the message that I was not the author of the article she wanted.

If you are writing a book or an article, you definitely need an attractive title. Consider this one: 'Distinct Recruitment of Temporo-Parietal Junction and Medial Prefrontal Cortex in Behavior Understanding and Trait Identification.' I found it in an article by Tom Bartlett on the *Chronicle of Higher Education* blog; the article was about titles and, appropriately, the article itself was entitled 'Getting on Top Through Mass Murder'. The title was suggestive but Bartlett didn't lay down any rules or make recommendations. His blog-entry began with the following sentence: 'If you spend a chunk of time each day reading academic abstracts, you learn to appreciate good titles.' But *what* is a good title?*

A good title gives a sense of the research presented, sure, but it does so by evoking the subject rather than giving a comprehensive

---

*Titles aren't a matter of debate only in universities. After Philip Roth's death, I was amused to read this in the *Times*:

> Roth, who never won the Nobel Prize many predicted for him, once said, 'I wonder if I had called *Portnoy's Complaint* 'The Orgasm Under Rapacious Capitalism,' if I would thereby have earned the favor of the Swedish Academy.'

See Dwight Garner, 'Philip Roth, A Born Spellbinder and Peerless Chronicler of Sex and Death', *New York Times*, 23 May 2018.

or exhaustive account of it. *Fear of Small Numbers* is snappier, more intelligent and inviting, and therefore undoubtedly superior, to *An Analysis of the Violent Relationship Between Majorities and Minorities In The Age of Globalization.*

Each New Year's Day, I read *The Great Gatsby*. (This is an annual ritual, albeit of fairly recent vintage.) I'm aware that F. Scott Fitzgerald had seriously considered other titles: *Trimalchio in West Egg*; *Among Ash-Heaps and Millionaires*; *The High-Bouncing Lover*; *On the Road to West Egg*. The last alternative title that the writer had favoured, *Under the Red, White and Blue*, was rejected by his editor Maxwell Perkins. And after the novel's publication, Fitzgerald declared that 'the title is only fair, rather bad than good'. Each bad title proposed by Fitzgerald was bad in its own way; as a title, *The Great Gatsby* is not only the shortest, it also has the right balance of specificity and mystery.

A good thing about academic publishing is that in the matter of titles we command a strong degree of autonomy. In the journalism I have done over more than two decades I have only been able to give my own title to a small fraction of my work; on the other hand, not once has a journal editor or an editor at an academic press rejected a title I have provided for what I have written. This ought to give us a sense of freedom, and encourage us to be inventive. I find this freedom demonstrated in the titles used by a few of the scholars I talked to about academic writing while writing this book. Examples: *Friction. Walter Benjamin's Grave. Night Haunts. Lose Your Mother. The Law is a White Dog.*

CAMPUS CRITICISM

In an interview, the novelist and critic Zadie Smith was asked about the readings she most regularly taught in class.* In her response, Smith mentioned writers like the young James Baldwin and Muriel Spark and then added this bit of memoir: 'When I was a student I was assigned *Mythologies* and *A Lover's Discourse*, by Roland Barthes, and felt at once that something momentous had happened to me, that I had met a writer who had changed my course in life somehow; and looking back now, I think he did.' When I read those words, I was reminded of an earlier essay of Smith's titled 'Rereading Barthes and Nabokov'.** In that essay, Smith describes her tussle with what she frames as the two opposites: on the one hand, from Barthes, a 'radical invocation of reader's rights', and, on the other, from Nabokov, a 'bold assertion of authorial privilege'. As a published author herself, Smith finds refuge in Nabokov's notion of authorial design and the reader's search for it. This stance makes her feel lonely; it is possible to entertain the idea of communication, 'a genuine link between the person who writes and the person who reads'. But what Smith also remembers, not without fondness, is her younger, more isolated self in college, when she 'wanted to tear down the icon of the author and abolish, too, the idea of a privileged reader—the text was to be a free, wild thing, open to everyone, belonging to no one, refusing an ultimate meaning.'

---

*'Zadie Smith: By the Book,' *New York Times Book Review*, 17 November 2016.

**Zadie Smith, 'Rereading Barthes and Nabokov', in *Changing My Mind: Occasional Essays*. Ibid. See pp. 42-57.

I identify with Smith's argument because over the course of three decades in academia I too have 'changed my mind'. The two selves that Smith constructs are familiar to me and, even more, the phenomenon she calls 'the campus criticism that flowered on both sides of the pond during the eighties and nineties'. This is what she lists as the characteristics of the sort of theorizing that she also colloquially calls 'the overheated hustle of English departments': 'Wild analogy; aggressive reading against the grain and across codes and discourses; a fondness for cultural codes over textual particulars.' The prose that Smith now writes is a cocktail: a mix of Barthes (what is *White Teeth* but a rebellious rewriting, a wildly hilarious 'reading against the grain' of official, colonial history?) and also a well-measured pour of Nabokov (it is not in the irresistible punning or the puzzles of Smith's fiction but in the obscure details and affection in the story of her father, Harvey's life, that I catch an echo of Nabokov, a desire to fix in language the stable reality of a father's life). All those sometimes contrary spirits 'Barthes, Nabokov, and many others' are now part of Smith's fiction and criticism. Which is another way to say, I cannot but wish for myself and others equal access to all influences.

Early in Elif Batuman's novel *The Idiot*, her protagonist Selin, a freshman at Harvard, tries to get admission into a literature seminar.* During the interview, the professor says to her, 'From your application, you seem to be very creative. I enjoyed your creative application essay. My only concern is that you realize this seminar is an academic class, not a creative class.'

What are the differences between academic writing and creative writing?

I've wrestled with that question in the pages of this book, at times posting an opposition between those two categories, and at other times finding in the practice of several writers I admire a

*Elif Batuman, *The Idiot,* New York: Penguin Books, 2017. See p. 10.

blurring of the borders between them. Batuman belongs to the latter category. But Selin's story is of interest for another reason. It tells you about the ways in which learning—*and life*—happens in such unanticipated ways inside academe.

In *The Idiot*, we are in the fall semester of 1995. Selin is more or less a stand-in for her creator: not only does she want to be a writer, she also has some of the same experiences that Batuman has written about in earlier memoir-essays. The book is self-conscious about the uncertainties immanent in language: over and over again, Selin expresses her failure to interpret or understand. Selin's conversations, not least with her professors, sometimes verge on the absurd. Such episodes are funny or satirical but, in a more fundamental way, Batuman is interested in the mysteriousness of life and our struggle to give meaning. The novel's main plot evolves around an unsuccessful pursuit of love. Selin is filled with yearning for an older Math student named Ivan; he is Hungarian and already has a girlfriend. Our heroine finds the prospect of love confusing and, in time, even futile, but what makes this account engaging is that the real triangulation in her relationship with Ivan is with language.

In her foreign language class, Selin is given to read 'Nina in Siberia', a Russian text specifically for beginning students. The text advances in brief chapters and tells a story that seems to precisely match Selin's own—Nina's relationship with her lover, Ivan, isn't going well, and she seems peculiarly stuck in language, unable to pierce the gloomy opacity of words. For that reason alone, I found 'Nina in Siberia' a brilliant novelistic ploy. But there are further reasons for admiring such foreign language lessons. As Selin notes, 'The story was ingeniously written, using only the grammar that we had learned so far. Because we hadn't learned the dative case, Ivan's father, instead of handing the letter *to* Nina, had to say,

"There, on the table, is a letter."'*

When I read the above lines, I thought of the enormous difficulty of the rules of grammar. The difficulty of learning a new language. And then, by implication, but more distantly, about the difficulty of loving. I understood why Selin was struck by the foreign language lessons, seeing like her that 'the story had a stilted feel, and yet while you were reading you felt totally inside its world, a world where reality mirrored the grammar constraints, and what Slavic 101 couldn't name didn't exist.' The world that 'Nina in Siberia' had created—the goal of all fiction—Batuman's novel was trying to create, too. As a writer, I envied that, of course, but what I also envied was the artfulness of the foreign language instructors, the academic writers, who had designed such a textbook!

In an author's note at the end of *The Idiot*, Batuman notes that 'Nina in Siberia' is based on a real text, 'The Story of Vera', which she herself had encountered in 1995. 'The Story of Vera,' according to Batuman, 'was coauthored over the years by some number of Russian-language instructors working, as far as I have been able to determine, under a shroud of secrecy.'

All hail those anonymous authors! They teach us how to fall in love, and, to borrow a phrase from Selin, fall out of language.

When I wrote to Batuman to ask what had drawn her to 'The Story of Vera', she replied that she had been impressed by 'how closely the plot of the missing-person story corresponded to the progressive disclosure of grammar in a language text'. Batuman added that of all the texts that Selin reads in her first year at college, 'Nina in Siberia' most directly reflected the feeling of mystery and linguistic inadequacy that she herself was experiencing. Selin looked to it to explain her relationship with Ivan, though in the end it wasn't a hundred percent useful.

Batuman also reminded me that she had already written about

---

*Ibid, p. 28.

'The Story of Vera' in her introduction to her first book, *The Possessed*.* I had read that book but didn't remember any mention of the foreign language lessons. On taking down the book from my shelves, I found the passages easily enough. Batuman had described how Vera's story had progressed—new details accompanied by new examples of missing cases and tenses. 'In this way, introductory Russian manifested itself to me as a perfect language, in which form was an ideal reflection of content.'**

I read on, discovering over the next three or four pages of *The Posessed* all the details that were fresh to me from my reading of *The Idiot*: the autobiographical events Batuman had put down in the former had been turned into live fiction in the latter. This, too, was a lesson in language and writing. How one text, which had been composed as non-fiction, was paralleled by another text, with its own omissions and elaborations, into fiction. The task in both cases was to fashion a text that resembled life.

*Elif Batuman, *The Possessed*, New York: Farrar, Straus and Giroux, 2010.
**Ibid, p. 11.

COMMON SENSE

A friend told me of seeing someone on a university campus wearing a T-shirt that said: 'It works in practice, but does it work in theory?'

FARTHER AWAY

Why did I copy this out from a book I was reading?* Partly because like most writers in academia, I'm aware of the inordinate amount of time and energy expended on teaching, but partly also because of the fear, more particular to a fiction writer than a writer of non-fiction, that in academia you risk being shielded from so much in the world. (The limitations of the campus novel, etc.)

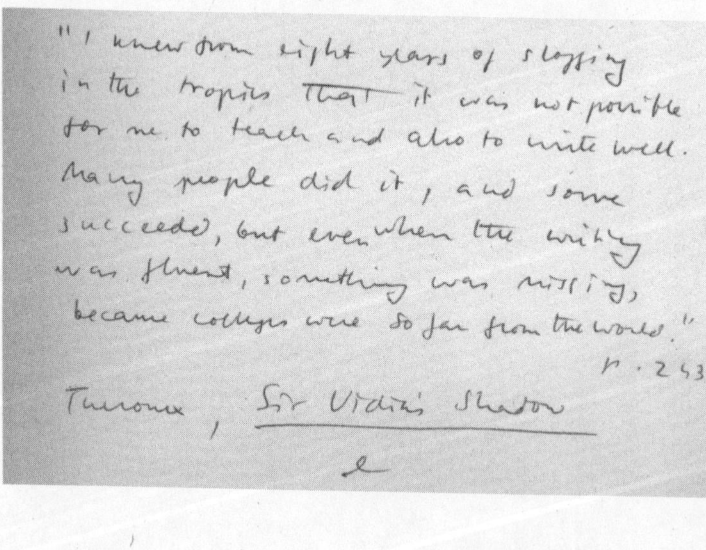

"I knew from eight years of slogging in the tropics that it was not possible for me to teach and also to write well. Many people did it, and some succeeded, but even when the writing was fluent, something was missing, because colleges were so far from the world."

p. 243

Theroux, Sir Vidia's Shadow

*Paul Theroux, *Sir Vidia's Shadow*, Boston: Houghton Mifflin, 1998. See p. 243. Also filed away in my notebook is a line from a magazine: 'Put a nation of writers in a cage, call it a university, and they'll start writing about their cage.' A Google search reveals that the author of this line is Christian Lorentzen, 'Considering the Novel in the Age of Obama', *Vulture*, 9 January 2017.

ACCOUNTABILITY

A campus-wide email was sent out to the faculty inviting attendance at a webinar entitled 'How to Develop a Daily Writing Practice'. This was a part of our programme for faculty development. About eight of us showed up and sat around a table looking at a large screen where slides would appear accompanied by the audio from the remote presenter. What struck me immediately from the moment the webinar started was how, in a discussion on writing, there was such a lack of sensitivity to language. 'Challenges to Writing Productivity' had the feel of a topic at a meeting of technical entrepreneurs. After the topic had been introduced the following text appeared on the next slide: 'The things that are least important to your evaluation have the greatest built-in accountability, while the most important factors in your tenure and promotion, your reputation as a scholar, and your mobility are the things that have the least built-in accountability.'* What the speaker meant was that on a day-to-day basis, an academic would have to answer questions if she didn't make her scheduled appearance in class. On the other hand, no one would be watching over her shoulder to find out if she had done any writing that day, or week, or month. With this matter laid to rest, we were told what to do. I agreed with the general practical advice (write daily, aim to be consistent, be prepared to write in small chunks

*When I read language like this, I can see the point of the line (see the closing line of the short paragraph circled on the following page) from Jeanette Winterson's review of Harold Bloom's *Falstaff* in the *New York Times Book Review*, 23 April 2017.

of time, etc.), but was often overwhelmed by the banality.* The repeated reference to 'the binge or bust train' (and the presenter's continued description of herself as the conductor on that train).

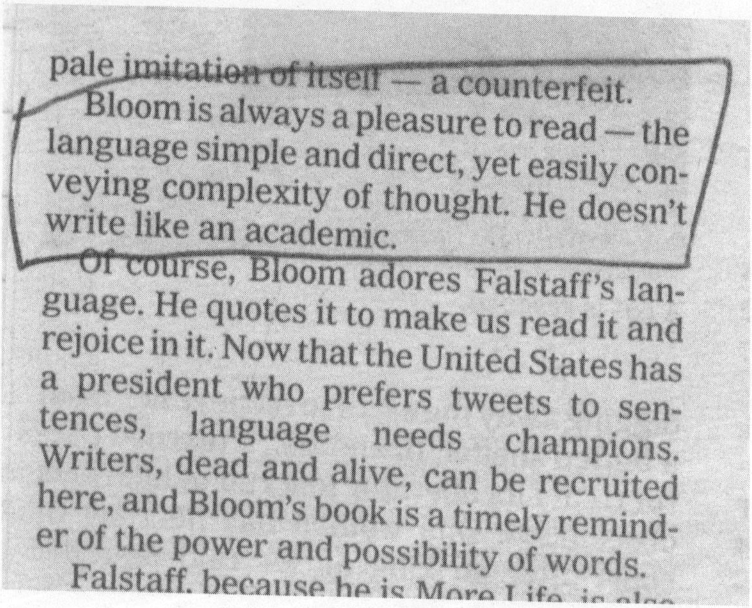

pale imitation of itself — a counterfeit.

Bloom is always a pleasure to read — the language simple and direct, yet easily conveying complexity of thought. He doesn't write like an academic.

Of course, Bloom adores Falstaff's language. He quotes it to make us read it and rejoice in it. Now that the United States has a president who prefers tweets to sentences, language needs champions. Writers, dead and alive, can be recruited here, and Bloom's book is a timely reminder of the power and possibility of words.

Falstaff, because he is More Life, is

---

*I'm not sure I've managed to evade banality myself. Among the books on writing I've read most recently, at least as far as language and understanding of craft is concerned, a book that succeeds is Colum McCann's *Letters to a Young Writer*, New York: Random House, 2017. (An early chapter offers the following advice: 'Don't write what you know, write toward what you *want to know*.') I've already mentioned Annie Dillard more than once. But the other enemy of banality is a non-chatty self-consciousness mixed with a precise form of expression on the page, a kind of heightened awareness of the foibles and prejudices of the world. Who do I have in mind? Janet Malcolm, of course. In my journalism classes, I regularly teach Malcolm's books. Even if the subject is crime, I believe the lesson on the page is also about how to write. See, for example, Janet Malcolm, *The Journalist and the Murderer*, New York: Vintage Books, 1990. (My copy of the book has on the cover the following quote from David Reiff's review in the *Los Angeles Times*: 'It is not with regard to journalism but with regard to the making of works of art that Malcolm's important book gathers its inspiration, its breathtaking rhetorical velocity, and its great truth.')

The exaggerated, melodramatic trick of giving the writing suggestions the name '12-Step Program'. Calling any resistance the writer experiences by a friendly name: Bill, the bodyguard. But, and this is the truth of academic culture, even the banal and the boring delivers kernels of valuable knowledge. The presenter was telling us why she had started talking about accountability. What startled me was the 'data' about the difference in 'writing productivity' when the writer in a group does two extra things: in the participating groups where the members didn't report to each other on the amount they had written, the participants wrote 17 pages over the year; in the participating groups where the members kept a daily record, the participants wrote 64 pages over the same period; and, most crucially, when the groups had members that wrote daily, recorded progress, and were 'accountable' to others, the participants produced (I think I'd have meekly accepted the phrase 'by comparison, a whopping') 157 pages.

JOURNALS

Editorial Vacancy

> The *London Review of Books* is looking for an editor, preferably one with an interest in politics and history. Would suit a young, disaffected academic.
>
> Please send applications—something more than a CV, something less than a full autobiography—by email to edit@lrb.co.uk by 14 January. An idea of why you would like to work for the *LRB* would be helpful.

I saw the above ad on Twitter and immediately posted it on my Facebook page. My friends who responded to the post were all academics; all claimed to be disaffected, and I had no reason to doubt them. In fact, the next morning, a fiction writer, also an academic, had posted the following question at the end of the thread: 'Isn't "*disaffected* academic" redundant?'

There are various reasons for being disaffected and these vary, of course, across institutions. Anxieties about tenure, bad pay, increasing corporatization of academic culture and also of the curriculum, lack of time for research and writing, marginalization of the humanities and general marginalization of intellectual life in this culture. But what I would add to that list is this: we always want to write, and we rarely do, or not enough. (If only the lines of the Elvis Costello song held true: 'And I'm giving you a longing look / Every day, every day, every day I write the book.') There is an enormous amount of intelligence and training available here, but very little writing gets done. And the writing that does get accomplished often lacks any expressive force. It is dull and turgid. And after you have written an article and submitted it for publication, a journal takes several months, and sometimes years, to publish it.* Often, even that doesn't happen. It would all be quite sad if it weren't also farcical. But the true saving grace lies elsewhere. Academics value smartness over everything else and they can be merciless when it comes to dealing with stupidity. That is what makes going for drinks after departmental meetings so much fun. But I'm getting off-track. The point I was making was more about the enormous frustration that can accompany the process of achieving academic publication. A friend of mine recently showed me the exchange from a few years ago between her and a journal of popular culture. I'm quoting the exchange here, partly because it cannot hurt to record the rot, but more than that, my friend's response reveals how liberating it is to find a release in language:

> Dear Dr. __________,
>
> In an effort to speed up the publication schedule and work through our backlog, we are attempting to collect any remaining permissions from authors who are moving up in line for publication. Our records indicate that we still require permissions for the image(s) contained in your article, '(redacted).' Please return these permissions as quickly as possible or update us as to the status of your attempts to obtain these permissions. If you have any questions or concerns, please contact us.
>
> Thank you for your interest in The Journal of ________,

*A good set of tips for publishing in academic journals appeared in a non-academic publication: Rowena Murray, 'Writing for an academic journal: 10 tips', *The Guardian*, 6 September 2013.

and congratulations again on the acceptance of your essay for publication.

Best regards,
The Journal of ________

Dear Journal of ________,

Thank you so much for your note. I was very grateful when you accepted my article for publication in your journal seven (7) years ago. Since that time, approximately five (5) years ago, you forgot that you had accepted the article and re-sent it through your review process, after which you sent me a rejection letter based on the insane rants of an inflamed tea-partier (anachronistic, I know, but it gives you an idea of what I mean). After I brought this imbalanced review to your attention, you rescinded your rejection and re-accepted the article for publication. A year later you sent me a letter similar to the one above. Since I had several years before supplied all the permissions, I grew tired of our little back and forth, stimulating though it had become, and rescinded my acceptance of your re-proferred acceptance. Soon after, I also lost the article in a devastating hard drive crash, and subsequently quit my academic career. Since I no longer had a stake in feverishly publishing my feeble pensées in poorly-run academic journals, I thought no more of the matter, until today.

Best wishes to you and the entire Journal of ________ family,

____

XI

Materials

PHOTOGRAPHS, ETC.

Just about when I began work on this book, I came across a quote from James Agee in the pages of the *New York Times*. 'If I could do it, I'd do no writing at all here,' James Agee declared in 'Let Us Now Praise Famous Men', his 1941 classic about tenant farmers in Alabama. 'It would be photographs; the rest would be fragments of cloth, bits of cotton, lumps of earth, records of speech, pieces of wood and iron.' When I sent out questions to various colleagues, asking them about their writing, I'd also ask at the end what they would have liked to put into their book. Not everyone responded to that question, but several did. Josh Kun, author of *Audiotopia*, wrote back: 'I would have filled *Audiotopia* with 78s and LPs and cassettes and CDs, scraps of ticket stubs and liner notes, faded photos and Basquiat shards, cowboy hats, bongos, Radio Shack mixing decks, green cards, and bowls of matzoh ball soup....'

But I ought to have pressed everyone to respond. Writing is a material practice. Our books can hold, like dirt, the marks of our struggle to put words on paper. I don't work in archives; all I have are my notes with clippings like the ones in this book, pasted on the page. Lines I heard on the radio or saw in a book, I've scribbled them down and they've sat in my mind like epigraphs. Each spring, when the many different kinds of flowers blossom on my college campus, I pluck one or two to put in the notebooks I'm using. Also pictures of my children and the drawings or badly-spelt notes they have written to me; I think I put these last things in my notebook to guard against misfortune but now, looking at the early pictures, I'm conscious only of how much time has passed in the putting together of this book.*

Maybe another thing I could put in here is the page photocopied from Dani Shapiro's *Still Writing: The Perils and Pleasures of a Creative Life*.** It's not even the entire page, it's a paragraph, and I see it every time I come to my desk because I've pasted it on my computer. This is what the paragraph says: 'One of my dearest friends began her last novel—one that went on to become a prizewinning best-seller—by telling herself that she was going to write a short, bad book. For a long time, she talked about the short, bad book she was writing. And she believed it. It released her from her fear of failure. It's a beautiful strategy. Anyone can write a short, bad book, right?'

Instead of bits of cotton and lumps of earth, would I put in here all the letters of rejection? What about the letters of acceptance? In writing, as in love, the acceptance might have more meaning, but it is rejection that is closer to the surface, always visible like a scar.

Also in these pages, the intangibles. The feeling of calm that is mine during long walks near my house, a pencil and an index card in my pocket. The memory of a month in Marfa, Texas, enjoying a writing residency, the daily question of how to best cultivate solitude in order to fetch something from deep inside me. Or when that work was done, the long wait, always the wait, for things to happen.

---

* A piece of advice that CLR James gave for writing: Keep a shoe box, collecting in it various ideas and thoughts. When the shoebox is filled, you have all that is needed for writing. Stefano Harney and Fred Moten, *The Undercommons: Fugitive Planning and Black Study*, New York: Minor Compositions, 2013. See p. 103.

**Dani Shapiro, *Still Writing: The Perils and Pleasures of a Creative Life*, New York: Atlantic Monthly Press, 2013. See p. 18.

An admiring quote about Samuel Beckett from a letter written by Harold Pinter in 1954: 'the most courageous, remorseless writer going, and the more he grinds my nose in the shit the more I am grateful to him.' When I read that quote my mind moved quickly from Beckett to the scholarly writers and I asked myself if I had experienced the same emotion as Pinter. A beautiful feature of academic writing is complexity; the best writing draws you into difficulty, and explains this difficult world to us. But the truth is I've never copied a passage from a book of academic writing to save in my journal. So nothing of that kind among my materials.

No one asked me the question I posed to others from the Agee quote but what I'd like to put in this book is a recipe for grilled shrimp.

A few years ago, an esteemed writer was coming to the town where I live, and he wanted a restaurant recommendation. I sent him a name but regretted I wasn't going to be around; if I were, I'd have grilled some shrimp for him, Indian-style. No worries, he wrote back, but do send me a recipe.

This is what you must know about this writer. I have never met him, but admire him immensely for his sentences. For their stab of taste. They surprise you with their wit, and they're always done just right. If you knew who I was talking about you'd read my recipe and think I was trying to sound casual like him, unaffected, but I so wish I also had his precision. Anyway, here's what I sent him:

To begin, marinate. The previous night, coat a pound of shrimp in yogurt and sprinkle a teaspoon each of turmeric, cumin, and coriander. A little less of salt, I think. Also a bit of chilli powder, or better still, chili oil. If there's scallion around, put that in. Or coriander, which is more authentic. But here's the important part: I get this ginger-garlic mix, from the Indian/Pak store, and add a heaping tablespoon of that. Now, using this bottled mix leads to a lot of guilt, so I also mince a couple of cloves of fresh garlic and mince an equal amount of ginger to go with it. The fresh stuff doesn't suffice, by the way; I have a near-scientific faith in what comes out of bottles. Which brings us to the final ingredient, even if it's only a spoon or two, and that is the dark matter that comes out of the bottle, again easily available at most stores, Patak's Vindaloo Curry Paste. This paste gives, among other things, the gift of colour.

The next afternoon or evening, when you're ready to eat, first pour yourself some gin and tonic. That must always be the first step.

An hour before you start, take the shrimp out of the refrigerator and allow it to return to room temperature. Heat a grill to around 300 or maybe less if the grill is small. I use these metal skewers I picked up at Stop & Shop; just baste the skewers and the shrimp with olive oil. They take about five minutes per side. I don't let anything other than the tail get singed. Serve it after sprinkling fresh lemon and pepper.

The dish should always be washed down with gin and tonic. For somewhat specious reasons, I only drink Bombay Sapphire.

ACKNOWLEDGEMENTS

In late March 2017, tweets with the hashtag #ThanksForTyping began appearing on my timeline. These tweets were from a graduate-school colleague of mine, Bruce Holsinger, now a professor of English at the University of Virginia. Holsinger's tweets highlighted what till not too long ago had been a part of the convention of acknowledgements in academic books: male professors thanking their wives for typing their manuscripts. Below are a few of the examples that Holsinger posted on Twitter, rightly calling them 'an archive of women's academic labor':

> 'I am most grateful to…my wife for typing, retyping and typing yet again the manuscript.'
>
> 'With two aching fingers my wife typed out the whole manuscript.'
>
> 'I have to thank my wife for typing the whole of this difficult manuscript in spite of the heavy burden laid on housewives by a six years' war and its oppressive aftermath.'
>
> 'Immediately after the war ended I resigned my alumni duties and devoted all my free time to my dissertation. After a year of research I started writing in the fall of 1946 and finished in the spring of 1947. My chairman, H. Clay Reed, helped me by arranging a very convenient schedule and my wife typed my manuscript drafts as soon as I gave them to her, even though she was caring for our first child, born in June 1946,

and was also teaching part time in the chemistry department.'

'I wish here to express my thanks to my wife for typing and retyping most of the manuscript 15 or more times; and I thank her and my editor, Miss Estelle Nachbar, for much constructive criticism.'

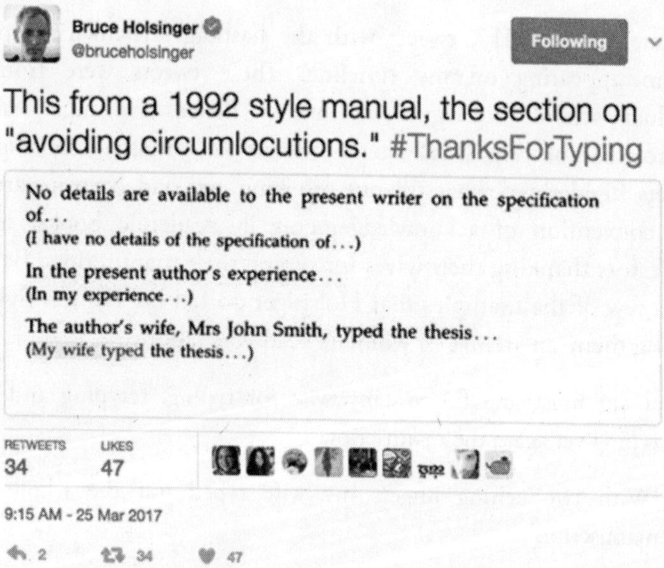

In addition to the burden of unpaid labour, in each of the examples, the female spouses bear the burden also of anonymity. Just by itself this would have been a striking fact but the omission of the names turned out to be embedded also in the ideology of style: this was revealed by another tweet of Holsinger's quoting from a manual of style:

What did this rule of style erase? Here's Holsinger: 'A number of responses that came in talked about the politics of academic labor and writing, the role of women as collaborators, often even unacknowledged co-authors of academic work.'* A seemingly simple injunction about style naturalizing, with a deliberative intent, the naming of women as writers, proofreaders, editors, typists, or translators.

The examples that Holsinger tweeted are extremely unlikely to appear on the acknowledgement pages of scholarly books—but the above discussion serves as a reminder to me to thank the Vassar College students who have been assigned to me over the years as research assistants on work-study. In particular, I want to thank Mikko Harvey, Danielle Bukowski, Noah Johnson, Faith Hill, and Hadley Seufert.

One more thing that I'm thankful for. It cannot be denied that for the most part what the reader usually encounters in this particular section in a book is the necessary, courteous, but quite routine enactment of gratitude. Therefore, I was very pleased to encounter a disavowal of that conventional feeling in the following acknowledgement by Brendan Pietsch, an assistant professor of religious studies at Nazarbayev University, in his book titled *Dispensational Modernism*: 'I blame all of you. Writing this book has been an exercise in sustained suffering. The casual reader may, perhaps, exempt herself from excessive guilt, but for those of you who have played the larger role in prolonging my agonies with your encouragement and support, well…you know who you are, and you owe me.'** This candour struck a chord in other hearts too and *Inside Higher Ed* reported that a blog post that Pietsch made about his acknowledgement page resulted in drawing attention to a book that had 'previously had about nine readers'.*** I'm happy for him and want to borrow his idea—and his luck—by heaping

*Cecilia Mazanec, '#ThanksForTyping Spotlights Unnamed Women in Literary Acknowledgments', *NPR*, 30 March 2017.

**Brendan Pietsch, *Dispensational Modernism*, New York: Oxford University Press, 2015.

***https://www.timeshighereducation.com/blog/best-book-acknowledgement-ever

blame on those who were my enablers. You know who you are, but guilt only goes so far—in fact, it goes in both directions, and I owe you.

APPENDIX A

TEN RULES FOR WRITING*

When I was promoted to the rank of professor, the library at the university where I was then employed asked me to send them the name of a book that had been useful to me in my career. I chose V. S. Naipaul's *Finding the Center*.** The library then purchased a copy, which was duly displayed in one of its rooms, with a statement I had written about the book:

This was one of the first literary autobiographies that I read. Its very first sentence established in my mind the idea of writing as an opening in time or a beginning: that sentence conveyed to me, with its movement and rhythm, a history of repeated striving, and of things coming together, at last, in the achievement of the printed word: 'It is now nearly thirty years since, in a BBC room in London, on an old BBC typewriter, and on smooth, "non-rustle" BBC script paper, I wrote the first sentence of my first publishable book.' This first sentence—about a first sentence—created an echo in my head. It has lasted through the twenty years of my writing life. The ambition and the anxiety of the beginner is there at the beginning of each book. Every time I start to write, I am reminded of Naipaul's book.

But that wasn't the whole truth, neither about Naipaul, nor about beginnings. The sentence I had quoted had mattered to

---

*First published in Kumar, *Lunch with a Bigot*. See pp. 119-24.

**V. S. Naipaul, *Finding the Center*, New York: Knopf, 1984. The quote appears on p. 3.

me, yes, and so had the book, but what had really helped was Naipaul's telling an interviewer that in an effort to write clearly he had turned himself into a beginner: 'It took a lot of work to do it. In the beginning I had to forget everything I had written by the age of 22. I abandoned everything and began to write like a child at school. Almost writing "the cat sat on the mat." I almost began like that.'*

And I did that too, almost. About a decade ago, soon after I had received tenure, *Tehelka* asked me to come aboard as a writer. I was visiting my parents in India at that time; it was winter, and I went to the *Tehelka* office to talk to the editors. Later, when we were done, I was taken around for a tour of the place. There was a pen-and-ink portrait of Naipaul on the wall because he was one of the paper's trustees. And high above someone's computer was a sheet of paper that said 'V. S. Naipaul's Rules for Beginners'. These were rules for writing. It was explained to me that Naipaul was asked by the *Tehelka* reporters if he could give them some basic suggestions for improving their language. Naipaul had come up with some rules. He had fussed over their formulation, corrected them, and then faxed back the corrections. I was told that I could take the sheet if I wanted. A few days later I left India and the sheet travelled with me, folded in the pages of a book that I was reading. In the weeks that followed, I began writing a regular literary column for *Tehelka*, and, in those pieces, I tried to work by Naipaul's rules.

On the night that the world received news that V. S. Naipaul had died I wrote an obituary for CNN. In it I noted that I had once sent Naipaul a piece I had written for the *New Statesman* about a visit to Kashmir. On my last day there, I had gone looking for a hotel named Leeward where Naipaul had stayed in the sixties and written about in one of his earlier India books. The hotel was

---

*V.S. Naipaul interviewed by Ahmed Rashid, 'The Last Lion', *Far Eastern Economic Review*, 30 November 1995. See pp. 49-50.

now a military bunker. Soon I received a fax from Naipaul. His letter began: 'The Leeward was a doghouse, really. Better for it to be turned into the bunker you describe.'

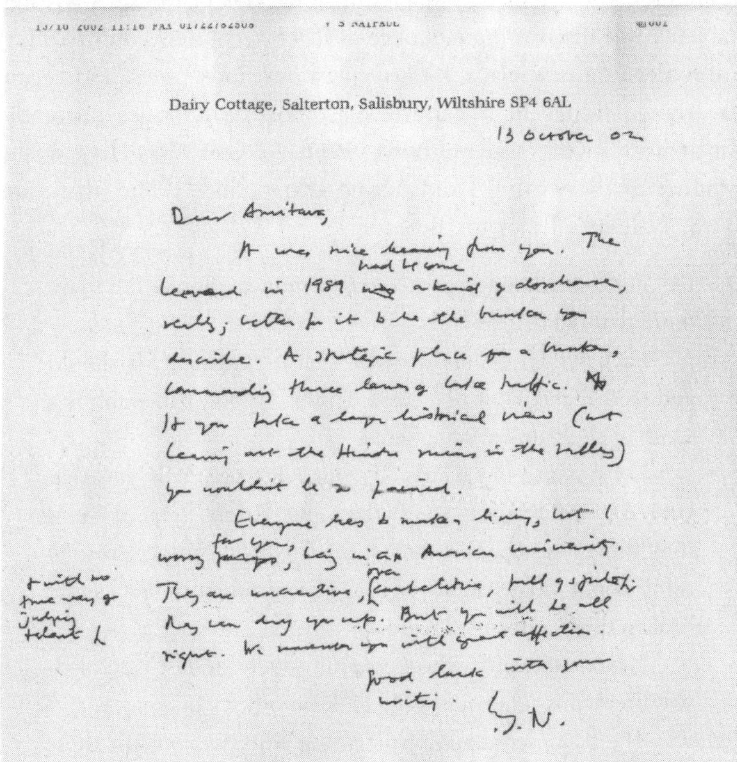

Dairy Cottage, Salterton, Salisbury, Wiltshire SP4 6AL

13 October 02

Dear Amitava,

It was nice hearing from you. The Leeward in 1989 had become a kind of dosshouse, really; better for it to be the bunker you describe. A strategic place for a bunker, commanding three lanes of lake traffic. If you take a large historical view (not leaving out the Hindu ruins in the valley) you wouldn't be so pained.

Everyone has to make a living, but I worry for you, being in an American university. They are unsecure, even cannibalistic, full of spite + with no true way of judging talent; they can chew you up. But you will be all right. We remember you with great affection.

Good luck with your writing. V.N.

Naipaul then proceeded to offer me a brief history lesson about the ruins in Kashmir. He was merciless, but also wrong, and perhaps more than a bit bigoted. But the real thing I want to tell you is that I lost the fax. And yet, until I found it many months later, I could recall each word of it. That is the real importance of Naipaul's talent as a writer: to find in deceptively simple prose, an arresting syntactic rhythm that fixed for his reader an image of the world as it was.

Rereading the letter now, I'm reminded also of the number of times I have read—with mixed emotions—in Naipaul's small, tight script, his acerbic views on the American academy.

The rules were a wonderful antidote to my practice of using academic jargon, and they made me conscious of my own writing habits. I was discovering language as if it were a new country. Like a traveller in a new place, I asked questions, took notes, and began to arrange things in a narrative. I followed the rules diligently for at least a year, and my book *Bombay-London-New York* was a product of the writing I did during that period.* Here, then, are 'V. S. Naipaul's Rules for Beginners':

> Do not write long sentences. A sentence should not have more than 10 or 12 words.
>
> Each sentence should make a clear statement. It should add to the statement that went before. A good paragraph is a series of clear, linked statements.
>
> Do not use big words. If your computer tells you that your average word is more than five letters long, there is something wrong. The use of small words compels you to think about what you are writing. Even difficult ideas can be broken down into small words.
>
> Never use words whose meanings you are not sure of. If you break this rule you should look for other work.
>
> The beginner should avoid using adjectives, except those of colour, size and number. Use as few adverbs as possible.
>
> Avoid the abstract. Always go for the concrete.
>
> Every day, for six months at least, practice writing in this way. Small words; clear, concrete sentences. It may be awkward, but it's training you in the use of language. It may even be getting rid of the bad language habits you picked up at the university. You may go beyond these rules after you have thoroughly understood and mastered them.

---

*Amitava Kumar, *Bombay-London-New York*, New York: Routledge, 2002.

> In their simplicity and directness, I do not think the above rules can be improved upon. A beginner should take them daily, like a dose of much-needed vitamins. Of course, rules can never be a substitute for what a writer can learn, should learn, simply by sitting down and writing. But I offer my own students rules all the time. On the first day of my writing class this year, I handed out xeroxed sheets of rules by Ray Bradbury, not least because he offers the valuable advice that one should write a short story each week for a whole year. Why? 'It's not possible to write 52 bad short stories in a row.'*

I have also prepared my own list of rules for my students. My list isn't in any way a presumption of expertise and is offered only as evidence of experience. I tend to teach by example. These habits have worked for me and I want my students to use them to cultivate the practice of writing.

1. Write every day. This is a cliché, of course, but you will write more when you tell yourself that no day must pass without writing. At the back of a notebook I use in my writing class, I write down the date and then make a mark next to it after the day's work is done. I show the page to my students often, partly to motivate them, and partly to remind myself that I can't let my students down.
2. Have a modest goal. Aim to write 150 words each day. It is very difficult for me to find time on some days, and it is only this low demand that really makes it even possible to sit down and write. On better days, this goal is just a start; often, I end up writing more.
3. Try to write at the same time each day. I recently read a Toni Morrison interview in which she said: 'I tell my students one

*'Ray Bradbury Gives 12 Pieces of Advice to Young Authors', 2001. Available at http://www.openculture.com/2012/04/ray_bradbury_gives_12_pieces_of_writing_advice_to_young_authors_2001.html Accessed on 1 February 2019.

of the most important things they need to know is when they are at their best, creatively.'* It works best for me if I write at the same time each day—in my case, that hour or two that I get between the time I drop off my kids at school and go in to teach. I have my breakfast and walk up to my study with my coffee. In a wonderful little piece published on the *New Yorker* blog, Page Turner, the writer Roxana Robinson writes how she drinks coffee quickly and sits down to write—no fooling around reading the paper, or checking the news, or making calls to friends or trying to find out if the plumber is coming: 'One call and I'm done for. Entering into the daily world, where everything is complicated and requires decisions and conversation, means the end of everything. It means not getting to write.' I read Robinson's piece in January 2013, and alas, I have thought of it nearly every day since.

4. Turn off the Internet. The Web is a great resource and entirely unavoidable, but it will help you focus when you buy the Freedom app. Using a device like this not only rescues me from easy distraction, it also works as a timer. When you click on the icon, it asks you to choose the duration for which you want the computer to not have access to the Net. I choose sixty minutes, and this also helps me keep count of how long I have sat at my computer.
5. Walk for ten minutes. Or better yet, go running. If you do not exercise regularly, you will not write regularly. Or not for long. I haven't been good at doing this, and have paid the price with trouble in my back.
6. A bookshelf of your own. Choose one book, or five, but no

---

*Daily Routines Blog, Interview with Toni Morrison. Accessed at http://dailyroutines.typepad.com/daily_routines/2008/09/toni-morrison.html
See also Roxana Robinson, 'How I Get to Write', *New Yorker* Page Turner Blog, 4 January 2013. Accessed at http://www.newyorker.com/online/blogs/books/2013/01/on-writing-in-the-morning.html

more than ten, to guide you, not with research necessarily, but with the critical matter of method or style. Another way to think about this is to ask yourself who are the writers, or scholars, or artists that you are in conversation with. I use this question to help arrive at my own subject matter, but it also helps with voice.

7. Get rid of it if it sounds like grant talk. I don't know about you, but I routinely produce dead prose when I'm applying for a grant. The language used in applications must be abhorred. Stilted language, jargon, etc. I'm sure there is a psychological or sociological paper to be written about the syntax and tone common in such things—the appeal to power, lack of freedom—but in my case it might just be because, with the arrival of an application deadline, millions of my brain cells get busy committing mass suicide.
8. Learn to say no. The friendly editor who asks for a review or an essay. Even the friend who is editing an anthology. Say no if it takes you away from the writing you want to do. My children are small and don't take no for an answer, but everyone who is older is pretty understanding. And if they're understanding, they'll know that for you occasional drinks or dinner together are more acceptable distractions.
9. Finish one thing before taking up another. Keep a notebook handy to jot down ideas for any future book, but complete the one you are working on first. This rule has been useful to me. I followed it after seeing it on top of the list of Henry Miller's 'Commandments'. It has been more difficult to follow another of Miller's rules: 'Don't be nervous. Work calmly, joyously, recklessly on whatever is in hand.'*
10. The above rule needs to be repeated. I have done shocking

*Henry Miller, 'Work Schedule 1932-33,' in Henry Miller, *Henry Miller on Writing*, New York: New Directions, 1964. Accessed at http://www.brainpickings.org/index.php/2012/02/22/henry-miller-on-writing/

> little work when I have tried to write two books at once. Half-finished projects seek the company of their own and are bad for morale. Shut off the inner editor and complete the task at hand.

If you have read this essay so far, you are probably a writer. That is what you should write in the blank space where you are asked to identify your occupation. I say this also for another reason. Annie Dillard wrote, 'How we spend our days is, of course, how we spend our lives.'* Those words scared the living daylights out of me. I thought of the days passing, days filled with my wanting to write, but not actually writing. I had wasted years. Each day is a struggle, and the outcome is always uncertain, but I feel as if I have reversed destiny when I have sat down and written my quota for the day. Once that work is done, it seems okay to assume that I will spend my life writing.

---

*Annie Dillard, *The Writing Life*. The quote appears on p. 32.

APPENDIX B

PEN TEN INTERVIEW*

When did being a writer begin to inform your sense of identity?

I must have been sixteen or seventeen. In a vague way, I began to think of myself as a writer. Except, and this is the odd thing, the Bhopal gas-leak took place when I was an undergrad and it didn't occur to me that I could take a train down there and write about it. Instead, I wrote poems about the girl who used to take the same bus to the university. Her jawline stirred me more than anything else in the world.

Whose work would you like to steal without attribution or consequences?

I'm sure I already have. A phrase or two, maybe a line. Certainly ways of looking. I'm thinking here of John Berger but I'm sure there are others too.

Where is your favourite place to write?

I was once on a transatlantic flight, going to judge a literary prize and therefore being flown business class. The unexpected luxury, not to mention Jimmy Cliff singing 'You Can Get It If You Really Want', released something in me. I wrote a short story which I later published with Cliff's title. But one can't be flying every day, and

*Published online on 14 October 2014. Available at www.pen.org.

certainly not in luxury, so I write in my study with the books and songs I like within easy reach.

Have you ever been arrested? Care to discuss?
I have but I can't talk about it. I could get deported.

Obsessions are influences—what are yours?
Failure. I'm obsessed with failure because I think of it as our common fate and material. Every time he puts a sheet in the typewriter, Naipaul's Mr. Biswas types out the following: 'At the age of thirty-three, when he was already the father of four children....' The half-finished sentence lights up a whole dark universe of desire and futility. I want to write about failure the way others write about sex or death.

What's the most daring thing you've ever put into words?
My mother died recently. In my last book, which came out in India a few months before she died, I had written about anticipating my parents' death. Was it courage on my part? Or was it only fear? An incantation against the inevitable.

My mother had more courage. A few years ago, on a visit to my hometown in India, I was asking her about her early days—what happened when she married my father, someone she hadn't met till the day of their wedding? I asked her what was it that my father had loved about her. We had never talked like this before. She said that there had been love, but didn't say anything else. When I got back to the States, I saw a letter tucked into my notebook. My mother must have put it there. It had been written by my father around the time of my birth. The letter was full of love and physical ache. I found it difficult to even read that letter. I tried to honour my mother's daring and smuggled a part of it into a novel I was then writing.

What is the responsibility of the writer?
Our responsibility is only to be honest, even if it means being base

or wrong. I fear it is fashionable for many writers to think that they have to be right. I want to be wrong but true. Our task is to be human.

While the notion of the public intellectual has fallen out of fashion, do you believe writers have a collective purpose?
I confess I'm always uncertain when I'm asked to sign petitions. But I like very much reading writers who—more as writers than as citizens—address an issue of broader concern. If writers have a collective purpose, it is only to be singular in approaching any social issue.

What book would you send to the leader of a government that imprisons writers?
The banality of evil is not that there is no interest in culture. No, the leader can read and be moved by a fine book and still imprison writers. I wouldn't want to instruct but I could share. I'd share whatever I was reading at that time. I'm at last reading right now Sonali Deraniyagala's *Wave*. Her sadness has seeped into every part of my waking consciousness.

Where is the line between observation and surveillance?
I'm always haunted by a scene: Chinese kids during the Cultural Revolution denouncing their parents and teachers. 'My parents like to read poetry.' 'My mother tore up the picture of Chairman Mao.' 'Our teacher is a class enemy.' An oppressive system wants you to draw the line between you and the enemy. Who is the enemy? Where is the line between seeing and judging? Forget children. When is it not a violation to observe? Writers have always known this, but they own up to it. The state disowns it, unless it is utterly brazen and corrupt, and that is its greater violence.

APPENDIX C

EYE OF THE BEHOLDER*

Your first film-related obsession?

I was six or seven. I'd cut out pictures of actors from the *Illustrated Weekly Of India*—a memorable one had Pran, with rosy cheeks, peeling an apple—and stick them in a scrapbook. Jeetendra at the bottom of the stairs, Rajesh Khanna driving a red car, stuff like that. I learned I was doing something wrong when one of my parents threw the scrapbook away.

One thing you miss about the way in which you saw movies as a child?

We'd be visiting relatives in one of Bihar's small towns and we would pile into rickshaws and go to a cinema-hall to watch a film. Each town had its own special offering of food during the interval. My favourite was seekh kebab in Bettiah.

The worst book to film adaptation?

I know that the film *Guide* has many admirers. I love many of its songs myself, but I'm sorry, in almost every sequence we are witness to Bollywood pissing on everything quiet or contemplative about (R. K.) Narayan's writing.

---

*The Big Indian Picture Interview, September 2012: http://thebigindianpicture.com/2012/09/eye-of-the-beholder-amitava-kumar/

If you were to adapt a film to a book, it would be...
Vishal Bhardwaj's *Maqbool* might well have been based on Shakespeare's *Macbeth*, but it is inventive enough, rich enough, to be turned into an absorbing work of literature.

A sequence/ character/ plot in any of your books that has been inspired by cinema?
My novel *Home Products* was very much inspired by the Manoj Bajpai character in Ram Gopal Varma's *Satya*.

Do you read film reviews? What do you look for in a film review?
You need a good critic to tell you about the ways in which a work of literature or a film is in conversation with other works. I read good reviews, say by Namrata Joshi in *Outlook*, because she is good at sketching a quick family tree. There are other reasons for reading reviews, when critics are successful in presenting an attitude, or outlining what is elusive or unexpressed in a powerful film.

In a movie version of your life who would play you?
Manoj Bajpai.

What book of yours could be made into a film?
I once wrote a story for Mahesh Bhatt and when it wasn't used I put it in the novel I was writing at that point. I had tried to set a Chekhov story in India. But once I started thinking in terms of Bhatt, I began to invent a storyline for a new film and put that in the novel too. The imagined film was called 'Prithvi'. All of this is in *Home Products*.

Who would you like it to be directed by?
The director I really like is Dibakar Banerjee. Also, of course, Vishal Bhardwaj and Anurag Kashyap. But I have to tell you, I grew up wanting to write a story for the likes of Shyam Benegal and Govind Nihalani. Films like *Nishant* or *Aakrosh* are seared into my memory.

Who would you cast ?
In *Home Products*, while writing about a man named Rabinder dreaming of making a film when he came out of prison, I imagined Manoj Bajpai playing that role. I spent some time with Manoj and it allowed me to flesh out the character. And Tabu! Tabu as the demure but strong woman whom he discards.

One male actor you've always loved?
Naseeruddin Shah and Om Puri. I can't choose one over the other. I'd lay down my life for either of them. I hope that last statement has a nice filmi ring to it.

One actress you absolutely adore?
Oh, this is difficult. It is a glittering galaxy. Those trips I took to Bihar's small towns were lit up with encounters with Madhubala and Waheeda. In those days, theatres screened old classics all the time. Later, when I was a student in Delhi, Shabana (Azmi) and Smita (Patil) fired my imagination. Tabu ever since.

What fictional characters would you like to see your favourite actor/actress play?
I remember a Satyajit Ray adaptation of a Premchand story, *Sadgati*, in which Om Puri had starred. It would be wonderful if some of our most powerful stories received a similar treatment.

One writer whose biopic would definitely be A-Rated?
Saadat Hasan Manto. It would be wonderful not only because it would involve the upheaval of the Partition but also the story of Hindi films.

A writer whose biopic you want to see?
Other than Manto? You know, I was always fascinated by a writer like Nirmal Verma, going out of India at a time when it was rarer, living in Europe, and then coming back with new sensibilities. A refined filmmaker would shine a light on the mysteries and make

the mystery deepen.

One non-fiction title that could make for a good film?
Good question. Anurag Kashyap made tremendous use of my friend S. Hussain Zaidi's *Black Friday*. Aman Sethi's book *A Free Man* could have tremendous dialogue. Biharis spouting abuse in Delhi is an underrated cinematic resource!

One thing that the novel can do which a film can't?
I think films are to be watched with others, while a novel is to be consumed alone. I take that as a given. A novel guarantees you solitude. A film ushers you into a broader collective experience. Which is to say, I go to novels for inwardness.

One thing that cinema can do that a novel can't?
Technically speaking I find that films can do collage so much more successfully. Transitions are easier too. So many jumps, so many cuts, are accomplished so much more seamlessly. You don't need too much back-story because the eye can take in so much at once.

A film that made you very happy?
There was a time—I'm talking here of thirty years ago—when films like *Chashme Buddoor* and *Jaane Bhi Do Yaaro* lit up my life with laughter. I watched *3 Idiots* in a theatre in Washington DC. It was a very fun experience.

A film that made you cry?
This is embarrassing. Even bad films make me cry. *Chak De* wasn't a bad film at all, but yes, I remember bawling when I watched it.

A film you keep re-watching?
I have watched *Shakespeare Wallah* many times. Many early Shyam Benegal movies too. When working on *Home Products*, I watched *Satya* several times. *Maqbool* I have seen often too.

A film you would recommend for its dialogues?
I have just watched *Gangs of Wasseypur*. The dialogue there flows like hot lava.

A film every writer must see?
Writers are drawn to films that show characters finding their artistic selves. I recommend Shyam Benegal's *Bhumika*. Smita Patil is unforgettable. It is a gem of a film.

Your favourite film on writing/ a writer?
Il Postino (*The Postman*), which featured Pablo Neruda, on the side of the frame as it were, was a film with great charm.

If you ever made a film it would be...
A film in which the visual image would be streaked with the light of verbal poetry.

A film script you would like to read?
Monsoon Wedding.

A film you wish you had written?
Maybe I should say something like *Deewaar* but I'll say *Monsoon Wedding*.

One underrated film?
Why isn't the film *Party* better known? Prakash Jha's *Damul* won a national award but does it occupy a place in the national consciousness?

One highly rated film that did not work for you?
Sanjay Leela Bhansali's *Black* was voted among the ten best films of the year by TIME Magazine. It won many Filmfare awards. Really? I don't need to inform you that filmmakers can take a complicated story and turn it into sentimental garbage flecked with psychological pap.

Name one male and one female character from the movies whom you could imagine having an interesting conversation with?

Salim Mirza, the character played by Balraj Sahni, in M. S. Sathyu's *Garam Hava*. And the girl played by Sreela Majumdar in Mrinal Sen's *Khandhar*. I suspect there wouldn't be much said during dinner but I'd want very much to share a meal with them and, for a while, stand inside their circle of sadness.

LIST OF ILLUSTRATIONS

Page viii © Cy Twombly Foundation. Image courtesy of Sotheby's.

Page 223 *Fray Hortensio Félix Paravacinoi*, 1609 © Museum of Fine Arts, Boston by El Greco (Domenikos Theotokopoulos), Greek (active in Spain), 1541–1614. Oil on Canvas.

Page 221 © The Estate of A.K. Ramanujan
The A. K. Ramanujan Papers, Special Collections Research Center, Regenstein Library of the University of Chicago. Published in Guillermo Rodriguez, *When Mirrors Are Windows*, New Delhi: Oxford University Press, 2016.